CHASING
SACHIN

CHASING
SACHIN

By Adam Carroll-Smith

Pitch Publishing Ltd
A2 Yeoman Gate
Yeoman Way
Durrington
BN13 3QZ

Email: info@pitchpublishing.co.uk
Web: www.pitchpublishing.co.uk

Published by Pitch Publishing 2011
Text © 2011 Adam Carroll-Smith

The publisher makes no representation, express or implied, with regard to the accuracy of
the information contained in this book and cannot accept any legal responsibility
for any errors or omissions that may be made.

A CIP catalogue record for this book is available from the British Library.

13-digit ISBN: 9781908051516
Cover design by Brilliant Orange Creative Services.
Typesetting and origination by Pitch Publishing. Printed in Great Britain.
Manufacturing managed by Jellyfish Print Solutions Ltd.

For Mum, Dad, Josh, Grandma
and especially you, Gramps.

Some names have been changed to protect the innocent/unhelpful/lazy/dangerous.

No animals were harmed in the making of this book, although one wasp came close.

PART ONE

It was Saturday 8 June 1996, when I had my first encounter with cricket. I cycled straight into a thin, barely visible rope surrounding the square at my local park and ended up spread-eagled on the pitch. As introductions go, it was some way short of ideal. Not many great cricketing careers began with a near-decapitation. Most at least had a bat or ball in hand and hardly *any* were on a bike. Even fewer were wearing a Transformers t-shirt with the sleeves cut off and singing the rap sections of 'Killing Me Softly' by the Fugees.

The unkempt playing fields at the park were the exclusive domain of mad, mumbling men who drank cheap beer and swore at strangers, dog walkers with incontinent pets and enormous teenagers playing terrifyingly aggressive five-a-side football, while their girlfriends smoked funny-smelling cigarettes by the swings. It was a bit like a warzone with a cycle path and monkey bars.

Generally speaking, it was the sort of place to avoid, but swept up in the euphoria of the upcoming Euro '96 football tournament, just hours from starting at a sun-drenched Wembley 80-odd miles away, my brother Josh and I cycled down for a kickabout. After finding a postage stamp-sized patch of turf free from dog shit, fag-butts and half-crushed lager cans, I began pedalling aimlessly while Josh hoofed and toe-punted the ball at me to try and knock me off the saddle.

It was the sort of masochistic practise session of which Brian Clough would have approved. It was also, self-evidently, about as pointless as Mike Gatting's completely spherical head (seriously, look at it; it's like someone has drawn an angry little goatee and some beady eyes on a volleyball).

After one effort fizzed past my nose, I wearily chased the stray ball. As I raced further away, a golden strip of land inched into view through waves of summer heat. Well, through waves of summer sort-of-heat. It was June in England, after all. Come to think of it, it was probably more like tsunamis of torrential summer rain.

If the rest of the park echoed with the clatter and chatter of creaking swings and agricultural swearing, this part of the fields was green, pleasant land. Even the smell was different – a fresher, healthier smell than the 'after-party at a Snoop Dogg concert' aroma of the cigarettes being smoked by the girls near the swings. It was the first time I had ever seen a cricket pitch up close.

Seconds later, I felt the hot friction of wiry rope cutting painfully across my midriff and forearms, sending my bike and I cart-wheeling apart. I lay on the dusty surface for a few seconds; arms and legs jutting in opposite directions like a miniature John Travolta (except for the Transformers t-shirt) in *Saturday Night Fever*.

"Get off the bloody square!"

A man's voice boomed at me from my right. I sucked in humid June air and rubbed my arms in pain as I scanned the park to see exactly whose square – whatever one of *those* was – I found myself lying upon. I hauled myself to my feet gingerly brushing dust and loose blades of grass from my clothes. A man in his early sixties and wearing a faded white flowerpot hat, cream knitted jumper and dark blue shorts, was breaking into a semi-jog towards me. He looked a bit like Worzel Gummidge on his way to a squash match.

"Get off the bloody square you little shit!" he hollered once more.

It almost definitely wasn't Worzel Gummidge. I'm not sure Worzel Gummidge ever used language like that, (certainly not towards a child, he might have told the odd crow to piss off, but then he was a scarecrow, so fair enough) but whoever it was, his voice, at first croaky and smoke-damaged, was now clearer and biting with anger. Panicked and still in some discomfort, I propped my bike up, hopped into the saddle and fled, my feet whirring at a Road Runner-esque, smoke-producing speed. I sped past my brother and out of the park, only stopping to catch my breath once the man's shouting had faded into silence. I didn't want to go back to the park ever again. There was no point; our football was probably slowly deflating on the prongs of a gardening fork.

But even so, the image of that cricket pitch stayed with me for weeks, inflaming my interest in the game. A fascination began – springing like a post-traumatic reflex from the shock of riding into the rope and the threat of a walloping from a drunken middle-aged man – with all things cricket.

That day, while England limped to a 1-1 draw with Switzerland (and I gingerly limped around the house rubbing the rope burn on my arm), within the relative quiet of Edgbaston cricket ground in Birmingham, an impish-looking batsman called Sachin Tendulkar was scoring a flawless century against England's cricketers, smashing 122 out of a meagre total of 219. The best any of his team-mates could manage was 18. It was a display of utter genius that not only transcended the mediocrity around him but highlighted it, too. It was the cricketing equivalent of Alan Shearer scoring a double hat-trick, but England losing 7-6. To the Germans. On St George's Day.

Like most people in the country, I was oblivious not only to the supreme achievement of Tendulkar that day, but entirely unaware of what a phenomenon he already was. I was more interested in Gary Neville's long-throws than Sachin's back-foot cover drive, which is a bit like saying you preferred ready salted crisps to cheese and onion or that your favourite Beatle was Ringo. It was sporting sacrilege.

The rope burn healed, but my interest in cricket grew exponentially over the coming weeks. Rosh, a short boy from Malaysia, was the only friend I knew at school who liked cricket. A mutual love of professional wrestling (the sort where American men called 'Randy' in luminous, skin-tight lycra hit each other with metal chairs) had brought us close in the classroom, and it seemed only natural to turn to Rosh for an introduction to cricket. Not that he knew that, of course, when I invited myself over to his house to watch a video of an old Wrestlemania.

"I'm thinking about playing cricket, Rosh," I said as we stared at the TV.

"Cool."

He didn't bat an eyelid. In his defence, ex-*Baywatch* star Pamela Anderson was escorting a wrestler to the ring. My attempts to strike up a conversation were no match for Rosh's raging pre-teen hormones, but I persisted. Well, actually I joined in with the ogling for a bit and then I persisted.

"Yeah, so I was wondering if you could help me get into it, Rosh."

"What?"

"Cricket."

"What about it?"

"I want to start playing cricket."

"Cool." Pamela was jiggling about. I left him to it and gazed out of the window. Oh alright, I leered at Pammy too. 'Pamela' seemed an unlikely name for her to have. I only knew one other lady called Pam, and she was a 70-year-old lady who lived on our street. She didn't like wrestling, had never starred in *Baywatch* and as far as I remember, never wore anything as revealing as Pamela Anderson did, which was a relief. Although she certainly would have got people talking at the next Neighbourhood Watch meeting (probably about not inviting her to the next meeting if she insisted on wearing the red swimsuit and carrying that flotation device) if she did.

Rosh's father, near-identical to his son save for the fact he always seemed to be wearing slippers, shuffled silently into the room as we gawped at the screen. Within seconds the wrestling tape was whisked from the VCR on the grounds of its 'puerility'. I wasn't sure quite what it meant, but it sounded mucky. Neither Rosh nor I protested too much. We quickly snapped out of our hormonal reverie.

"Adam wants to start playing cricket, Dad."

Rosh's father's bright white eyes peered over the top of his glasses at me as I sat on the floor. He always reminded me of Kermit the Frog, if Kermit wore tank tops three sizes too big for him and worked as a business trouble-shooter, which as any Muppet fan knows, he did not. He didn't have time for anything like that. And if he did, any business that thinks a small, furry frog with a man's hand up its arse is the answer to its problems should probably just shut up shop anyway.

"That is wonderful, Adam," he said. "Rosh has lots of cricket videos. Rosh; why don't you both watch one?"

Begrudgingly, Rosh agreed and thrust a tatty-looking VHS into the player with a petulant pre-teen huff. After the tape adjusted to the tracking mechanism and the mangled images bobbed into focus, we both sat cross-legged in close attention. A tall man with jet-black hair started his run-up from the bottom of the screen, his clumping, leaden-footed charge ending in a flurry of arms and legs. At the other end was a tiny man whose bat appeared to be two-thirds as big as him. One elegant, effortless swing and a pleasingly bassy clunk off his bat later, the ball zipped away. The contrast between the bowler – his every limb seemingly at war with the other as he bowled – and the balletic movement of the batsman could not have been more marked. It was all rather lovely.

"That's Sachin Tendulkar, the greatest batsman in the world."

I turned to see Rosh's dad watching the video intently, his beady eyes wide – or at least wider than normal – with excitement.

"I taped this for Rosh, he must study how Tendulkar bats if he wants to get better as a batsman. Nobody else can hold a candle to Tendulkar's talent."

We watched again as Tendulkar elegantly clubbed the bowler, the curiously named Ronnie Irani, twice more. The bowler grinned and shook his head in begrudging appreciation for the shots being played. The little batsman's balance, timing and power were incredible, almost otherworldly. From beneath his blue helmet he seemed a picture of quiet, brooding confidence, and yet he looked no more than a few years older than me; a cherubim-faced boy surrounded by the grizzled features of the England fielders.

In between deliveries he shuffled nervously with his gloves, adjusted his pads obsessively and scanned his dark brown eyes around the ground, anxiously seeking gaps between the scattered fielders. But the moment an English bowler began his run-up, a calm descended as Tendulkar stood statue-still, upright and unflinching, his bat hovering perfectly perpendicular to the ground. Even through layers of tape fuzz he transmitted an intangible quality that marked him out from the other players on display. It was sporting love at first sight.

India, the commentators said, were under the cosh, battered and beaten into near submission by England. The young batter was the only player holding firm. So began a fascination with Sachin Tendulkar.

Punctuating each of his boundary-bound shots were the giddy celebrations of the English bowlers as they claimed Indian wickets with ease. The crowd cheered every dismissal – a nicer, less taunting sound than a football cheer – but incredibly, rapturously celebrated each breathtaking shot Tendulkar played, too. The camera panned to the spectators irregularly throughout, and most were patently English; all pale skin, nylon football shirts and half-empty plastic pint pots. Yet they cheered each graceful blow by the young Indian like it was a German penalty soaring over the crossbar, their eyes fixed in awe on Sachin as though he were a 5ft 5in tall Pukka pie.

Rosh and I continued to watch as Tendulkar reached 50, raising his bat with little fanfare to all corners of the ground. He continued imperiously towards his century, removing his helmet when he did so to salute the crowd. He barely cracked a smile, merely raising his arms aloft before adjusting his equipment and readying himself for the next ball.

Finally, he was dismissed, a simple BBC graphic undermining the beauty of his innings: 'S.R. Tendulkar 122, c. Thorpe b. Lewis'. His dismissal drew a huge cheer from the English contingent in the stadium, a belching, late-in-the-day roar of relief that slowly mutated into a standing ovation for his efforts. As he walked off, even the umpire, a portly, ruddy-faced man, acknowledged Tendulkar's brilliance with a nod of congratulations to him. I had never seen sport – or sportsmanship – like it. The tape ended. I was transfixed.

For the rest of that afternoon, I sat entranced as an uninterrupted succession of cricket videos flew in and out of the video player; England's cricketers toiling on impossibly fast and bouncy pitches in Australia, the West Indian, Brian Lara, wristily smashing hot and bothered-looking England bowlers around dusty, sun-baked Caribbean grounds and a pair of Pakistani bowlers called Wasim and Waqar splaying stumps with balls seemingly hurled at the speed of light. I was amazed by the endless different types and characters of players; from the dour grittiness and permanently furrowed brow of England's Mike Atherton to the shrill, peroxide-coloured exuberance of Australia's Shane Warne. But among the myriad of new faces and techniques, no one came close to the calm, almost divine simplicity of Tendulkar's batting.

Over the remainder of the summer, Rosh and I walled ourselves off – literally, in his enormous back garden – from football's iron grasp on the sporting schedules. With a tennis ball half-covered in sellotape ('it makes the ball swing', according to Rosh), a tatty Gray-Nicolls bat and a plant-pot for stumps, we played for hours on the uneven sun-faded pink paving slabs, mimicking the batsmen and bowlers we admired.

Throughout those balmy few months, I perfected cutting and driving with a flourish as a replica (albeit right-handed) Lara, and could bowl loopy leg-breaks like a pint-sized, mousey-haired Warne. But most impressive was Rosh's impression of Tendulkar. Upright in his stance, technically perfect and naturally as short as Tendulkar himself, bowling at Rosh was as close as it got to bowling at the great man. We watched and studied that video of Tendulkar at Edgbaston until the tape warped and perished from the strain of repeated viewings. We dreamed of one day meeting our hero, perhaps even playing against him.

Such thoughts were extinguished early and in resounding fashion. I made my cricketing debut later that summer. This, I told myself, was the first step towards emulating Tendulkar's career. True to my prediction, I, like the Little Master, was dismissed in my very first game for a duck. So far, so on course to emulate my hero.

But doubts began to surface soon after. I discovered Sachin's next run of scores after that maiden zero included a pair of triple centuries. *Triple centuries*. I'm not sure I've scored 300 runs in my life.

By the end of his first year in junior cricket, Sachin was averaging over a thousand runs per innings. After my first four games, my average was zero, and the backyard bowling skills I had developed were not serving me very well on real pitches either. My best moment came when I athletically stopped a smashed cover drive in a school game. Well, I say 'stopped' – it was more a case of it smashing into my knee. I hobbled off with tears in my eyes.

Already, the signs were clear; I would never dazzle my hero with my batting talents, nor get the chance to bore him out with my slow-medium bowling. It is a sad day when a boy realises he will not play for England – even now I am realistic enough to acknowledge it would take at least two or three injuries to key England players for me to get a call-up (or the discovery of a South African grandfather).

Rosh and I drifted apart over the years too, as we swapped afternoons inside watching cricket videos for nights down the pub with mates, and substituted ball games in the garden for days at the beach with our girlfriends. My boyish idolisation of Tendulkar turned into a more adult, sober appreciation of his talents.

And that is how things could have stayed. The tape of Tendulkar's 122 disappeared and Rosh's near-perfect Sachin impressions became a memory. Life moved on.

****

I had not seen Rosh for more than a year when we bumped into each other at a party one early May evening in London. Like recovering drunks recalling hedonistic days gone-by, our conversation soon turned to cricket, and back to those sun-dappled days playing with the taped-up tennis ball. Empty beer bottles soon snaked around us as we relived our childhood cricketing adventures. Praise pinged elastically between us for our ability to ape Lara's high back-lift or defend like Michael Atherton; we even talked about digging our whites out and playing some proper cricket again. Standout backyard innings came flooding back to us like Technicolor highlight reels. It was a nice jog (we were too drunk to have driven) down memory lane.

"My Tendulkar impression was the best, wasn't it, Ad?" Rosh suggested. I nodded in agreement and sipped my beer.

Warm memories rushed back of the boyish excitement we both felt about Tendulkar.

"In fact, did you ever even bowl me out when I was batting as Tendulkar?" he asked. "I don't think you ever did."

It was a ridiculous thing to say – in backyard cricket, wickets fell about every three seconds. My reply lacked subtlety.

"Bollocks. Of course I did," I spluttered. Rosh sipped his beer and smirked. No one likes a smirker.

"*I bloody did*," I persisted, "I remember bowling you a big inswinger which hit the very top of the plant pot."

I didn't remember it exactly, but it was a punt worth taking. If I threw him some invented specifics about the incident, maybe he would assume I was right.

"I think it went just over. It was given not out on referral." *Clever bastard*. He'd called my bluff.

"No, no," I insisted. "I definitely got you out when you were batting as Sachin. I remember celebrating the wicket in a big way."

"Rubbish. You never bowled Sachin." Rosh was adamant. He sipped at his beer again and swallowed his mouthful with another irritating smirk.

Red mist descended. I went 'postal' as the Americans say. By which I mean I got incredibly irate, rather than I started trying to stuff his stamp-covered face through a letterbox, although the thought did occur to me. But stamps are expensive.

"Rosh, this is crazy," I whined, "I definitely bowled you. It was an incredible delivery. I can still remember it clearly, it dipped and swung and you tried to defend it, but it went between the bat and your leg and knocked you over. It was good enough to get the real Sachin Tendulkar, let alone you doing an impression."

Whether we agreed to disagree or bemused onlookers were forced to intervene at this point in our frankly ridiculous conversation, I don't remember. But as I woke in my bed with a hangover the following morning, a seed had been sown.

Tendulkar, for the first time since I was 13 years old, was at the forefront of my mind. Burying my head into my pillow and groping for my phone on my bedside table, I fished it closer to check the time. The screen displayed an unfinished text message.

'*Track dwn sachnin tendulkar n bowl him out*'.

Ignoring my terrible spelling, snatched fragments of another conversation immediately came wobbling back into focus. I closed the message draft down and called Rosh. Perhaps he knew why I had left this cryptic, drunken note for my sober self to pick up the next morning.

"Ugh, what," he groaned, answering the phone.

"I just found a text I wrote to myself on my phone," I said "It's about Sachin Tendulkar."

Rosh said nothing. Clearly, he had no idea what I was on about. This bizarre memo was obviously of my own doing.

"I don't know what you're on about," he yawned. "Have you just woken me up to talk about a text?"

"Well, it said: '*track down Sachin Tendulkar and bowl him out*'. It just sounded like something you might know about."

Saying it out loud made me sound a bit mad, like I'd woken up with a piece of toast or a signed photo of Sir Ian McKellen under my pillow and then called him demanding to know who had put it there. Neither of us said anything for a few seconds.

"So how are you going to do it?" he yawned.

I felt a bizarre rush of adrenaline fizz through my stomach. The same sort of rush I would have got if I'd woken up with a picture of Sir Ian, probably.

"No, I'm not going to do it," I replied instinctively. "I just wondered why it was on my phone this morning."

"What?" Rosh replied, suddenly sounding wide-awake. "Why the hell wouldn't you do it?"

"Why *would* I do it?"

"Well, fairly obviously, because you might get the opportunity to bowl at Sachin Tendulkar," Rosh countered immediately.

It was hard to fault his logic. It was flawless. We said our goodbyes and both went back to sleeping our hangovers off. I closed the text message down.

I have never run a marathon, climbed a mountain, or cycled from Lands End to John O'Groats and until that moment I had never understood why anyone – charity fundraising aside – ever felt the need to, either. Such tasks are hard work mentally, physically draining and yet ultimately, entirely pointless. *I climbed the mountain because it's there,* mad adventurers always seemed to bleat when any right-thinking person asked why on earth they were doing it. All that adventuring felt like something other people did; people who didn't have satellite television, wore Birkenstocks and enjoyed herbal tea (it *all* tastes like sweat – it lures you in by smelling lovely, but then the taste – *ugh!*). I had always preferred to go to the pub or eat dry cereal from the box, because they, conveniently, were *there*. I didn't need a Sherpa or an anti-malaria jab to go to The Yorkshire Grey (unless it was over-45s singles night, in which either might come in useful at some point).

But bowling to Sachin had always been a dream since childhood – and did I need any other reason to do this than that? I *would* track down Sachin Tendulkar and bowl him out, simply because he was there – or more specifically because he was *here*, in England, on probably his last tour of the country with India. Was this a plan? It felt like a plan.

I got up and made myself a cup of tea. (Earl Grey. With milk. And sugar. And a malted milk biscuit with a picture of someone playing hockey, I think. Or maybe it was horse racing. It was hard to tell.) I thought about pulling myself together. *This is a ridiculous idea,* I thought. Only it wasn't what I thought at all. '*Oh my word this is the best idea ever and I absolutely have to at least try*' would have been closer to my actual inner monologue. Like a tunnel-visioned sprinter dashing towards the finish line, I had seen my goal and now nothing would throw me off my stride. I would travel far and wide to get the chance to bowl one delivery at my hero. I would bowl a ball of such judicious accuracy and deceiving guile it would fox the great Tendulkar.

Amazingly, none of that sounded the least bit farcical to me any more. Tendulkar would be in England for the summer. He would be playing cricket. I might be able to find a way to bowl a few balls at him. It all seemed simple enough. It was no longer an idea, now it was a *project*. I called Rosh back.

"I'm going to do it," I announced grandly.

"What?"

"Track down Sachin and bowl him out," I panted excitedly.

"Ha," Rosh chuckled, dismissively, "don't be stupid."

What? Where was this negativity coming from? Not long ago he was convincing me I *had* to do this. I sipped my tea and angrily bit the hockey player/jockey on my biscuit in half.

"What do you mean?" I moaned, meekly.

"Well," Rosh huffed, derisively, "you'll never bowl him out. You never even got me out when I was batting as Tendulkar in my back garden. And you never will, either."

This time I let it go. I knew he was wrong and even if he wasn't it didn't matter. The endless viewings of Tendulkar's 122 at Edgbaston had taught me one thing – besides the fact that Sachin was as close to cricketing infallibility as it got – that eventually, after the highlights reel of thundering shots, it took just one ball to get Sachin out. And get out he did, just like every other batsman. All I needed was the opportunity. If Ronnie Irani could have a go, so could I. No offence, Ronnie.

For the next few days, I pored over hundreds of online videos of Tendulkar's best innings and read countless quotes from the great and good of the game on the Little Master. One from Shane Warne, spoken after Tendulkar had clobbered the great leg-spinner to all parts, read:

> *"I'll be going to bed having nightmares of Sachin just running down the wicket and belting me back over my head for six."*

For Warne, the thought of Sachin Tendulkar smashing one of his deliveries into the stratosphere inspired nightmares – but for me, just being there, ball in hand, watching Sachin poised in readiness at the other end of a cricket pitch was the stuff of fantasy; it would be a dream just to watch him clobber one of my dreadful deliveries at such close quarters.

Not that he would of course, because I was going to knock his off stump over.

Probably.

PART TWO

It was late May – a typical English month full of sun, rain, hail, a growing obsession with a posh girl's bum (yes *you*, Pippa Middleton), a little bit more sun, a lot more rain and Manchester U-flipping-nited (as they are known in my household) winning another league title. But more importantly than all that (with the possible exception of Pippa's derriere, which by the time you read this will probably be designated as an area of outstanding natural beauty by Unesco) in less than two months' time, Sachin Tendulkar would begin his final tour of England with the Indian cricket team. My summer chasing Sach would soon be under way.

Anticipation about India's arrival was already bubbling away, with pundits predicting how well the great man would deal with England's bowling attack, which just a few months previously had destroyed the Australians in their own back yard. Excitement abounded that the Little Master might notch his 100th international century while on the tour.

Strangely, my name appeared not to have been mentioned at all (it may have been; I didn't check *every* paper) as one of the bowlers who might prevent Sachin reaching that historical landmark during the coming months. Perhaps – like similarly mercurial talents Graeme Hick and Mark Ramprakash before me – the experts were giving me a rough ride. Or perhaps word had reached the cricketing press about my lack of training so far towards my goal of bowling Tendulkar.

Three weeks had passed since the party with Rosh in London. I had watched a few more videos of Sachin's batting and become a 'fan' of the great man on Facebook. I discovered via one website that he collected watches. Another webpage told me his favourite film was *Coming to America* and his favourite band was 'The Eagles'. Both seemed too low-brow for an icon like Sach. It was like discovering David Gower didn't actually sit around reading Proust (who is the *spit* of Alastair Cook, if Cookie ever grew a 'tache) and being fed grapes by his butler, but actually loved 'The Doobie Brothers' and regularly 'LOL-ed' at the films of Adam Sandler.

The Sachin trivia available online was never-ending. I found out his favourite actress was Demi Moore and that he was a huge John McEnroe fan. Strangely, his favourite cricketer was apparently *Brain* Lara, whom I assumed was a close (and highly intelligent) relative of the more-famous Brian. I even learned that Sachin had never learned to swim. I could challenge him to a few lengths in the pool if I didn't manage to bowl him. Or at least threaten to push him in the deep end if he didn't have a net with me.

But while all that was interesting (to me, at least) in reality, I had achieved nothing. Well, maybe not technically *nothing*. I had re-watched *Coming to America*, listened to 'Hotel California' and been swimming a few times, but if you want to be pernickety, it wasn't much. If only I shared Sachin's passion for timepieces, I might have realised how much of the stuff I was wasting.

I had form for this sort of procrastination. Every so often, I would fire a group email or text round to my friends threatening some grand day out or gibbering enthusiastically about some hastily cobbled-together scheme. Normally, it would fizzle out. If it did take place – after somebody else had taken over the organisational reins – I would invariably fail to show up, normally on the grounds of having already arranged to sit in my boxer shorts eating popcorn, drinking milkshakes and watching repeats of *The Simpsons*. I very rarely broke *those* arrangements. I didn't pull my trousers up and put my milkshake down for any old thing.

I had returned to my hometown of Portsmouth for the weekend. I got up late on the Saturday morning to find my Dad sat on the corner sofa, with one eye on his newspaper and the other on his laptop. Technically speaking, he was multi-tasking. More accurately, he was going cross-eyed.

So was Mum, though rather more vigourously (the multi-tasking, not the going cross-eyed bit), dusting and scrubbing and cleaning every inch of the house. If I didn't know better, I could have sworn she had even suped-up the vacuum cleaner. It looked like she had fitted a spoiler to aid the aerodynamics and it sounded like it had more horsepower than next-door's Volvo. It was a sound system and a few neon lights away from being the sort of vehicle you see spotty lads in baseball caps gathered around at McDonald's drive-thrus.

I had returned home to tell my parents about my plan to bowl Sachin. Surprisingly, I was a bit nervous. Maybe it was because my Mum has never seen the appeal of cricket. Despite her background as a junior tennis champion (I have never beaten her at *any* racket sport. I suggested she take a drug test after one defeat, but that just got me a painful, almost *performance-enhanced* clip around the ear) the only time I had ever seen her wield a bat in anger was when she swung for a wasp during a picnic in our back garden. She missed and knocked over a bottle of orange Lucozade, which ironically attracted rather more wasps. She washed her hands of the game (and the sticky soft drink, obviously) there and then. Mum also once donned a set of batting pads to 'save her knees' while she cleaned the kitchen floor – the only time I have ever seen a set of Gray-Nicolls pads teamed with a floral skirt outside of one pretty niche-interest stag do – but those incidents aside, mum was a cricketing novice.

Dad was roughly of the same mind, dismissing cricket as 'boring to watch' and 'a bit pointless' – pretty rich coming from someone who has supported Southampton Football Club for fifty years and watches the anti-virus scan on his computer with the same spellbound, priapic excitement most men reserve for films with the word 'spank-a-thon' in the title.

But between ear-splitting blasts of turbo-powered vacuuming and the occasional rustles of broadsheet pages, I tentatively began to talk them both through the highlights of Sachin's career. Mum 'ooh-ed' and 'aah-ed' with seemingly genuine interest as I splurged a mass of facts and figures at her. I mentioned that Sachin's wife, Anjali, becomes so nervous when he is batting that she cannot move, eat or even sip a glass of water. Mum tutted in disapproval. I told her of Sachin's miraculous feats of batting; of his 99 international hundreds; of the hero worship his talent inspired back in India; of the apocryphal tale of the trains grinding to a halt across India when Sachin is approaching a century. More 'oohs' and 'aahs' followed.

Finally, I explained my mission to bamboozle Tendulkar. Mum coo-ed with the same tentative approval she used to whenever I brought a shoddy painting home from primary school (or a shoddy girlfriend home from university, for that matter) and demanded to know her opinion (the paintings were always better received than the girlfriends). Dad's laptop – or maybe it was just Dad – whirred away quietly in the background. They had heard plans like this before. They were conserving their enthusiasm.

I continued regaling them both with tales of Sachin's debut for India as a 16-year-old schoolboy and his heroic double centuries against the Australians, until Mum stopped suddenly, leaning like a cruise ship stand-up comedian on the handle of her vacuum cleaner. The room was quiet, with just the distant buzz of a lawnmower oscillating in the air. She looked deep in concentration, as though she was internally wrestling with the proper pronunciation of Tender-cat or Ten-car-doors or whatever it was.

"Sorry, I'm confused," she said, her brow furrowed. "I thought you went to school with this… What's his name again?"

"Ten-dul-kar," I replied, emphasising each syllable deliberately. Mum mouthed the name again silently.

"Who was that boy you used to play cricket with?" she asked, her forehead creasing even more intensely in confusion.

"Whoever it was," I replied, "it *definitely* wasn't Sachin Tendulkar, Mum…"

"He lived with his parents and grandparents in that big house on the hill…and he was quite tall; had as much facial hair at 14 as you do now…Actually, probably even more, because he had a *proper* moustache. You still can't quite manage one…"

"Mum…" I said softly.

"He always used to have his finger up his nose as well, and…"

"Mum," I blurted out, impatiently, "I don't know who this bloke you're describing is, but it's not Sachin. We have never given Sachin Tendulkar a lift home from school. Sachin Tendulkar is an Indian cricketer. He's more than ten years older than me. He's also just about the most famous person in the whole of India and one of the greatest batsmen to have ever lived."

The message finally seemed to have gotten through. Mum paused again, deep in thought once more.

"OK," she smiled. "So you're going to bowl this Indian batsman out this summer?"

"Yes. I have no idea how, and even if I do get the chance, he'll probably just smash the ball 25 miles, but there we are."

Mum shooed my feet off of the floor, pushing the vacuum past me as she did. I stretched out across the sofa, resting my feet and head on opposite arms. The wheels of the hoover gently squeaked past me. I closed my eyes and envisaged running in and bowling to Sachin. I imagined watching as the ball landed and arrowed neatly past his pad, the movement off the pitch completely deceiving him. I could hear the sweet sound of leather clattering into the stumps and see the bails fluttering artfully to the ground, like little wooden butterflies. That was how it would happen. I could see it all unfolding so perfectly.

Only it wasn't Sachin Tendulkar I was bowling to in my daydream. It was Eddie Murphy. Eddie Murphy dressed as Prince Akeem, the character he played in *Coming to America*. And he wasn't holding a cricket bat. No, he was swinging a guitar and singing the chorus to The Eagles' 'Hotel California'. Maybe I'd overdone it with my Sachin research.

"Well," Mum began, snapping me out of my bizarre fantasy. "Top-level sport is about skill up to a point, but a lot of it is about good luck, better timing and the best preparation."

My Mum, hair tied back, marigolds tucked into her trousers, had suddenly become a sports psychologist, with me, lying prone on our leatherette two-seater, her first client.

"It's only one ball, isn't it?" she mused. "Anything can happen in one ball. That's the beauty of it."

I nodded in agreement.

"Anyone who can bowl a ball half-decently could – given the opportunity – feasibly bowl the best player to have ever played the game," she continued. "It's like if you and Tiger Woods were both given short putts, he *might* miss and you *might* get it in. If you played one point against Roger Federer, he *might* hit your serve into the net or serve a double-fault. It's a 50-50 chance. This cricketer will probably hit your ball, but he *might* miss it."

All of a sudden, the likelihood of me bowling Sachin had leapt from 'about as probable as Ravi Bopara winning Sports Personality of the Year' to a 50-50 chance. Thank goodness for a mother's confidence in her son. That same belief had allowed her to convince me I was cool enough to wear a cowboy hat to my first ever date with a girl (there was no second date, presumably because the poor girl thought I might take her to a barn dance or to Texas for the state-sanctioned execution of a felon or something), but on this occasion, it was helpful.

"Exactly," I beamed. "You're right."

I leapt to my feet and instinctively tumbled through my rusty bowling action, muscle memory from years gone by taking over as my arms and legs twirled with awkward familiarity. I felt twinges in parts of my back and shoulders I had not used in years. Muscles I had forgotten about creaked as I swung my arms around. My face twisted into a painful grimace. Mum's reaction mirrored mine, squirming sympathetically. I could have sworn I saw her visibly adjust her '50 percent chance' prediction downwards by a few decimal points. I rubbed my back and grinned half-heartedly as I slumped back onto the sofa.

"What do you think, Martyn?"

Mum bellowed over to my Dad, who angled the corners of his paper down and peered over the top of the pages. His glasses fell from their perch on top of his head and thumped down onto the bridge of his nose, with enough force to make most people jump. My Dad isn't 'most people', though. I'm not sure he even noticed.

"I'm going to track down the best batsman in the world, Sachin Tendulkar, and bowl him out this summer, Dad," I explained.

He made an elongated, high-pitched noise of general approval and semi-interest, then flipped the pages of his paper back upright noisily, obscuring his face.

"Weren't you more of a batsman though?" His voice floated over the top of his paper.

"Yes, I was. Or rather I still am. But it's only one ball. There's always a chance with one ball. He might miss it. And if he doesn't, it would be a thrill to watch him smash the ball up close," I reasoned.

Dad let out a small 'hmm' of agreement before returning to his paper.

"Didn't you get hit for three sixes in a row in a school game once, Ad?" he chirped up suddenly. *No,* I told him emphatically. *I definitely did **not** get hit for three sixes in a row.*

"Was it four?"

It bloody well *was* four. Two of the balls were lost. One of them is officially orbiting the planet. The other one has probably just about landed on Mars by now. If man ever colonises the Red Planet, chances are the Martians will probably already have a half-decent cricket team set up (probably with a couple of South African ringers of questionable Martian ancestry thrown in, as is the norm), all thanks to my buffet bowling. Either that or they will think Earth is populated by small, red leather beings called 'Readers Extra Special'. That, I should point out, was the logo on the cricket ball – although it sounds oddly like a top-shelf magazine catering exclusively for cricketers (full of *maidens* letting a bit of *leg slip*, probably). It went so far, so quickly, that even the umpire was moved to exclaim 'bloody hell!' as it whooshed away.

Dad laughed. Then Mum laughed. Then I laughed. Then my back twinged again. Perhaps it was time for some practise. Or at least some stretching. Unfortunately, I already had a date with some repeats of a certain animated American comedy and Mum and Dad's local corner shop had a two-for-one offer on banana-flavoured milk-based beverages. Like any self-respecting elite athlete, I fell asleep that night with popcorn kernels in my chest hair, halfway through an old episode of *Murder, She Wrote*. I was living the dream.

"Howwwzzzaaattt!"

I woke the next morning to the sound of my brother, Josh, loudly appealing at the foot of my bed with all the ferocity of wee Stuey Broad throwing a tantrum when Andy Flower tells him he can't watch *Dragon's Den* because its past his bedtime.

I pulled the covers over my head and impolitely told Josh to leave me alone. He impolitely told me he would not. In fact, his response was so impolite it even contained a swear word I have not heard before or since. It sounded like it had an 'X' or two in it. Maybe even a stray '7' and one of those upside-down Spanish question marks, too. It seemed to rhyme with everything! Imagine Matt Hayden's response if you sledged him from slip about how supple and 'willing to experiment' his wife was. Then imagine all the violent and inventive oral daggers you'd throw at Piers Morgan's enormous smug face (I've bagsied 'epic twunt') if you ever got the chance. Multiply the two. *That* rude.

"Tendulkar, Ad?" Josh squealed. "*Tendulkar?*"

Mum and Dad had obviously filled Josh in on my plans. And obviously he was fairly unconvinced about the likelihood of me succeeding. He was, after all, the bowler in the family.

"He'll smash you about 200 miles!" he roared. "You're the batsman and *I'm* the bloody bowler in the family, remember? (Told you). Don't you remember that school game? Wasn't it *five* six… "

"Four," I interrupted him abruptly, pulling myself upright in bed.

I sat staring at him, bleary-eyed for a few moments. I brushed some popcorn crumbs from my chest and let out an early morning burp. At times like this, I wondered how it was that I was still single.

Josh stared back, his face full of joy and excitement, eyes wide with glee, like wee Stuey Broad being told by Andy Flower that actually he *could* stay up to watch *Dragon's Den*, if he promised not to call any more umpires 'bumheads' or 'bollock-faces'. His enthusiasm was all very motivating and uplifting, until he did another inventive curse at me. This one sounded all sharp and pointy and angular – like the curse word equivalent of Nasser Hussain's schnozz.

"We should go to the nets today, get you practising that rusty bowling action," Josh suggested. "The last thing you want to do is embarrass yourself in front of Tendulkar. I mean, going down there today will mean embarrassing yourself in front of any people walking in the park, and embarrassing yourself in front of me, but it's a start. All great journeys begin with one step. Well, except that guy who broke the world record for moonwalking. That started with more of a slide."

He was right. I couldn't drag my heels like a record-breaking moonwalker; I needed to get started right away. If I was going to do this, I would need to dedicate myself to the task. I would need to spend every waking hour working towards fulfilling my boyhood dream.

"Dogs too," Josh added, as I began to ease myself out from under the covers.

"What?" I said, raising an eyebrow quizzically.

"Any dogs in the park, too. You'll embarrass yourself in front of them as well," Josh clarified. "And any birds in the trees, cats that have wandered in, babies in prams…"

"I get it, Josh. I am going to be so crap that even newborn infants, with no frame of reference for how good or bad my bowling is, will instinctively be able to tell I'm not very good."

"No, it's much worse than that," he scoffed, "they'll instinctively be able to tell that you're *absolutely crap*. As will the dogs and birds and everything else that happens to be watching and doesn't necessarily know anything about the mechanics of bowling a cricket ball."

He was probably right, but he had at least given me the first target on my road to Tendulkar – to prove my bowling was professional enough not to draw mocking laughter from newborns or howls of derision from animals who were stupid enough to be startled by the sight of their own wagging tail. I was no more than quietly confident.

Reluctantly, I hauled myself out of bed and lugged my cricket bag down from the top of my wardrobe, bringing a torrent of dust down with it. Everything smelt musty, but pleasingly nostalgic. A bit like my great-grandmother, but with added notes of linseed oil and less of that 'damp cat and chip fat' aroma. Memories of long bus trips with school teams and hungover car journeys to village grounds with club team-mates flooded back. I half-expected to find an old cheese sandwich and a doughnut from a lovely village tea in one of the pockets.

I pulled my bat from its holder and practised a few strokes. It was lighter than I remembered, and felt smaller in my hands. I found a ball too, rolling around among crispy, decaying gloves, two startlingly enormous boxes and a jockstrap I never remembered owning in the first place.

I picked the ball up between my thumb and forefinger, careful to avoid brushing against the ancient-looking underwear. It felt bloody *enormous* in my hand. (The cricket ball I mean, not the jockstrap. Although that was pretty big. It definitely wasn't mine.) Had cricket balls always been this size? And this bloody heavy? As I held it in my hand, I genuinely doubted I could even chuck this thing 22 yards down a cricket pitch. It looked like someone had painted a medicine ball red and stitched a seam across it. It felt like I was about to try and bowl Graeme Smith's enormous melon of a head.

"You ready?" Josh panted as he bounded into my room, dressed head-to-toe in his old cricket whites, sunscreen smeared across his cheeks.

"That's a bit serious, isn't it, getting the old whites out?" I said as I looked down at my faded football shorts and baggy hooded jumper combo. It didn't scream 'serious cricketer'. In fact, if it screamed anything, it was 'I am a single man who does his weekly shop at the petrol station and eats his dinner from the pan it was cooked in.' Which I was.

"Not at all," Josh replied. "Whites are essential. If people see me playing cricket with you, they are going to assume I am as crap as you are. But by wearing my whites, I will alert any passing spectators to the fact that, while *you* may look like you are playing the game for the first time, I am quite obviously a bit more of a pro."

I nodded. It was sound enough reasoning.

"At the very worst, Ad, people might just think you are some under-privileged kid that I am offering some free coaching to. Or maybe they might think you're a young offender who has been let out of the Institute for an afternoon of exercise."

With that crumb of encouragement ringing in my ears, I heaved my bag onto my shoulder (I should have taken the ten-tonne cricket ball out first) and we set off for the park; the very same place we had cycled to more than 15 years ago.

Much had changed. Everything was cleaner and newer. The swings and slides were still there, but the chain-smoking teens were not. Nor were the rambling drunks. I had even managed to take five paces onto the grass without even *seeing* a dog turd, let alone stepping in one.

We schlepped over to the cricket nets in the top-right corner of the park, which were relievably at a point furthest away from any footpaths or entrances. A railway line ran behind a row of trees at the back of the nets, but any train passing would be travelling too quickly to notice anything untoward. I was on pretty safe ground. I could shame myself in almost complete isolation (something I imagine happens a lot in parks around the country, actually. Although hopefully nothing I did would result in a police caution for public lewdness. My bowling wasn't that bad. I'm not Paul Harris, whose bowling is sometimes so filthy it does look a bit X-rated).

Josh had a strange look in his eye as he began to pad up; a cruel sort of delight about what was to come. I could tell he was expecting something spectacularly bad; a sort of live-action greatest hits package of cricketing bloopers. Basically a typical Mitchell Johnson over, if you like.

"Don't forget the arm guard and the thigh pad," I told him, as he velcroed the second of his two pads on.

"You're joking aren't you?" he giggled. "I'm not even going to wear a box."

"That's a bit risky, isn't it?" I countered, trying in vain to touch my toes by way of a warm-up. I got nowhere near. If humans were meant to touch their toes, man would never have invented the chair. "Don't you remember what happened to Tim Cummings at my school?"

Poor Tim copped a cricket ball right in the crown jewels during practise. He didn't walk straight for a few weeks and it took him years to shake the nickname 'Eunuch'.

"Nah, I'm not worried about that," Josh laughed, "not at the speed you bowl, which I imagine is even slower than it used to be – and it was slow back then. If you manage to hit me in the 'nads it'll probably be closer to pleasurable than painful."

Bollocks to that (as we used to say to Tim in hilariously high-pitched voices). I would show him. I would punish him for this lack of respect. I did a few loosening exercises, whirling my arms around; lunging forward to stretch my legs; arching my back to warm those bowling muscles up. I windmilled through my action. It felt *good*. Maybe it was the fresh air. Maybe it was last night's popcorn kernels I'd eaten off of my chest hair that morning. Whatever it was, I felt *ready*.

Josh, 30 yards away at the end of the net, took his guard. This felt gladiatorial, like two great warriors preparing to do battle. He noisily thumped his bat into the ground in readiness. Before now, all I had done was talk. Actually, all I had done for three weeks was sit around listening to The Eagles. Now, I was taking some serious *action*. This was the start of things. This delivery to Josh was the very moment that my plan to bowl Sachin Tendulkar moved from the realms of fantasy and started, tentatively, to become a reality. This was huge. As huge as that jockstrap in my bag.

"Ready?" I bellowed, shaking the image of the enormous jockies (not the kind that sit on horses, but enormous jockeys would also be quite terrifying) from my mind. I began my run-up; a dozen or so paces, increasing in speed with each step. My mind was oddly clear of thoughts, the gentlest of breezes blowing my hair across my forehead. I focused on the stumps at the other end of the net as I pounded in, my muscles tightening in readiness. I leapt into my bowling action…

"Go Grease Lightning, you're burning up the…"

Josh leapt away from the stumps, frantically waving his hands and gesticulating wildly with this bat, yelling at me not to bowl. Was that the theme from *Grease*?

"Sorry bro…my phone," he said, flinging his batting glove from his right hand before pulling his ringing mobile from his pocket. It was *definitely* the theme from 'Grease'. He took the call.

"Sorry Ad," he added, throwing the handset to me after finishing his conversation. "Here, hold onto this for me. I've put it on silent now."

"Was that the theme from *Grease*, Josh?" I asked tentatively.

"Yeah."

He clearly saw nothing odd about it, and trudged back to the end of the net. *Maybe he'd joined a gang,* I thought. *Or maybe he was a closet John Travolta fan…or Olivia Newton-John?*

"Come on, get bowling," Josh yelled, snapping me back to my senses.

Refocused, I ran in again, huffing and puffing noisily. For some reason, 'Let's Get Physical' by Olivia Newton-John was in my head. I hurled myself forwards, the muscles in my arms flexing and relaxing as I tried to sling the ball towards Josh as quickly as possible. It felt good – a bit awkward, but good, like getting off with your girlfriend's sister (apparently). My head dipped as my momentum took me forward. In an instant, I looked up to see where the ball was headed. It wasn't a pretty sight.

The ball appeared to be floating; just gently floating in the air and not moving. If it was making its way towards Josh, it was doing so at about three miles per hour. It arced and dipped slowly, like a child's balloon bobbing serenely to the earth, and with about as much venom. It finally landed on the turf, with all the force of a proud granny kissing her newborn grandchild for the first time. Josh calmly plonked his bat behind it, sending the ball rolling gently into the side of the net.

"Not a bad loosener," Josh said, tossing the ball back to me.

I stood halfway down the net, my hands on my knees, panting like I had just run a marathon. In fancy dress. Carrying a half-tonne backpack. On the hottest day of the year. I appeared to have broken into a sweat after one ball.

"Come on Ad, maybe the next one will reach 30 miles per hour," Josh laughed. *Excellent.* Now my pride hurt, too.

I slowly trudged back to the end of the net. I took a deep breath and began jogging back towards the crease. Everything ached. Unbelievably, I had totally forgotten just how *physical, physical* (damn you, Olivia Newton-John) an action bowling a cricket ball was. I flung myself towards the crease once more. A passing train honked its horn mockingly – or so it seemed – as I jumped into my bowling stride. Even public transport was taking the mickey now. I felt the eyes of dozens of commuters on me as the ball left my hand.

If anything, it was slower. Slower *and* less accurate. Josh slapped it dismissively into the side netting with some force. More than force, it felt distinctly like it had some gusto behind it.

"That was shit mate!"

I turned around to see two boys, neither more than 12 years old. They were about 20 yards away, and both wearing football shirts and baseball caps. Being a level-headed, mature-thinking man in his mid-20s, I ignored them. I would not stoop to their level and trade insults. I was a man with a degree, my cycling proficiency certificate and a 25-metre breaststroke swimming badge. I was above rising to the insults of stupid, ugly, smelly, rubbish *children*. They'd probably never even kissed a girl. I'd kissed literally *some* women (fifteen, but who's counting…oh right, *I am*) in my time. And I had a car – my own bloody car! I was unequivocally better than them. And taller. Just. In a display of immense maturity, I decided to turn the other cheek.

Actually, I ignored them because they looked utterly terrifying and I didn't want to suffer the indignity of being beaten up by two children whose combined ages were less than mine. But they didn't know that.

"Piss off, you little wankers!" Josh bellowed from away in the distance.

He obviously didn't share my concerns about getting a kicking from a pair of pre-teens, but then he was 20 yards further away with a bat in his hand and head-to-toe in protective clothing.

This was a nightmare. I wanted to turn around immediately and run away from the pain of bowling, but if I wimped out now, the devil children would laugh me all the way home. And if I told Josh I wanted to pack up and head home to escape these loathsome little tykes, I would have looked pathetic. There was only one thing to do. Suck it up, charge in, and bowl a brilliant ball that would prove to them I was *not* shit.

The problem was, I was knackered. I felt like a baddie in a *Scooby Doo* cartoon; my carefully laid plans had been ruined by the unwanted interference of some pre-teen oiks. I would have got away with being crap at cricket if it weren't for these pesky, meddling kids.

I had to bowl again. I returned to my run-up mark and prepared to sprint in, mentally adding my shins to the list of body parts aching from ever-exertion as I did. This must be how Shane Watson felt during every over, I thought to myself. No wonder he always looks like he's in the middle of a back, crack and sack wax.

The kids started a long *'oooooooh'* which got louder as I got closer to the bowling crease. I gritted my teeth and threw every ounce of my energy into getting the ball down to Josh's end of the net as quickly as possible, my fingernails digging into the leather in determination. I grunted loudly with genuine effort as I let go of the ball.

The jeering started a split-second later. My radar had failed me, the ball angling harmlessly wide of Josh and rippling quietly down the side netting, before spinning to a stop beside him. My three deliveries had each been progressively worse than the last. I was, to use a technical cricketing term, *bowling shit.* Or like Mitchell Johnson, if you like.

The youngsters' laughter echoed all around me. But still, I was a man. I remembered all the women I had kissed (fifteen, as I mentioned earlier; keep up). What would they say if they saw me getting bullied by these simple children? I had to stand up for myself. I had to deal with these punks, right here, right now. I strode over, purposefully, with the calm composure of Sachin walking out to the wicket.

"You're shit mate," one of them laughed.

I laughed, dismissively. "Now listen, you two can…"

"Go Grease Lightning, you're burning up the…"

Josh's phone chirruped into action once more, cutting me off mid-sentence. The tracksuited little runts (I said *runts*) exploded, sadly not literally, into violent fits of laughter.

I said nothing. Any pretence I had of standing up to these

pre-pubescents was ebbing away with every extra second the phone rang. If the song got to the bit with all the handclaps, their giggling would break the sound barrier. The smaller, angrier-looking of the two flicked me a one-fingered salute, as the pair of them walked off into the distance. Either that or he was showing me how many brain cells/illegitimate children/ASBOs he had.

"Mate, you're shit at cricket and you've got a shit ringtone too," he bellowed over his shoulder, as the pair of them disappeared into the distance.

He was half right.

PART THREE

Things had undoubtedly got off to a poor start. If my first net session with Josh had been a movie, it would have been *Speed 2: Cruise Control*. You know, the one set on a cruise liner. The one where baddies hid explosive golf balls (yes, *really*) around the ship and refused to open the onboard duty-free shop (not really, they weren't *that* evil). The one that was so terrible, even Keanu Reeves wouldn't star in it.

A week had passed since my dreadful showing in the park. I'd had some time to reflect on what had gone wrong. Unfortunately, and through no fault of my own, I had not magically transformed from 'unremarkable teenage cricketer' to 'world-class 26-year-old bowler' in the years since I had stopped playing competitively. This in spite of maintaining a sportsman's diet of booze and crisps and spending countless hours lying around in the sun. It was hard to know what more I could have done. After all, it had been enough for Phil Tufnell and he'd ended up King of the Jungle, for goodness sake. They gave him a crown and everything.

But more worrying was exactly how bad I was. Bowling, I thought, would be like riding a bike – a painful, largely pointless, outdoor activity I had not done for donkey's years, but one which, after a few moments of uncertainty and a few hours of discomfort, would become second nature again. But in reality, bowling was *exactly* like riding a bike. Both hurt my thighs, bruised my ego and made me look like an idiot. In cricketing terms, my training wheels were back on. My confidence in my bowling was flimsier than Luke Wright's (clearly bogus) claim that he honestly is a professional cricketer and not just some competition winner who keeps getting asked back.

India's tour was due to start in little more than six weeks. I needed urgent help to turn me from a village cricket trundler into something approaching a decent bowler – but it was already June and time was short. I couldn't afford to waste all my time in the nets. Even if I just focused on becoming the best bowler I could be, it could still take weeks or even months before people in the park realised I was actually a decent bowler and not just rehearsing some bizarre interpretive dance or doing my best Ronnie Irani impression (no offence, again, Ronnie).

But likewise, I couldn't just rely on emotion to succeed in this task. I thought back to my days as an obsessive computer gamer; had I completed Resident Evil on the PlayStation (another boyhood dream, for about three weeks) by relying on poxy emotions to get me through? No. I had knuckled down, zoned out and killed some mother-flippin' zombies. Bowling to Sachin was a bit like that. Minus the guns and zombies. Hopefully. I couldn't just wing it. I needed a plan.

In the past, my approach to organising anything in my life had always been a bit *jazz*; all free form and meandering, revelling in the detours and tangents but forgetting where I had started and what I was trying to do. I was the Miles Davis of organisational skills, minus the trumpet and the heroin addiction. Although even he got more done than me when he was getting higher than Chris Tremlett on a pogo stick on the top of the Empire State Building.

My history of organisational cock-ups would have to change. This wasn't my physics GCSE exam (crammed the night before, snuck away with a B grade) or my driving theory test (crammed the night before, failed miserably, *twice*). This was proper. This was the dawn of the new me, the updated and improved, organised and diligent Adam who made plans and then followed through on them.

I sat down at my desk at home that lunchtime, pulled a notepad from the bottom drawer and grabbed a pen in hand. This, I thought to myself, was how some of the most world-changing documents ever written began – the Magna Carta; the Treaty of Versailles; the contract for Graham Gooch to advertise that hair replacement company – they all probably started with just one man and a pen. I slid a mass of papers and receipts to the edge of the desk and threw away an old Mars bar wrapper. It was planning time.

My chewed-up biro hovered over the crisp, white page, like an explorer's muddy boot poised over an untapped plane of snow, ready to make the first footprint on uncharted land. Instinctively, I wrote my name at the top, followed by the date and the number '1'. It seemed the best place to start. Something of a maverick though I am (I make turkey sandwiches using hot cross buns as the bread, for example. I just do not give a shit about the rules), sometimes it's best to stick with convention. This list, like all the best lists, would start at number one.

I stared at the neat '1' in the paper's margin. I leaned back in my chair and eyed the paper curiously, tilting my head to one side to check the neatness of my handwriting. It was, indeed, *very* neat. But somehow, the page still looked a bit empty. I mean, it *was* largely empty, save for my name, the date and a solitary number in the margin, but even so, it still didn't look quite ready to receive a whole flurry of fantastic plans and ideas. I needed a title for this momentous document, something short, pithy and attention-grabbing to really stir the blood and inspire me every time I looked at it. This was important. If the Declaration of Independence had been called 'The Announcement of America's Lovely New

Independence', America would probably have been invaded by Canada by now (which I guess would mean fewer guns but more people speaking French. You really can't win them all).

I pulled a tatty sheet of paper from the drawer beside me and began jotting potential names for my plan down.

'My plan to bowl Tendulkar': No; too simplistic.
'Sachin and Me: How to Bowl out a Legend': Oof, no way. Too dramatic.
'A step-by-step guide to bowling Tendulkar': Nope; too self-help-manual.
'A Nine-Point Plan to Bowl Sachin Tendulkar'…BINGO.

That was it. That was the one. A nine-point plan just sounded right. It looked right on the page. Ten would have been clichéd and any less than nine a bit wishy-washy and unrealistic. No, nine sounded perfect. It sounded official. It just sounded very…*plannish.*

"*Hey, Adam,*" people would say, "*I hear you're trying to bowl out Sachin Tendulkar. Won't that be nearly impossible?*"

"*Not really,*" I would reply, chuckling quietly to myself, "*…because I have a nine-point plan.*" Boom. Straight away, they would know I meant business. I was a man with a plan – a man with a nine-point plan.

I neatly added the remaining eight numbers to the margin and paused to look at the paper again. It looked brilliant; so uniform and organised. I thought about all the years I had wasted thinking only weird people planned things. Planning, I thought, was a relic of the pre-internet age. How could I be expected to diligently organise things in advance when there were videos of cats that can play the piano and skateboarding dogs online? But as it turned out, I was a natural at this planning lark. I treated myself to lunch and looked forward to finishing my epic plan in the afternoon.

I woke up some hours later, my face resting on my hands and a pool of drool attractively forming on the page. I had sat staring at the nearly blank sheet of paper for what seemed like days after lunch, but I had nothing. No ideas. Not one. So far, my plan to bowl Sachin was to, well, just, sort of, bowl him. Somehow. I had the broad concept, but the details were hazy. Actually, the details were non-existent. Either it was writer's block or I had no bloody idea what I was doing. It felt more like the latter. I briefly considered turning to heroin like dear old Miles, but apparently it's a right tough habit to break. I had enough of a problem cutting down on Jaffa Cakes and apparently heroin is way worse than that (and less appetising with a cuppa). Instead, I simply had to face the fact that maybe I wasn't a natural planner, after all. But luckily enough for me, I knew someone who was.

****

The pub was dimly lit but cosy, a quintessentially English boozer where the music and conversations stopped whenever a non-regular walked through the door and, for example, dared to ask for a bottle of pear cider.

As I sat tucked away in the corner of the pub, hesitantly sipping a tepid pint of real ale that really wasn't the crisp, fruity beverage I had tried to order (seriously, I could have walked in and asked for a *hand shandy* and got less of a dirty look – and probably better – ahem – *service*), the doors to the pub swung open suddenly, spearing a shaft of brilliant sunlight through the darkness and stirring the beer-soaked fixtures at the bar into life.

"Hello Dad," said Jono, bouncing over to my table.

Before you start worrying: I am not Jono's dad. Jono is my friend, not my son. I wouldn't even consider adopting him, to be honest. He has very expensive tastes and his real parents would probably be a bit put out that I was trying to usurp them, although after 27 years they may have had their fill. Jono is in fact more than eight months older than me, but for some reason, he insists on calling me 'Dad', which almost certainly is a pretty good sign he is one bobble short of a bobble hat. But right now, I needed his help.

Jono (or 'Dad' to his friends) is a planner at an advertising agency. When he wasn't eating carbon-neutral sushi from an upturned top hat or sitting on an invisible beanbag playing Sonic the Hedgehog on a retro Sega Mega-Drive (I don't know for certain that's what ad agency workers do, but I suspect its basically that every day), his job was to plan things and then make sure those plans were closely followed and completed.

This was perfect. I needed a plan. More than that, I needed a good one and I needed help making sure I got it completed. He must have been alright at his job because he had been doing it for a few years and still hadn't been sacked or forced to relocate or sued for incompetence. That was good enough for me. Jono was my man.

He sat down and took an enormous gulp of his drink. It smelt divine, like a fresh, fruity Swedish forest, or at least the finest synthetic pear flavouring known to man.

"What's that?" I asked.

"Pear cider, Dad," he replied.

"They told me they didn't have any…" I whined, gesturing towards my horrible pint.

"Yeah, you've got to know what to ask for. It's that sort of place."

Already he was showing his worth. His organisational skills meant he actually got served the drinks he wanted in pubs, while I had to sit cradling a glass of 'Old Jimmy's Arsewater' that smelt like it was still fermenting, or possibly even a little bit alive, in my hands.

"Right," Jono said, rubbing his hands together eagerly, "what can I help with?"

"Well, I need you to help me plan something. Something quite big and potentially impossible, but hopefully quite fun, in the end," I told him cautiously.

"Oh. You want to get married," Jono deadpanned, a look

of concern on his face.

"What?" I shrieked. "No. I mean, yes, at some point probably, but no, that's not why..."

"Oh good," he interrupted. "Because I don't think I could help with that."

"No it's not that," I continued, before belatedly, Jono's insult landed. "Hold on Jono; why couldn't you help me find a wife?"

He looked sheepish and sipped his drink. "Well," he muttered, "it's just all the girls I know are a bit...too fit for you." Ouch. My self-esteem. How shallow of him, to think that the girls he knew wouldn't be interested in a dude like me.

"It's not all about looks, Jono," I sniped back through gritted teeth.

"I know," he said apologetically, "but they're all really nice and interesting and successful too."

I thought for a moment. Maybe he was right. They didn't sound like my type at all.

"So," Jono sighed, "what is it that you *really* need my help with?"

I sipped my beer and winced. Jono was a planning expert. If he scoffed at the words *'I want to bowl Sachin Tendulkar'*, it almost certainly meant this was a stupid, un-plannable task. If he thought it was impossible, it probably was.

"Well," I began, "I want to try and bowl Sachin Tendulkar this summer. Because I think I can. Well, I think anyone could, if they could bowl a half-decent ball and just happened to get lucky and..."

"Brilliant," Jono interrupted. "That's amazing. So what's the plan?"

"Ah, right," I stuttered. "Well, to be honest, I don't have one. At all. I'm not much of a planner. Well, I had a nine-point plan, but..."

"What was the nine-point plan?" Jono asked enthusiastically.

"Well it was just an idea," I said, using the word 'idea' very loosely, "but then I realised I didn't have the first point of the nine-point plan sorted yet, or actually *any* of the points, so…" I tailed off. I sounded like an idiot. "I just thought it sounded good. It sounded official. *Nine points*…" I held up nine fingers to illustrate my point. "It just sounded quite… *plannish*."

"*Plannish*?" Jono arched an eyebrow at me. "Yeah. You're right," he chuckled, picking his drink up.

"I *knew* it," I said confidently, "it does sound professional!"

"No," Jono interrupted. "I meant you're right that you definitely need my help." He guzzled down the last dregs of his pint, the ice tinkling merrily around the bottom of the glass as he put it back onto the table.

"Come on, let's go," he said, jumping to his feet.

"Where are we going?" I asked, quite reasonably, I thought.

"To the *Ideas Chamber!*"

Oh no. *Oh no, no, no.* I didn't want to go to the Ideas Chamber, or sit in the Creativity Chair or take a ride down the Innovation Slide; I just wanted a plan.

"Jono mate, I don't…"

"Come on!" he bellowed. "To the *Ideas Chamber!*" he grinned maniacally at me.

My heart dropped. Jono wasn't the answer to my planning problems; he was the harbinger of a fresh kind of hell where everyone rode tiny bikes around the office and read graphic novels about anatomically unrealistic crime-fighting Japanese schoolgirls to get their 'creative juices flowing'. These weren't my people. They didn't watch World War II documentaries or know where Ambridge was.

Suddenly, he broke into gales of laughter.

"I'm joking, Dad! No, we've got to go to another pub because Jim says he won't serve you a pear cider until you've drunk that ale he poured you. He says you have an 'attitude'."

"What?" I scoffed. "He can't do that…"

"Yes, I can!" a voice boomed from some distance behind me.

"He can," added Jono.

"The danger for most of us," Jono whispered, *"is not that our aim is too high and we miss it, but that it is too low and we reach it."*

Happily ensconced in a new pub – a forward-thinking establishment that would actually serve me the drink I wanted – Jono had suddenly turned into a philosopher. He'd always struck me as the sort of bloke who thought 'deep-thinking' was something to do with trying to do long division while snorkelling but apparently, I was wrong.

"Amazing," I smiled. "That's exactly how I feel about bowling Sachin. Obviously, it's a pie in the sky dream, but at least I am trying to achieve something miraculous."

"Michelangelo said that," he replied, proudly.

Jono – a man I once saw urinate in the corner of his own room after a particularly boozy night out – was quoting Michelangelo to me. This was impressive and highly unexpected. He'd even thrown a cheeky Italian accent on to pronounce his name properly, like a real, cultured man of the world. He'd be critiquing America's foreign policy and recommending obscure French films from the 1960s next. It was startling, but I hadn't even seen all the Harry Potter films yet. I didn't want French film recommendations. I wanted a plan to help me bowl Sachin Tendulkar. He sipped his drink and burped loudly. Maybe he hadn't changed that much after all.

"People who say it cannot be done," he continued, *"should not interrupt those who are doing it."* I nodded sagely and sipped my drink. "George Bernard Shaw said that. He won an Oscar, a Nobel prize and helped found the London School of Economics."

An Oscar and a Nobel prize? It put the third-place in Court Lane junior school's long jump competition into a new and depressing context. Maybe it was time to take down the rosette and certificate from above my bed.

Jono narrowed his eyes and looked at me, raising the index finger of his right hand and pointing with purpose at my face.

"Last one," he said intensely, "and it's the best one: *Don't just stand there*; ***do** something*."

It was a very neat, pithy quote. I liked it.

"Goethe?" I asked, groping for the name of *any* philosopher I could think of who might have given the world such a neat quotation.

"No," Jono said, shaking his head.

"Leonardo da Vinci?"

"No."

"Cant?"

"*Dick Dastardly,*" Jono whispered.

"The cartoon character? With the dog?" I squawked back in shock.

"Yeah, Muttley," Jono grinned.

My phone vibrated to life on the table. It was Josh. I ignored the call.

"*I am impressed by…*" began Jono once more, his esoteric pep talk far from finished, before my phone rattled noisily once more on the table. Josh was calling again. I picked up the phone, made my apologies and walked through the pub doors out into the damp central London streets.

"Hello Joshua," I said, curtly.

"Ad, I've got good news!" he raved. "I think I know how you can bowl Sachin!"

Good old Josh; he might have relished how bad I had been in the nets, but here he was finding me a way to bowl Sachin Tendulkar. How brotherly of him. Perhaps he had found a chink in Sachin's game I could exploit? Or maybe he had been thinking about my bowling action and stumbled upon an improvement he thought could change my game overnight?

"I've just been reading about someone called Renate Neufeld," he said. "She was an East German sprinter in the 1970s. She fled from East Germany to West Germany because she said her coaches made her take performance-enhancing drugs."

My mind boggled at the thought of what he had googled to accidentally end up on a page about an East German sprinter from the 1970s.

"Apparently the drugs made her grow a moustache," he continued breathlessly. "And then she married a *Bulgarian* it says here. I wonder if he met her before the moustache or after, because if it was after…"

I tried to interrupt him. I failed.

"I can just picture them standing and both shaving their 'taches off, first thing on a Monday morning…"

I tried to interrupt him again. I failed once more.

"*Do you think we should have matching goatees, darling?*" he trilled in what I guess was the voice of an East German sprinter.

I gave up trying to interrupt him.

"*No!*" he boomed, in a cod-Bulgarian accent. "*I think we should both go with the handlebar moustache my love! It brings out your eyes! You're lovely, manly eyes!*"

"Josh!" I shouted. "What is your point?"

"Oh right yeah, sorry; well its obvious isn't it? The only way you can bowl Sachin is to cheat."

"What?" I snapped angrily. "Are you bloody kidding?"

Josh has always been a creative thinker, but this was taking the piss somewhat. Performance-enhancing drugs? What the hell would he recommend next? What the hell could be worse than this? I had to nip this in the bud and quick, too. I furiously told him that in no way, shape or form would I ever consider taking performance-enhancing drugs. That simply would not happen, ever.

"Calm down, calm down, Ad," Josh said patronisingly. "Of course I'm not suggesting that you take performance-enhancing drugs. That would be illegal, dangerous and just plain wrong. Although your performance is *so* bad that you could take them and people *still* wouldn't notice. And you've never been able to grow a proper moustache, so maybe you should consider it."

I sighed and played with the stubble on my top lip. He was right about the 'tache.

"And maybe you might meet a nice Bulgarian man…" he laughed. I sighed once more.

"Alright," he continued, "joking aside: while that stuff is obviously unforgivable, it did get me thinking about gamesmanship – you know, giving yourself a competitive advantage but within the rules of the game and the laws of the land."

"Like what?" I asked, my interest suddenly piqued.

"I don't know, maybe you could arrange for a streaker to run behind you when you bowl so he gets distracted. That sort of thing. It's not illegal but it gives you an advantage."

"I don't know Josh," I said, shaking my head. "This is cricket. It's a gentleman's game. I either bowl him fairly and squarely, or I don't." But Josh was undeterred.

"What if you made him bat with a really small bat?"

"No, Josh," I said sternly.

"Or use bigger stumps so you have more to aim at?"

"Bye, Joshy," I said matter-of-factly.

"I don't mind being the streaker!" he yelled, as I put the phone down.

I laughed, shook the image of Josh streaking from my head and walked back into the pub. I entered to find Jono sat, head down, feverishly scribbling on a piece of paper. I watched closely as the pen skidded across the page at ferocious speed, his biro circling and crossing out various blocks of text, as his brow became ever more wrinkled in concentration. Whatever he was doing, it looked intense.

"What are you doing, mate?" I asked as I sat down opposite him. He didn't bat an eyelid. It was definitely some very intense work. An angry look of concentration was etched on his face; the same look displayed by Ricky Ponting when he spent a whole net session trying to work out why the formerly bald Dougie Bollinger had turned up to training with Shane Watson's off-cuts perched on his head.

I sat quietly sipping my drink until Jono suddenly emerged from his writing trance, slapping his hand on the table and exhaling loudly as he did.

"Done," he gasped. "Your plan. All finished and ready for your perusal."

He slid the dog-eared sheet of paper across the table towards me. It was littered with scribbles, but through the scrawled, undulating sea of blue biro ink bobbed a list of points, each circled and underlined for clarity's sake.

"It's a bit messy, but that's you," he puffed, "you're not the most organised and we can't change that overnight, so let's work with what we have." I studied the piece of paper carefully. It was the greatest (i.e. only) plan I had ever seen.

1. Just get it done, you dickhead
2. Buy Jono a pint

This was amazing. And look! Only two points! Perhaps nine had been a bit ambitious.

"I haven't made this a prescriptive list of things you have to do – you know, I haven't said '*Monday: Go to the nets and practise bowling*' or anything like that," Jono added. "You need to work out exactly how you are going to get him out, how much you need to practise and how you are going to meet him, all those very important specifics – but this list will make sure you keep on the right path and not jack it all in at the first sign of a setback. Its brilliance is its simplicity. The whole ethos of this idea of yours is that it's impossible and yet possible at the same time, right? So your plan has to reflect that. This plan effectively reminds you that, somehow, by hook or by crook, you just *have* to find a way to do it. That's the only thing you have to remember. You have to take every opportunity that comes your way, exploit every little chance that arises. You need to tell everyone you meet about your Tendulkar quest because you need all the help you can get. But most of all," he said as he ran his finger under the first point of the plan. "you have to '*Just get it done, you dickhead*'. Just somehow make sure you do it. Don't give up like you normally do."

"Is the '*you dickhead*' bit at the end really necessary?" I asked.

"Yeah, definitely," he replied assertively. "You're a bit of a dickhead. Another reason why I couldn't set you up with any women I know." Ah yes, of course.

"Oh, and by the way," he added, "point two applies at all times. It's more of a general rule for life. But that can wait: now you have to sign it."

"Absolutely…" I replied.

"…In **blood**." He said menacingly, his eyes wide.

Blood? Why blood? Why had things suddenly taken a turn for the pagan? This seemed a bit much. That *Twilight* franchise had a lot to answer for.

"Nah, only joking," said Jono, snapping back to his normal, jovial self, "red pen is fine. Unless you want to?" He pulled a Swiss Army knife from his jacket pocket. A look of panic and confusion shot across my face.

"It would only be a little prick," he promised, "something I'm sure you're familiar with…"

"No, really mate," I chuckled anxiously. "Pen is fine."

And with that, I signed. Jono and I shook hands. This was definitely a hand-shaking moment. I was now contractually obliged to try my darnedest to bowl out Sachin Tendulkar. My phone vibrated in my pocket with an incoming text message. I pulled it from my jeans and inspected the screen:

"How about you make Sachin bat with a blindfold on?"

It was from Josh. I quickly tapped out a reply.

"Josh, how is Sachin going to see you streaking if he is wearing a blindfold?"

He didn't text back.

PART FOUR

"Slowly but surely, I think the hard work is starting to pay off," I told Josh as we sat in our local after yet another excellent training session.

He nodded in fairly insincere agreement, his normally perfect hair matted with sweat. I guzzled down my energy drink – yes, an *energy drink;* the only choice for pro sportsmen like me – and felt a warm ripple of self-satisfaction surge through me. Josh took a sip of his drink – a humble, distinctly non-isotonic pint of lager; the preferred choice of most recreational sportsmen – and said nothing. I took it as a cue that he wanted to hear more of my theories on my sudden and substantial improvement from rank amateur to world-beater. That's right. I was, all of a sudden, a flippin' world-beater! I beat worlds like so many eggs in a tub or a dish or whatever it is you beat eggs in (I don't cook. I've never beaten an egg).

It had been seven days since my meeting with Jono, and it was fair to say the events of the previous week had left me feeling quietly confident. Well, I say *quietly* confident. To the untrained ear, my newfound and supposedly low-key self-assurance sounded a lot like noisy, absurdly arrogant bragging. I was a bit like a Home Counties Kanye West in a brand-new cricket jumper, loudly telling the world of my greatness. I was days away from changing my name to 'LL

Cool A' and referring to myself in the third person.

But things were undoubtedly heading in the right direction since Jono thrust 'the plan' into my hands. My bowling had improved immeasurably over the course of just a few net sessions. You know how Liz Hurley famously blossomed from being a scruffy punk in her teens into a glamorous international sex symbol? Well it was exactly like that with my bowling, only thankfully without any of the 'sleeping with Shane Warne' bit. He's not my type. I don't normally go for blondes. Or Australians.

My whole demeanour had changed, too. No longer did I run, huffing and puffing inelegantly to the crease anymore; now I glided along smoothly, with all the grace and power of a champion horse, or at the very least, a well-maintained mid-range Volvo. My action was smooth and rhythmical, like a bald man playing the bongos. I was regularly bamboozling Josh with deliveries that were trickier than a sudoku puzzle printed on a Rubik's cube, tucked inside a bumper book of *Times* crosswords.

"I really think my bowling is in a groove now," I told Josh between sips of my luminous energy drink. "I feel like I understand my action. I think I am really developing as a bowler at the perfect time. Sachin will be here soon and I've never been more confident."

Josh nodded again, adding a non-committal 'hmm' into the bargain.

"I knew I would never be able to develop into a genuinely fast bowler and be able to trouble anyone with speed," I added self-assuredly, "but I think I have started honing some other skills. I mean, my pace is sort of slow-medium – so a bit faster than a normal spinner – but I am still getting some turn. It's sort of a new style of bowling that I'm doing, in a way."

Ah yes, did I fail to mention that, in addition to becoming a beater of worlds, I was also revolutionising the game? It must have slipped my mind. Turns out LL Cool A (oooh, there it is) was also a trailblazer; an innovator; a *genius,* some (mainly me) might say.

Suddenly cricket all felt very natural and obvious to me. At this rate, I'd probably end up bowling at Sachin for England in one of the actual bloody Test matches. By the end of September I would probably have skittled him a few times and cemented my place in the England set-up. The lucrative sponsorship deals would be flooding in before you could say 'Adam Carroll-Smith is the world's greatest bowler and a world-class lover'. Easy. After all, hadn't Michael Beer come from nowhere to bowl for the Aussies in the Ashes? If it could happen for Michael, it could happen for me. (An interesting fact about young Michael: I know for a fact he almost got sacked from his day job in McDonald's after he rang to tell his boss he needed five days off to play for Australia in a Test match. They thought he was lying and told him if he wasn't back in front of that milkshake machine he could hand back one of the stars from his name badge. In the end they took a star off him anyway, but not because he was off work without permission, but because he 'had a perfect chance to kick Shane Watson in the bollards, but didn't take it'. Apparently it was 'an opportunity many Australians would kill for' and he blew it. Poor Michael.)

"You shouldn't drink that after exercise," I told Josh, somewhat – alright, *very* – smugly, as he slurped away at his pint.

"Thanks for the tip," he replied curtly.

I am so professional, I thought to myself. I'd be having ice baths next. Maybe I'd finally find out what a squat thrust was. It had always sounded like an uncomfortable sexual position to me.

"Actually, while we're dispensing advice Ad," Josh said, interrupting my worrying daydream about myself doing something quite unsanitary (and possibly quite bad for my back), "do you know how many bowlers have ever actually bowled Sachin Tendulkar with their *very first ball* to him in his entire international career?"

I didn't, but I was pretty sure Josh didn't know either, so I bluffed.

"Yes, actually," I said dismissively, "it's a surprisingly high number, I think you'll find…"

"It's *one*," Josh spat out brusquely.

Damned brotherly intuition. He knew I was trying to pull a fast one. This was exactly like the time I borrowed his bike, rode it to the park and then got the bus back home, completely forgetting his treasured two-wheeler. My claim that I had 'taken it to a repair shop so they could fix the squeaky brakes' was quickly (and correctly) identified as complete and utter bullshizz.

"I did some research," Josh continued, a note of real relish in his voice. "One person, Ad. In twenty-two years. *One*. And do you know who it was?"

"Ashley Giles?" I said, hopefully. If it was Gilo, I was still in with a chance.

"No," smiled Josh.

"Better or worse than Gilo?" I asked.

"Better," Josh said, quick-as-a-flash. Better than Gilo? Surely such a thing was not possible, unless a cyborg cricketer from the future had travelled back in time and played a few Tests for the Aussies in the early 1990s. Craig McDermott maybe?

"It's Shoaib Akhtar," Josh whispered menacingly.

Oh balls. Not Shoaib Akhtar. Not the bloke who could bowl a cricket ball faster than my car could travel. Not the man responsible for the quickest recorded delivery (a whopping 100.2mph) in the history of cricket. Anyone but him.

"He clean bowled Sachin with his first ball to him, Ad," Josh continued. "It was a 90mph yorker, which was just about impossible to stop. So I think you might need to up your pace a bit."

Ah. Bollocks. This wasn't great news.

"And I'm sure you'll have already read a lot of those pieces on Tendulkar which say his only real weakness – if he even has one – might be against bowlers who are really, seriously quick."

I hadn't read any of those pieces. I'd been too busy watching *Coming to America* again whenever I had a moment to spare. It was fast becoming my favourite movie too. I'd even made a mental note to thank Sachin for converting me into a fan after I'd bowled him out. Maybe he could sign my DVD.

"And obviously being an Indian and growing up on spinning pitches, he's a pretty good player of slow bowlers, too," Josh continued. "But hey, I'm not being negative. I'm just saying my streaker idea isn't looking so bad now. Or the blindfold."

I gulped down the last of my energy drink. Suddenly, it wasn't filling me with a primal, barely containable energy. It looked like someone had emptied the contents of a glow-stick into a bottle. It tasted like it too.

"I'm just giving you some context, Ad," Josh grinned. "Do some research and you'll see not many people have even bowled Sachin out *at all* in the last twenty-or-so years, so don't go thinking a few energy drinks and some good balls that sneak past me will be good enough. Proper bowlers don't just turn up and think '*hmm, I think I'll just run in, bowl a half-decent ball at this batsman and hope he misses*' and they certainly don't rely on some hippie nonsense about leaving everything up to fate and chance – they scrutinise batsmen, look for areas where they're weak – and try to exploit them."

"Yeah, maybe," I responded, breezily.

But there was no *maybe* about it. Josh was right, but the thought of actually looking for weaknesses in Sachin's game made me feel sick. It was like looking for a needle in a haystack, or trying to find a single imperfection on Gemma Arterton (which to be honest, sounded more fun at least, and something I would happily dedicate myself to, if you're reading, Gemma).

"But Josh, if I look into all that, all I'm going to find is that bowling Sachin Tendulkar is basically impossible," I grumbled, accurately.

"That's because it is impossible," he replied. He wouldn't be getting work as a motivational guru anytime soon with shtick like this.

"So why bother then?" I moaned. "Why bother doing a load of research that is just going to confirm to me what I already know and leave me feeling depressed? Why not just put my faith in good luck?"

"Because," he said, suddenly assuming the air of some ancient mystic, "good luck only comes as a result of good preparation."

I scoffed. It sounded like a quote from a self-help manual.

"No, listen Ad, I'm totally right about this," he barked, firmly. "You've been training to give yourself the best chance of at least bowling one straight, right? Well now you need to stop thinking about what you're doing and start looking at what Sachin has done. You need to realise this is a duel, a battle, a *war,* between the two of you. It's time to get 'Rocky Balboa' on this thing."

A duel? Oh bollocks. I'd never even been in a fight before and the closest I'd got to a war was meeting Australia's *Steve* during the 1997 Ashes Test at Headingley. I thought about Rocky Balboa, getting up at 4am, drinking his raw eggs for breakfast and running up all those stairs. I usually preferred a lie-in followed by a Pop Tart. I *always* took the escalator. This wasn't going to work.

It took me two days to muster the courage to turn my laptop on and start analysing Sachin's game. I needed to know more about Sachin's game. I needed to look at the bowlers who had got him out the most and learn from them. I needed to get inside Tendulkar's mind, past all the gibberish about

Eddie Murphy and to the nitty-gritty of his (unparalleled) cricketing strengths and (non-existent) weaknesses. Most of all, I needed to find some proof, some tiny, redeemable shred of evidence that bowling Sachin wasn't completely impossible. Deep down, I knew it was going to be a futile, soul-destroying exercise, but so was listening to Coldplay or watching Formula One and plenty of people did that.

I navigated to Sachin's page on Cricinfo, a veritable treasure trove of statistics on just about every player to have played the game to a meaningful level. There he was, smiling back at me. A mocking, cocky smile of a man who knows he is a genius. It was the sort of smile LL Cool A gave himself in the mirror, before his cruel brother robbed him of his confidence.

Sachin's figures, fairly obviously, were astounding – too staggering to take in all at once. The numbers were just too big; bigger than Xavier Doherty's Test match bowling average and larger even than Inzamam-ul-Haq's body mass index. Almost 15,000 Test match runs, with a mammoth 51 Test Match centuries; more than 18,000 one-day international runs and a gargantuan 48 one-day International centuries. Each of those is a world record, by the way.

I slammed the lid of my laptop shut. What the bloody hell was I thinking? I couldn't argue with figures like that. There was *zero* chance of me succeeding. Even on my best day and Sachin's worst, even if he was holding a cocktail stick and I were bowling at him from six yards away at the speed of light, he'd still manage to keep me at bay. He was *Sachin Tendulkar*, for goodness sake. It *was* impossible. I was wasting my time.

But as I sat softly banging my head on the closed lid of the computer, a strange feeling came over me. I wanted to look at Sachin's figures again. For some reason – probably the same morbid fascination that makes people slow down at the scene of road accidents or support Tottenham Hotspur – I couldn't tear myself away. Maybe it was all those bangs of my head on the computer.

I flipped open the laptop and found my way to a page listing the names of every player who had ever dismissed Tendulkar during his international career. It was like an encyclopaedia of the great and good of the game over the last two decades. And Ronnie Irani (sorry again Ronnie, I just can't help myself).

Familiar performers dominated the top of the list – Brett Lee, in the lead with 14 dismissals in 40 games, was closely followed by legendary name after legendary name. Muttiah Muralitharan, Shaun Pollock, Glenn McGrath and Allan Donald were all among the bowlers who had troubled the Little Master the most during his career. Clearly, it took a high-class performer to trouble Sachin. My heart sank a little more. The closest I had come to a 'high class performer' was when a lady approached me near King's Cross train station in London and told me she could show me 'a good time'. I politely declined and told her I was on my way to see *Stomp*. She laughed and walked off. I can only imagine she knew what I had coming. I felt dirtier after watching those rhythmic binmen than I would have done after an hour in her company, that's for certain.

As I stared at the reams of statistics, I realised Josh was right; hardly anyone had managed to clean bowl Sachin in more than 20 years. King of the gingers Shaun Pollock led the way, but he'd only managed to hit Sachin's stumps three times. *Three.* Knocking Tendulkar's off stump over, as a strange old English teacher of mine used to say about the Moon landings, just did not happen. Oh dear.

My phone vibrated loudly on the table, waking me from a stats-induced snooze a few hours later. The never-ending names of bowlers had hypnotised me to sleep. My phone buzzed again. It was an incoming call from an unknown number.

"Hello?" I said timidly.

"Hello," a calm, monotonous-sounding voice replied.

"Yes, hi…"

"*This is a pre-recorded message from your mobile phone provider,*" it blurted. "*Your bill is now overdue. Please pay…*"

I re-loaded the page of bowler's names as I half-listened to the robot on the phone. "*Press THREE if you would like more information on changing to online statements only*" she bleated. "*Press FOUR if…*"

And then it happened.

I slammed the phone down immediately.

There he was; second from bottom of the entire list.

Number 254 out of the 255 bowlers to have dismissed Sachin.

There he bloody well was!

Roger Whelan.

One match played against Tendulkar, for Ireland.

One dismissal.

Cleanbowled.

And it only took him three balls.

It wasn't one; but it was close enough.

He was my proof that Sachin was human.

He was my proof that just turning up and bowling Sach was possible.

He was also proof that Josh was right, but I could forgive him that.

Roger Whelan, you *beauty*.

I clicked through to his profile on the Cricinfo site. Roger, it turned out, had only played two international games for Ireland, both in 2007, and taken two wickets. I chuckled at the thought that Sachin Tendulkar accounted for fifty per cent of his wickets at the highest level. The briefest of biographies had been written beneath his figures.

"*Roger Whelan, a brisk opening bowler, made his ODI debut for Ireland against India in 2007 and claimed Sachin Tendulkar as his first scalp.*"

So far, so impressive.

"...But at the end of the summer he announced his retirement, not only from international cricket but from the game entirely."

What? Retired?

"...When he's not on the field he's the lead singer for The Stimulants."

This had to be a wind-up; an elaborate practical joke set up by my brother, or something. What sort of cricketer quits the game just months after dismissing the greatest batsman of the modern age to start a band? I'm pretty sure Geoffrey Boycott never took a sabbatical from the game in the late 1970s to play bass guitar in *The Stranglers*, and David Gower definitely did not moonlight as the drummer in *Squeeze* when he wasn't captaining England. Lead singer? *The Stimulants?* It was fair to say Roger wasn't your typical cricketer.

But that, it struck me, was exactly the sort of cricketer I needed. Roger was just a chancer. He hadn't dedicated his entire life to cricket; that wasn't how he'd managed to bowl Sachin. He'd managed to bowl him because he was a talented guy – but mainly, because it was his lucky day. He was the missing piece of the puzzle. I had to find him.

By now, it was the early hours of the morning. Some gentle rain was tip-tapping against my window as I stared at my laptop. A pot of tea steamed away by my side, my face half-lit by my green anglepoise lamp. I felt like a modern-day Sherlock Holmes burning the midnight oil in pursuit of some vital clue. It was all very Dickensian and terribly romantic, if you ignored the fact I was also listening to Girls Aloud and eating a packet of Quavers. I doubt Sherlock ever ate Quavers. He was probably more of a Rib n' Saucy Nik Naks kinda guy.

If I wanted to find Roger, I had to find 'The Stimulants'.

I imagined they sounded a bit like an Irish Oasis (*O'Asis*, if you like. You don't? Fair enough) – all big choruses, laddish posturing and beer-soaked leather jackets. I preferred ponderous post-rock, pretentious hip-hop (and Girls Aloud) but nonetheless, it was a good name; a solid moniker for a rock n' roll band.

Unfortunately for me, literally 1,456,922 other bands (alright, not literally; it was about a dozen) thought so too, and had also decided to plump for '*The Stimulants*' as their name. I had no choice but to work my way through them.

The first, from a tiny town in Gloucestershire called Cinderford, described their music as sounding like 'shit hitting the fan', which must make their gigs an unpleasant experience, certainly for the people in the first few rows. A couple of the band members had Mohican haircuts. They all looked about 12 years old and not very much like former international cricketers. One of their songs was about a horse sedative called ketamine. This probably wasn't the band I was looking for.

The next batch of *Stimulants* described themselves as 'snot rock', which sounded less like a genre of music and more like something a particularly disgusting but organised schoolboy would amass over the course of a few weeks before throwing at his sister. A *snot rock*. A big rock made of his snot. Gross. I turned Girls Aloud up a bit louder. I was in uncharted waters. I clicked on their website; but these *Stimulants* were an all-girl group. My Sherlock-like detective instincts told me this probably wasn't the right band. None of the girls looked like a 'Roger'. Well, one of them did, but I'm not mean enough to say which. (Alright, the blonde one.) Satisfied at my powers of deduction, I moved on.

The third *Stimulants* were an African-American rap duo. Being a fairly bright, intelligent guy, I worked out this wasn't Roger's band within a paltry ten minutes. Too many things just didn't add up. But ever the professional, I played one of their songs just to be on the safe side.

The lyrics boomed out of my laptop speakers: *"Keep it tight within my clique / Know just who you fuckin' with…"*

My final doubts were gone. This was definitely not Roger's band. There isn't a great crossover between the rap world and the cricketing world. For a start, it's quite hard to look like a gangster in whites and it's almost impossible to pull the trigger on an AK-47 wearing wicket-keeping gloves. And very few words rhyme with 'googly'.

As I pondered starting a cricket rap band and wondered if anything actually did rhyme with googly (frugally? *'Batsmen score frugally off my googly?'*), I found them, buried away among hundreds of search results. The *real* Stimulants, an unsigned band from Dublin. It had to be them. I clicked a link, which took me to a plain white webpage.

The Stimulants is an unsigned Band from Dublin, Ireland. They focus on Rock / Indie / Acoustic music. Their band members include: Roj Whelan - Lead Guitar / Lead Vox…

There he was. I knew he wasn't a rapper. He couldn't have been a rapper. Not with a name like Roger.

I scanned the band's biography and sure enough, there was even a mention of a 'famous cricketer' being among their number. This was it, alright – this was *the* Roger Whelan. But what I needed now was an email, a telephone number, a Facebook page – anything that might help me to track down Roger. But how would I find that?

Well, quite easily, as it turned out. There in the corner of the page, winking provocatively at me was an email address for Roger's sister Babs Whelan, the band's manager.

This Sherlock Holmes investigative stuff was easy. I hadn't even had to smoke any opium or strike up a subtly homoerotic friendship with a sidekick called Watson to get to the bottom of the great 'Where is Roger Whelan?' mystery. Did that make me better than Sherlock Holmes? I guessed so.

I scribbled Babs' email address down furiously, opened my emails up and started elatedly writing her a message. I typed like a man possessed. Roger already felt like the missing piece of the puzzle.

"Hi Babs, my name is Adam.
Sorry for the randomness of this message, but I am trying to get in touch with your brother, Roger. I would really like to pick his brains about his cricket career, because I think he could help with something I'm trying to achieve. Basically, I am trying to bowl Sachin Tendulkar this summer. I'm not 100% sure why, but I definitely am now. I've signed a contract with my friend Jono and everything.

I need Roger's help – he's been there and done it. Everyone keeps telling me bowling Sachin Tendulkar is impossible, but Roger knows first-hand that it's not. I really feel like he could make all the difference between success and failure.

Anyway, thanks for reading. If you could pass my email address on, or point me in his direction on Facebook or something, that would be absolutely fantastic.
Cheers! Adam."

Sixty seconds later, an alert flashed up on my screen. It was a new email. Blimey. A new email, *already*. There was only one person it could be from, surely. This was a new email from Babs. I just knew it. It was a new email from Babs with Roger's contact details. It just had to be.

I started a little drum-roll with my fingers on the edge of the desk. This was it. This was the moment I would move one step closer to meeting Roger Whelan.

Ah, Roger, I thought, as my emails loaded.
Roger, my spiritual guide on this quest to bowl out Sachin;
Roger, my learned Sherpa who had already achieved the impossible;
Roger, who would tell me how I could follow in his footsteps;

Roger, the…

Ah, no.

Shit.

A bounce-back.

Babs' email address 'was not recognised'.

Bollocks.

This is like Christmas 1993 all over again.

(Dad broke my new Scalextric. He spilt Baileys on it.)

Spirit crushed.

Dreams dashed.

Teapot empty.

Laptop off.

Back to reality.

Damn you, Roger Whelan.

And you, Babs.

****

Fruitless email correspondence #1

TO: ONE OF SACHIN'S SPONSORS (names have been withheld to protect the unhelpful/unresponsive)

Dear Sir/Madam,

My name is Adam Carroll-Smith and I am emailing you to see if you may be able to help with a unique project I am undertaking this summer.

In a nutshell (figuratively speaking, of course), I am attempting to fulfil a childhood ambition to bowl one ball at the great Sachin Tendulkar. It really is as straightforward as that.

As one of Sachin's sponsors, I wondered if you might be able to help put me face-to-face with the Little

Master. I promise I shall endeavour to buy some* of your fine products in return (even though I must admit they are not to my normal taste).

Many thanks,

Adam

*I am not a wealthy man and by 'some' I mean roughly £10-£15 worth, though at a push I could go to £20.

RESPONSE: None. I think it was the sly dig at the quality of their products at the end.

****

PART FIVE

"Hey Ads, have you seen this?"

My flatmate Tim thrust a crumpled-looking newspaper under my nose, before dropping it onto the table in front of me. A dog-eared corner of the page slowly unfolded and flopped apologetically onto my plate, landing square in my freshly peanut-buttered toast.

I checked the date. It was June 26th. I had spent the past few weeks frantically emailing and calling anyone with the merest association with Sachin – from his sponsors to the Indian cricket board, and everyone in between – begging them to help me get closer to the great man. Sadly, no one was replying.

My bowling had plateaued, too. Somehow it all felt like Roger-bloody-Whelan's fault. My spiritual guide, my scientific proof that the impossible was possible was still proving painfully elusive.

But now, plonked in front of me, lay an enormous picture of Roger Federer, the five-time Wimbledon tennis champion. I wasn't sure quite why Tim had excitedly dropped it on top of my breakfast.

"Look!" he screeched, jabbing frantically at the page.

Federer (who really does look like the bastard lovechild of Andrew Strauss and alleged comedian Jimmy Carr) was talking to a short, doughy-looking Indian man in a suit and aviator shades. I recognised the smile instantly.

"It's bloody Sachin Tendulkar at Wimbledon, talking to Roger Federer," said Tim. "He's bloody here, in England. Here in bloody England right bloody now!"

"Yeh," I replied nonchalantly. "Great."

I could feel Tim's eager eyes peering intensely over the top of his glasses, boring into the side of my head, in expectation of an outpouring of emotion, or at the very least, some recognition of just what a momentous occasion this was. He could have been excused for expecting more of a reaction. This, after all, was my first sighting of Tendulkar on English soil. I cleared my throat, inhaled deeply and turned the page.

"Ah, snooker," I muttered quietly to myself. I furrowed my brow and skimmed my finger along the page, feigning interest in the story until Tim turned on his heel, shouted a half-hearted goodbye and left for work.

I craned my neck to listen for the sound of the front door slamming shut. As soon as I heard it crash closed, I snatched up the paper and turned back to the picture of Sachin and Roger.

I had seen thousands of pictures of Sachin, of course – his permanently cheerful grin was indelibly etched on my mind after so many years of hero worship. But as I stared intently at the photograph, I felt my face toughen into a scowl.

Somehow, it was as though a little switch had been flicked inside me. The cheeky, youthful face in the photograph was not that of my boyhood idol. I was no longer just a fan happily looking at a picture of his favourite batsman. This was a picture of a man who, very soon, I would be trying to bowl, a photo of my adversary for the next few weeks, whether he knew it yet or not. He was the Clubber Lang (minus the Mohawk) to my Rocky Balboa.

I felt a curious mixture of anxiety and excitement, as though this was the moment I had been both waiting for and dreading. Sachin had landed. His tanks were metaphorically parked on my lawn. Operation Bowl Out Tendulkar was now fully underway. This was T-Day. It'd be all over by Christmas (that's a World War II joke, ostensibly just for my Dad, so apologies to the rest of you for it), but now it was just starting in earnest. He was *here*.

Suddenly, everything was real. I pushed my toast away, disdainfully. This was no time for *toast*. I needed carbohydrates and protein. At the very least, I required something with the word 'Power' or 'Ultra' or 'Mega' in the brand name. Finally, it was the 'punching slabs of meat, drinking raw eggs and running up lots of steps like Rocky' stage of my training, or whatever the cricketing equivalent of that was. Maybe some bicep curls with a couple of cricket bats? Or star jumps wearing a batting helmet? Either way, that time was *now*. It was time to turn off the Toto and crank up some 'Eye of the Tiger'.

I drained the last dregs of my tea (it was still 'the time' for tea. The raw eggs could wait a little while) and sprinted upstairs. I rifled through my laundry basket in search of my cricket shirt, eventually pulling it free from a mass of tangled socks and boxer shorts. It smelt stale, festering as it was with the sweat from my last net session. It smelt like *victory*. I stuffed it, along with the rest of my kit, into an overnight bag. I picked up my phone and punched in Josh's number. I paced my room with all the angry impatience of Geoffrey Boycott waiting to voice a prejudice (probably against Michael Yardy) while Aggers does something as trifling as tell people the score.

"Hello?" Josh answered. It sounded as though he had just woken up.

"Josh, get your cricket stuff," I barked.

"What? Why?"

"Sachin is here," I said shrilly.

"In Portsmouth?" he said, sounding discombobulated.

"No, Wimbledon. He met Roger Federer," I explained.

"The tennis player?"

"No, the world-renowned fisherman," I scoffed, "...of course the tennis player!"

I could hear the gears whirring in his head. Maybe it had been too early for sarcasm.

"A fish...what?"

"Forget that Josh, just concentrate and listen to me," I growled. "It's *on*. It's happening. Sachin Tendulkar is finally in the country. I need to be ready to bowl at him at a moment's notice. Who knows when my opportunity might come? I need to become a finely-tuned cricketing machine, and I need to become one *right now*. It's like you said. It's time to break out the Rocky Balboa shit. It's time to move to Phase Two."

Phase Two? I wasn't even aware that there had been a Phase One of this scheme. Still, it sounded urgent and important. And these were urgent and important times.

"Sachin is here, Josh," I continued eagerly. "I need to be ready. Clear your schedule. It's time to get intense, like, like..." I groped for a comparison. "Like, you know that film, *A Clockwork Orange*?"

"Yeah..." Josh yawned.

"That film was intense, right?"

"Oh yeah, that film was *intense,*" Josh said, intensely. With intensity in his voice.

"Exactly. Well imagine that," I told him, "but with less milk and codpieces and weirdness and more cricket." Josh thought for a moment.

"Come on!" he yelled. "Let's do it! Let's put the petal to the metal!"

"The *petal* to the metal?" I spluttered.

"Yeah. It's a phrase, Ad," Josh said coolly. "It means like, now is the time to stop smelling the girly flowers and start squashing them...under some big manly metal. Grrr!"

I politely told Josh he might have been mistaken as to the meaning – and indeed, the wording of the phrase. I explained that, in actual fact, the phrase was '*put the pedal to the metal*'

– and that it referred to the action of putting one's foot right down on the accelerator pedal of a car, in an act of urgency, rather than to the strange practise of squishing flowers under non-descript blocks of metal.

The phone line temporarily went quiet.

"Is there really a famous fisherman called Roger Federer?" Josh asked, timidly.

I stifled a giggle. The line went quiet once more.

"There probably aren't that many rivers in Switzerland," he reasoned.

"The cricket nets in 45 minutes, Josh. Don't be late. I'm meeting someone later."

****

"Here you go mate," said Dave, plonking a pint of Guinness down in front of me, as I wiped the post-net session sweat from my brow. "Let's have a toast to Alfie Jacob. Ten weeks old today."

Dave, one of my best friends since the age of 11, had just had a baby. Well, if you want to be precise, his fiancée Stef had just had a baby, but from what I understand of the child-making process, he was quite heavily involved at one key point, at least. I'm almost certain Stef couldn't have realistically done it without him.

Understandably, Dave was excited. Stef was excited. I was excited. Alfie was less excited. He was asleep in his stroller, parked next to our table. But if he had been awake he would definitely have been excited by all the excitement he was creating. Although he might not have understood why his dad was quite so pleased to have got a pint of lager for under £2.50.

"Congratulations guys," I said, clinking my glass against Dave's and Stef's. "You must be so proud."

"Yeah. I can't believe it," Dave beamed. "Well, obviously I can believe it, because Stef has been pregnant for nine months, but you know what I mean…"

He sipped his beer and shook his head ruefully. I'd never seen him shake his head ruefully before. Perhaps this was a symptom of parenthood. Pretty soon he'd be wearing sensible shoes and moaning about the schools in his catchment area.

"So, what do you think of him then?" Stef asked.

I peered over the top of his buggy and looked down at little Alfie. There he was, sound asleep, his fists tightly clenched and his eyes firmly shut. He looked adorable, like someone had drawn a smiley face on a partially squeezed jam doughnut. A little smile spread across his tiny little pink face.

"That's probably him having a shit," Dave added, somewhat breaking the broody mood.

"He looks absolutely adorable, Stef," I cooed. "He looks like the best kid in the world."

And he really did. (And still does.) I'd seen kids before, but not one that anyone I knew had made. It felt like an actual achievement, a real feat of human construction and genetic engineering that this little chap was here at all. Stef beamed and coochy-cooed her little newborn boy's chubby cheeks. It was amazing how quickly they both seemed to have settled into their role as parents. It was all a bit emotional. Or maybe it was just how brilliantly cheap the booze was (£2.40!!!). We all clinked our pint glasses together again.

"He looks like me, doesn't he?" Dave said, proudly.

"He absolutely does," I agreed. "A very handsome young man."

Stef scoffed.

"Well, I meant that he's a bit chubby and bald, but thanks," said Dave.

"Right then Alfie," Stef said, "let's leave Daddy to it, shall we? He needs to get very drunk and then come home very late and wake us both up, doesn't he?"

Dave kissed Stef and Alfie goodbye and waved them off from the front of the pub. Now the proper celebrating would begin.

Dave and I had been drinking and laughing together for 15 years and over that period of time, nights out begin to follow a very precise but enjoyable formula. Shots of horrible, syrupy alcohol would be lined up and seen off. The ridiculous 'Lime-Eye' (don't ask) would be played at some point in the evening. We would stagger around the streets for a while, reminiscing about the time Dave had to be stopped from eating dog poo 'for a bet' or the time he stole a saxophone from the wall of a pub, before setting ourselves down in a curry house for a drunken dupiaza. This was our idea of fun.

We had celebrated news of new girlfriends, new jobs and new homes like this, but somehow, tonight felt different. It felt more significant, as though we should shun the routine of the past and instead settle down with a bottle of port and some cigars. Maybe even some olives or those nuts covered in that Japanese spice that sounds like a long-lost ninja discipline.

I began telling Dave this. He nodded silently, his eyes narrowing in concentration as I spoke about the importance of this moment. *What a good friend I am*, I thought to myself. Maybe this would even bag me favourite uncle status with baby Alfie.

We were toasting the most life-changing experience of his life, I told him. This was no time for bog-standard frivolity or the same old cheap booze and even cheaper thrills. This, I told him, was a time to really reflect on the enormity of what had just happened to him and celebrate in memorable fashion. Then he started snoring.

I gently jabbed the forearm he had fallen asleep on. He jolted awake noisily, almost knocking his beer flying.

"Sorry," he slurred. "Turns out it's *really* exhausting being a dad. He hasn't mastered the idea of a 'lie in' yet and shits almost constantly. I thought I was bad, but his poos smell like he's been eating fish-heads and pepperami. What were you saying?"

I told Dave of my epic little speech.

"Absolutely," Dave interrupted, as the phrase '*most life-changing experience of your life*' left my lips. "I really fancy a curry later…a dupiaza. But lets start with some shots first."

I stood up and began walking to the bar. Maybe Dave was right. Even though this was a big moment, perhaps it was best we stuck to what we knew best.

"Ad!" he bellowed.

I knew it. My stirring speech had punctured his subconscious as he dozed in front of me. I momentarily wondered if I had ever even drunk port before. I scanned the bar for olives or those spicy Japanese nuts – or were they actually peas? – either way, we would need such adult snacks now we were grown-ups. Gone were the days of cheesy Wotsits. I practised my pronunciation of 'pistachio'. *Piss-tash-ee-oh.* Textbook.

"Get some limes as well, yeah? Let's play Lime-Eye…"

Maybe I had been a bit premature.

"…And some Wotsits."

And so, in time-honoured fashion, we celebrated. Before long, our eyes were stinging from repeated exposure to jets of squirted lime juice (I told you not to ask) and our stomachs groaned for curry. Surprisingly, it all felt rather good.

"Who would have ever thought I would be a dad at 26?" Dave mumbled, grinning broadly.

"I know. It's insane. I still can't even use the washing machine," I hiccuped. "And to be honest, I'm still not entirely sure which one out of 'left-wing' politics and 'right-wing' politics is the nice one. I know one of them is broadly good and liberal, but it's also the one that Madonna likes, so swings and roundabouts. But I think all dads should at least know that. I don't think I'm ready for a kid."

"Nah, you're probably not," Dave agreed. "But it's alright; you probably won't have to worry about being a dad yet. You need to find a woman to have sex with you first if you want to have a kid," he joked.

Dave could make jokes like that now. He had fulfilled his biological function in the world. He was now so grown up, he probably didn't even giggle at the flavoured condom machines in pub toilets anymore.

As I returned to our table after a trip to the gents, chuckling to myself at the curry-flavoured condoms (and wondering why they weren't sold in a two-pack with 'rice' or 'poppadom' flavour – and if the person whose job it is to taste-test them has the worst job in the world) I noticed an old man with a silver beard and straggly silver hair had sloped over to our table. He looked a bit like Bruce Forsyth, if Bruce had spent the last thirty years taking strong hallucinogens and living in a tent in a forest, eating wild berries. So not much like Bruce Forsyth, really. He did have a big chin though, mind you. I think that was all it was. The chin.

Bruce (as we quickly christened him, imaginatively) stood staring at us for a moment or two, completely silent. I noticed he was wearing a reflective jacket underneath his heavy coat.

"Which one of you lads is celebrating?" he asked, in a surprisingly posh accent.

"He is," I replied, pointing at Dave. "Well, we both are, but he…"

"Ah, of course; happy birthday, son," he said warmly. "I knew from looking at you it was your birthday. You're a classic Gemini."

"It's not his birthday," I replied. "He's just had his…"

"DON'T…tell me," Bruce interrupted. "I don't want you to tell me. I'm a little bit psychic, you see, so I don't need you to tell me."

"OK," I replied, as neutrally as possible. I resisted every urge in my body to wipe away the fleck of spit he had just showered onto my forehead. All the same, I found him fascinating.

"Ah, I see now. *You* are the Gemini," Brucie continued, jabbing a wonky-looking finger in my direction.

"No, I'm not a Gemini," I smirked.

"Sagittarius?"

I shook my head.

"Libra?"

Another quick shake of the head followed.

"Ah, you're a Leo, then?" he mused, with unjustified self-satisfaction.

I nodded. Four guesses was three too many to qualify as a psychic in my book.

"And you're an only child, aren't you?" Brucie continued. He clearly thought he was on a roll now. Sadly he wasn't.

"Ah, but you're the youngest of three…four…only child?" he guessed, as I continued to shake my head with increasing agitation.

"I have one brother," I told him, putting him out of his misery.

"And he's an older brother, isn't he?" Brucie smiled.

He's not. He's three years younger than me. Brucie, I surmised, was no flippin' psychic.

"OK," he stroked his chin thoughtfully. Either that or he was sweeping it for the remnants of his dinner. "You're fluent in a foreign language, aren't you? Now don't tell me you're not fluent in anything. Is it French? German?"

"I'm not…" I stammered, but Brucie was on a roll.

"Spanish?" he asked hopefully.

I booted Dave under the table, stirring him awake with a jolt. He opened his eyes wide and looked at me quizzically.

"Cantonese, maybe?" Brucie pondered.

"Dupiaza!" Dave snapped. He'd taken Brucie's guess at my second language as an unwanted restaurant recommendation. Nothing was going to stand between Dave and a curry.

"Yes. Definitely, Dave," I said, standing up from the table. Dave followed suit. Brucie looked at me, with a look of genuine confusion on his face.

"Dupiaza, Brucie," I offered by way of explanation,

shrugging my shoulders.

"It's Italian for '*we have to leave*'," interrupted Dave, quick-as-a-flash. "We're both fluent."

"Are you?" Brucie asked, puzzled.

"Erm…*si,*" said Dave.

"Absolutamente," I added. It sounded Italian enough.

The local curry house had been there for decades and looked like it hadn't seen a new lick of paint since its grand opening. It was the sort of place that felt cramped even with no one inside. And nobody, besides Dave and I, was. We ordered our standard dupiazas, peshwari naan breads and poppadoms in almost complete silence, just the odd prang of cooking utensils and gentle Indian music from two tiny, tinny speakers filling the air. It had been a long, boozy night. Both our heads were swimming from ten too many.

"Hey, I saw Sachin was at Wimbledon yesterday," Dave said. "So he's really here now, eh? How's it all going?"

My net session with Josh earlier that day had been a *disaster.* It had been almost two weeks since my email to Babs had bounced back. My faith was wavering. My positive mental attitude had given way to a desire to forget all about cricket and sit in my boxer shorts watching *Columbo* and eating bag after bag of pretzels. I had stopped paying attention to Jono's plan. I hope you don't think any less of me, but faced with a bit of resistance, I was floundering. Things weren't going my way and I was sulking.

"Oh, I don't want to talk about it," I replied instinctively.

The sound of the chefs arguing suddenly blew into the room as the kitchen door swung open violently. We went back to drunken, sleepy silence.

"That old boy in the pub was funny, wasn't he?" Dave gargled, half-awake.

"He shouldn't be doing that sort of thing," I burbled, petulantly.

"What do you mean *that sort of thing?"* Dave chuckled.

This was embarrassing. Dave had spent the last two months changing nappies and building cots and learning how to be a father. I had spent them practising my bowling action in my bedroom while listening to 'Sultans of Swing' by Dire Straits (another Tendulkar favourite, natch) at full blast and annoying press officers at most of Sachin's sponsors. Now I was sulking because a strange man I had just met in a pub, who claimed to have psychic powers, had not magically told me I was going to play a sport he probably had no interest in, with a man he had almost certainly never heard of. But then, we've all been *there*.

"I thought he was going to say something about this Tendulkar thing," I hurriedly confided in Dave. I hated saying the words out loud, almost spitting them out in embarrassment.

"What, you thought he was going to ask you if the initials 'ST' meant something to you?" Dave laughed, sympathetically.

"Maybe. A bit. Yes. Exactly that, actually," I nodded. "I thought he might have been a sign from the universe that this Tendulkar thing is going to come off."

Dave scoffed.

"Listen," he said, sipping at his pint. "You can't sit around and expect the world to give you clues and signs that you're doing the right thing. It doesn't work like that. If I had waited for some proof that I was ready to be a dad, I would still be waiting, and waiting for a *long* time. Stef and I didn't take the plunge because we were both certain we were ready, or that we ever would be. We did it because we *wanted* to have children together and that is the *only* place to start from."

The waiter swooped into position, polishing plates and dumping huge mounds of steaming curry onto the table.

"Why are you sitting around getting uptight because you aren't getting enough nods and winks that you are doing the right thing?" Dave continued, ignoring the smouldering food in front of us. "If you really want to achieve this, you have to work for it. Happy coincidences don't always just fall into your lap. You are not going to bump into Sachin's mum in Tesco and have her hand over his mobile number. Mad old men in pubs are not the answer either. Sachin is here now. He is in the country. Now is when it all properly starts. You've done the build-up, now the fun starts. *Just get it done.*"

The gentle Bhangra music in the restaurant rose to a rousing crescendo as Dave's tub-thumping speech reached its stirring apex. Actually, they'd switched the radio onto Heart FM, and 'Dancing Queen' by Abba was playing. But you get the point. I sipped my beer, astonished. I almost welled up a bit – although that may have been the after-effects of one too many games of Lime-Eye.

"Jono said something very similar, actually," I admitted. "Only he called me a dickhead at the end."

Dave *hmm*-ed irritatedly. "Yeah," he chortled to himself, "I probably should have done that too: *Just get it done, you stupid dickhead.*"

"Jono just called me a dickhead," I moaned quietly, "not a *stupid* dickhead."

"Yeah," nodded Dave, "but I've known you longer."

We loaded up our plates and got stuck into the meal. After a few silent mouthfuls, I told Dave about Jono's dismissive reaction when he thought I was trying to enlist his help in finding me a wife.

"It was weird," I said, chomping through a gobful of food, "but he said he was relieved I *wasn't* asking for his, because…"

"…Because all his female mates are *really* good-looking?" Dave interrupted. "And interesting and successful?"

"Yeah…" I said meekly.

"Yeah, not your type. But anyway, what are the latest developments, Sachin-wise?" Dave asked enthusiastically.

I shrugged off the slur against the fifteen women (remember?) I'd snogged in my life and began to tell Dave about Roger Whelan – about how this wonderful man had played one game against Tendulkar for Ireland and managed to bowl him with his third ball. I eulogised about rock star Roger like I was his biggest fan. In some ways, I probably was. I told Dave of my hopes that some day soon, Roger – a man who had been there and done what hoped to do – might be my Sherpa on this impossible task.

"The only trouble is," I said, pulling my phone from my jeans and opening up my emails, "I emailed his sister but the email bounced back, see?"

I handed Dave the phone.

"I feel like I really need to speak to him," I added desperately. "I don't think I can do this without his help."

Dave chewed another mouthful and read the email. He cleared his throat and passed the phone back to me.

"W-E-H-L-A-N." Dave spelled the letters out methodically.

"What?" I muttered.

"You can practise your bowling as much as you want," Dave said jocularly, "but finding Sachin and working out how to bowl him is going to be much harder if you can't spell. You spelt Babs' email address wrong."

I held the phone in my hand, open-mouthed in shock. The waiter swooped over to our table, a Cheshire cat grin plastered across his face.

"Is everything alright for you, sirs?" he asked, imploringly.

I sat, stock-still, staring into space. I turned my head to meet the smiling waiter's gaze.

"Is everything to your liking, sir?" he asked again.

"I'm going to bowl Sachin Tendulkar this summer," I said, utterly gormlessly, but correctly. I bloody well *was* going to bowl him.

PART SIX

It was the morning after the night before. My bedroom was sweleringly hot, the air thick and stale. I felt like I had been zipped up all night in a cricket bag that had been left out in the middle of the Wankhede Stadium in 100-degree heat. I smelt a bit like I had, too. My bed sheets were damp with sweat and my hair was plastered across my forehead in a style that has not been fashionable since the days of the Third Reich. My mouth was drier than Steven Wright telling a joke about the Sahara with a mouthful of Ryvita, and tasted like pure regret, too (a mixture of Blue WKD, cold chips and a cola-flavoured Chupa-Chups lolly bought from a nightclub toilet attendant for about £11.40). I felt like I'd gone ten rounds (of triple vodkas) with Andrew Symonds. It felt like a futuristic dog made entirely of hammers and cannons (it could happen – people thought the iPod would never happen) was running around my hungover head. Even my eyelashes felt sore.

Put simply, it was a hangover and a half and it was, of course, nobody's fault but my own. Actually, technically it was *Alfie's* fault for stirring Dave and I into such a celebratory lather. I thought about calling Dave and telling him to give his son a ticking off but it didn't feel right to blame a ten-week-old baby for this predicament. I'd have to find a way to pin the blame on Ravi Bopara, as I normally did with most things.

I hauled myself out of bed, tip-toeing around a makeshift hopscotch court of abandoned clothes and empty bottles of water. I kicked at each container in the hope of hearing the splish-splosh of liquid inside, but none obliged. Hot and bothered, I wrenched my curtains apart. A dazzling rush of sunlight streamed into the room and the roaring heat of a beautiful day surged uncomfortably over my face. I gingerly heaved open my window and dropped to my knees to allow a rush of cool air to lap at my face. I exhaled noisily in relief, much to the surprise of the woman walking her dog on the pavement below. It's not often you see a half-naked man with his head out of his bedroom window, panting like an over-heated puppy. Even in Brighton.

The seagulls, a permanent squawking menace outside, swooped and danced past my window, each angry 'ka-kaw' rattling my hungover head. I hadn't felt this uncomfortable since I went inter-railing as a teenager and had to share a carriage on an overnight train with an enormous Russian man (shaved head; ominous chipped front tooth; looked like a strategically-shaved grizzly bear) and his fierce-looking girlfriend (bigger biceps than me; evil laugh; spitting image of Daniel Craig with breasts). They fed each other an assortment of pickled meats and appeared to be on the verge of having full-blown intercourse at any moment. It was a tense 14 hours, but somehow, this was worse.

A gentle rat-a-tat-tat sounded on my door.

"Can I come in?" It was Tim. I forced out a vaguely affirmative groan.

"Is that a yes?" he asked softly in his dulcet (ha!) Lancashire tones.

"Yes," I replied, half-heartedly, clearing my throat.

"Pardon?" he squeaked. (He has a very squeaky voice, does Tim. Sorry mate.)

"Just come in," I growled, the effort wobbling my unsettled stomach.

"Are you decent?" he asked, sounding not a little worried.

"I've still got the gimp mask on," I groaned, "but I'm not naked, if that's what you mean."

I eased myself to my feet and stood waiting for Tim to enter. But the door remained firmly closed. I cleared my throat, loudly enough so he would hear.

"Was that a joke about the gimp mask?" he whined, northernly.

"What do you think, Tim?" I sighed.

"I'll come back later then," he snapped, wittily.

Slowly, my bedroom door creaked ajar and Tim's cheeky, inquisitive face peeped in, the frames of his glasses catching the light for an instant. He looked like Harry Potter's long -lost, unshaven, pie-obsessed and gravy-guzzling northern cousin. Basically, he was rotund former England all-rounder Ian Austin in spectacles. He scanned the room quickly, his eyes darting into every corner.

"Where is she, then?" he hissed, excitedly. I was too hungover to try and second-guess him.

"Who?" I replied wearily, slumping back down onto the edge of my bed.

"Barbra!" Tim squealed. "You were shouting her name when you fell through the front door last night. I assumed you might have met a lady while you were out."

This made no sense. I was always more of a 'not on the first date, let's just have a goodnight kiss on the doorstep and see where it leads' kind of chap. I approached relationships with the same clinical, methodical mindset with which Jonathan Trott constructed an innings. I preferred to play myself in and build a solid foundation and then look for opportunities to – *ahem* – 'score' once I was well set. Either that or I would scratch around for ages, seemingly getting nowhere fast and then proceed to bore the poor girl to tears. But either way, I wasn't some Chris Gayle type, swinging wildly from the off. I was a gentleman.

"I don't think I did bring anyone home Tim," I admitted. "I wasn't so drunk that I wouldn't remember meeting a girl and inviting her back here."

"You were *pretty* drunk," Tim said ominously. "You were singing Fleetwood Mac songs in your room after you came in. I assumed you might have been serenading this Barbra."

"What Fleetwood Mac song was it?" I questioned nervously. "*The Chain*?"

Tim shook his head.

"*Rhiannon*?"

"Nope, not that either," Tim said with another brisk headshake. "*Oh, I…I wanna be with you everywhere!*" He belted out the chorus to Fleetwood Mac's 'Everywhere'.

Oh bugger. That was a sure sign I really was *very* drunk. Still, I thanked my lucky stars I hadn't been singing 'Little Lies' too.

"And that *Little Lies* song too," Tim said suddenly. "And you were even singing all…"

"All the little guitar and synth parts?" I guessed. Tim nodded and smiled. "Well then I apologise Timothy. But I am sorry to disappoint you on the lady front, as I didn't bring anyone home. This mysterious Barbra…"

And then it hit me. If this were a cartoon, an enormous light bulb would have pinged brightly and harmoniously above my head. I grabbed Tim by the shoulders and shook him excitedly.

"BABS! Not Barbra…*BABS!*"

I leapt back onto my bed and snatched my phone up from my bedside table. There on the screen was a familiar indicator. I had one new e-mail.

"Hey mate, it's me, Roger."

No way. No bloody way. Roger! Roger Whelan, at long, long last! I frantically read through the remainder of the email.

"Babs forwarded me your email this morning. I'll help you out as much as I can, no bother. I like the way you think – you're right to have a go at bowling him, even if people tell you it's impossible. It's funny, because I have the same attitude and it seemed to culminate with me getting Sach out, which really opened my eyes to what is possible. Anyway, this is my number – it'd be good to chat sometime. Cheers, Roj"

Not only had I somehow managed to send a half-coherent drunken message to Babs' proper email address, but now I had an actual reply from Roger, the man who single-handedly proved this stupid venture wasn't, perhaps, so stupid after all. I had Roger's number and his patronage. He was on board. Next stop, Sachin's off stump.

I let out a high-pitched 'woo-hoo' and felt a broad grin creep across my face. I couldn't have been happier if Sienna Miller had just given me the key to her hotel room, a copy of the Kama Sutra and told me to book the week off work. I looked up to find Tim looking at me quizzically.

"Hooray!" I cheered again, raising my hand into the air in expectation of a high five from Tim. He looked at my hand, dangling in front of him. He ignored it.

"So you *do* know someone called Babs?" Tim looked at me with a mixture of fear and confusion. The same look my Dad gets whenever Russell Brand dances onto the television in his impossibly tight trousers.

"Yes!" I cheered. "Babs and Roger!"

Tim took a deep breath and peered at me over the top of his glasses.

"Ad, be honest with me…" he said, his voice quiet with concern. "Are you meeting couples from the internet? You never know with those online dating things, they might be something horrible…"

Silence hung in the area for a moment.

"No, Tim," I chuckled. "I've not been on those online

things. It's nothing like that. For a start, they're not even a couple. Babs and Roger are brother and sister."

"They could be axe-murderers…" Tim continued, seemingly in a world of his own. "Cat people…or Manchester United fans," he added softly, his brow slowly furrowing. "Hold on. Did you say they are brother and sister?"

It was all too much for little Timmy to take in. He shuffled off back to his bedroom in a state of shock. I didn't feel the need to explain who Babs and Roger Whelan actually were; if I allowed his imagination to run riot, he might stop nicking my Tropicana.

With Tim gone, I was free to make one of the most important phone calls I had made in a long time. I punched in Roger's number and pressed dial. Soon, I would be listening to my spiritual guide telling me all the secrets that would help me to bowl the Little Master just like he had. My pen and pad were poised in anticipation. Well my pen was poised, my pad was just sort of lying there, as pads do. Bloody pads.

"Hello?" Roger picked up the phone almost instantly. I was still daydreaming.

"Hi, is that Roger?" I spluttered nervously.

"It is," Roger replied in his calming Irish brogue.

"Roger, it's Adam, the idiot who is trying to bowl Sachin Tendulkar."

My mouth was suddenly dry with nerves. Drier than a freeze-dried rice cake or an Andy Flower press conference. Somehow, I began to tell Roger about what I'd been up to so far in my quest to track down the Little Master.

"Well I've been practising and planning loads," I told him confidently, "and I've been badgering everyone from Sachin's agent and his sponsors to try and get a bit of face time, I've been researching Sachin's weaknesses – I know, there aren't any – but despite doing all that, what I really need is to speak to someone who, against all the odds, has managed to bowl Sachin. I need someone who has been there, done it and got the t-shirt. That's where I was hoping you might come in handy. Basically," I panted, "I need to know how you did it."

"How I did it?" Roger said thoughtfully. "I've never really thought about that before."

He'd *never* thought about how he'd managed to bowl the world's greatest living batsman? It was like asking Gordon Brown what shoes he would most like to wear if he got the chance to kick Tony Blair in the delicates and him replying *'kick Tony in the goolies? I've never really given it a thought!'*

"Well," Roger began. "It was my first international match for Ireland and I just wanted to be in the best mental and physical shape I could. It really didn't dawn on me at the time that I was about to play India. I mean, I knew I was going to be opening the bowling and I knew Sachin Tendulkar would be opening the batting for India. But somehow I didn't put two and two together and think *'oh shit, that means I'm going to be bowling at Sachin Tendulkar'*. Honestly, the first time it hit me what I was about to do was when I was standing at the start of my run-up and we were just getting ready to start. I had bowled a few warm-ups to mid-on and I was ready. There was a big crowd in and I felt good. But then I looked down the wicket to see Sourav Ganguly waiting at the striker's end. Sachin Tendulkar – *Sachin bloody Tendulkar* – was leaning on his bat at the other end and looking at me. The umpire, Billy Bowden, was looking around to see if I was ready. Suddenly, everything felt unbelievably surreal. I just stood there thinking: 'What the fuck is going on?' It was mad."

Bloody hell. Just hearing that scenario made me feel nervous. I put myself in Roger's shoes. I felt a bit sick at the thought of it. And not just because other people's feet and shoes totally gross me out.

"Ganguly faced the first three balls and then Sachin was on strike," Roj continued. "I tended to get a lot of wickets by beating the batsman with pace but I knew that wasn't going to work with Sachin. But really, I had no idea how I was going to get him out. I just ran in and tried to put the ball in a good area and get my rhythm. Sachin defended the first ball I bowled to him, but the next one was terrible – a low full toss which he smashed through the covers for four. I remember thinking that this was my first over in international cricket and it wasn't going well. I wasn't happy with myself at all, but I suddenly felt really angry and determined that I would make the last ball of the over count."

And count it certainly flippin' well did.

"I can remember the ball perfectly, even now," he said, his voice quietening to a gentle hush. "It was a straight ball angling slightly into his pads. It wasn't too fast, only about 80mph; nothing he couldn't deal with or hadn't hit for four a thousand times before. But this time, he tried to flick it through mid-wicket and he missed it. He just…missed it. The rest is just a blur. It was just my lucky day and that's why I think you can do this. Every dream is just a succession of choices one makes. It just needs to be your lucky day, too."

I was blown away. I didn't know what to say, but all this was music to my ears. I felt about ten feet tall. Roger totally got what I was trying to do. I had been right to think he was the perfect mentor. Because he was. This was exactly the glimmer of hope, the tiny slice of encouragement pie I had been craving. I wolfed it down appreciatively. All Roger had done was run up and bowl a normal, run-of-the-mill ball, and Sachin had missed it. This was my proof. It *was* possible!

"One thing I would say though, is this," Roj said, suddenly sounding more serious, "make sure you work out your celebration beforehand."

Roger was a man after my own heart; he was so confident I could succeed that he was already discussing how I'd celebrate.

Silence hung between us as I pondered my options. I'd perfected the Beyonce 'Single Ladies' dance weeks ago (what a cracking/frightening time in The Yorkshire Grey's over-45s singles night *that* was). Maybe I could 'do the Bartman?' Or what about the Soulja Boy dance? (Google it. Seriously. It trumps 'The Sprinkler' by a distance. You'll be shocked you've never seen Graeme Swann doing it after a wicket.)

"When I heard the stumps go and realised what had happened," Roj laughed, "my first reaction was relief, but when I realised what I had done, I immediately broke out into the 'Hot Coals' dance; I sort of hopped from one foot to the other and waved my arms about. I looked bloody ridiculous. Afterwards, I kept thinking that I should have done a 'Pete Townshend' windmill celebration."

The shrill sound of the front doorbell broke my concentration.

"Sorry Roger, my front doorbell is ringing; can you wait there for a minute?"

I scurried down the stairs and down to the front door. Whoever it was outside was very impatient – the sort of wilfully annoying person who thinks it's funny to keep ringing the bell until the very moment the poor person inside finally opens up. I swung the door open.

"Alright, bro?" Josh was stood in my doorway, clutching an enormous bag. "I'm desperate for a piss," he said, barging past me and into the bathroom.

I left him to it and bounded back up the stairs to my room, only for him to barge noisily up the stairs behind me not long later, dropping his bag onto the floor with an almighty crash as he careered through the door. He plonked himself on the edge of my bed and picked up my laptop, doing his best to eavesdrop on my conversation. Suddenly, a burst of aggressive noise interrupted my concentration.

"Go Grease Lightning you're burning up the…"

Not again. Josh's phone had sprung into life once more. Helpfully, he held it right next to me, blaring the song directly into the receiver.

"Sorry Roger mate, I've got to go…" I shouted over the

tinny music. I'm sure I heard him ask '*is that the 'Grease' soundtrack?*' as I hurriedly ended the call..

"What are you doing here, Josh?" I asked, with more than a hint of exasperation once his ridiculous ringtone had thundered to a halt. But Josh, my laptop perched on his knees, ignored me. I verbally prodded him again.

"Sorry," he said, coming to his senses, "I've got some big Sachin Tendulkar news. Do you want to hear it?" he asked. I nodded impatiently, in anattempt to be both annoyed with him, but also grateful that he was at least still trying to help me succeed.

"Well," he said confidently, "I've found that an anagram of 'Sachin Tendulkar' is 'AND I LACK THE RUNS'."

"Is that it?" I shrugged. I was tempted to tell him his own name was an anagram of '*Lo, Josh – Armchair Slut*', or '*Rumor: Ho Jilts Rascal*' but I left it.

"It's a sign!" he yelped.

"How, exactly?" I asked, confused that this simple anagram had warranted a trip down to Brighton and not just a short phone call.

But Josh ignored me, instead inching his face closer to my laptop screen and squinting slightly in what looked like concentration but may have been a bad case of wind. He looked genuinely perplexed.

"Ad," Josh asked boldly, "who the *hell* is Professor Shetty?"

Don't get me wrong; I've received exciting emails before. A couple containing jobs offers, one telling me I had won the Lichtenstein national lottery and plenty offering me the chance to 'improve' my manhood. But this was huge; huger even than the frankly unrealistic and impractical results promised by those manhood emails. Apparently. I don't know; I've never had cause to read them (alright, I did once, but that was a rare crisis of confidence). But this email, from the exotically-named Professor Shetty, trumped the lot of them. And this was the reason why:

Dear Mr Carroll-Smith,

We are forwarding your email to the Manager of the Indian Cricket Team, Mr Chaudhary with a request that he do the needful for you. You may call him on his UK mobile number: 07xxxxxxxxx.

Regards,
Prof. R S Shetty
Chief Administrative Officer
BCCI

I quickly thrust the email under Josh's nose and asked him to confirm what it said. My hands were shaking with exhilaration.

"Am I going mad, Josh," I wheezed nervously, "or does this email look like one of the big cheeses in the BCCI is telling me to call the Indian cricket team's manager and arrange when I can bowl at Sachin Tendulkar? Have I basically emailed one of the biggest organisations in world cricket and asked if I could have a bit of a net session with the star of their national team, and they've replied saying '*yeah, sure*' and then handed over the telephone number of the manager of their national cricket team? Is that what this is?" Josh read the email again.

"Yes!" he screeched. "And they've promised this Mr Chaudhary will '*do the needful*' for you too! Whatever that means."

I jumped into the air and squealed with barely contained delight. I high-fived Josh, then high-tenned him, then mid-fifteened him before giving up the whole pretence and scooping him up into a bear hug. I ran in ever-decreasing circles around my room, pumping my fists in celebration. I did the first few steps of the Soulja Boy dance (it all went to pot after the 'Superman' bit) and the Beyonce 'Single Ladies' handshakey bit. This. Was. **Mega!** I was happier than Murali (officially the world's smiliest man) playing naked Twister with Shakira at a Chris Gayle party that Shane Watson *hadn't* been invited to. Which is the happiest it is possible for anyone to be, I believe.

Professor Shetty worked for the Board of Control for Cricket in India. In fact, he was the chief administrative officer of the whole frigging BCCI. I'd dropped him a frankly bonkers email weeks and weeks ago, telling him about my Tendulkar quest.

I fully expected that a 'spam' filter would sweep up the email before it got anywhere near someone of importance at the BCCI. At best, I hoped for an automated reply along the lines of '*I am sorry, we get millions of emails from nutjobs like you and we would rather eat a deep-fried copy of Hello! magazine than reply to each individually*'. I hadn't been this pleasantly surprised since I accidentally ate tzatziki and discovered that, despite appearances, it didn't actually taste like seagull poo. This was like emailing the Football Association and asking if Wayne Rooney could play for your Sunday League team at the weekend, and them replying and saying: '*Yeah, fine. Is it OK if Rio Ferdinand, Steven Gerrard and Gareth Barry tag along as well? They're at a bit of a loose end*'. Not that Gareth Barry would get in many Sunday League teams, mind you.

I read the email again and again. I double and triple-checked the email address to make sure this wasn't a cruel practical joke played by Rosh. It was the sort of thing he'd do. But no, it was indisputably a genuine BCCI email address. I could not believe what I was seeing. I had gone from being ignored by almost everyone to being given permission to call the Indian team manager – the equally wonderful-sounding Mr Chaudhary – and organise bowling at Sachin Tendulkar.

"What are you going to say to Professor Shetty?" asked Josh, interrupting my millionth re-reading of the message. "Hey, you should ask him about my blindfold idea!" he screeched. I tried to ignore him. "Actually, whatever you do," he added, "Do **not** mention my streaking idea. I want that to be a *big* surprise for Sachin."

I nodded and made a guttural noise of general agreement.

"A *big* surprise, yeah? Get it?" Josh raised his eyebrows and grinned.

"Yes," I said. "I get it."

"I'm talking about my cock…"

"Josh," I snapped. "Trust me. I got the joke."

Josh smiled. I smiled. It was a smiley sort of moment. Bowling at Sachin was within my grasp and the tour hadn't even started yet. First Roger Whelan had got back to me, and now Professor Shetty. I needed a bit of a lie-down.

Whelan and *Shetty*. They sounded like a crime-fighting duo from the 1970s. *Shetty* would be the older, stuck-in-his-ways cop, and *Whelan* would be his younger, more cavalier partner. *Shetty* would always be trying to make *Whelan* play by the rules, but Roj just wouldn't listen. It had the makings of a classic. I made a mental note to run the idea by them both at some point. Maybe I could do a *Life on Mars* type thing and set it in the past! Either Roman times, or 1995, when 'Don't Stop (Wiggle Wiggle)' by the Outhere Brothers was at number one. We could get them in to play a pair of criminals who speak entirely in rap. The Beeb would lap that nonsense up, surely.

"It really is amazing what you get if you just ask," I said, stretching out triumphantly on my bed.

"That reminds me, actually," Josh replied. "In the spirit of '*it's amazing what you get if you just ask*' - and bear in mind that you have just been the recipient of some great generosity yourself today…can I borrow 200 quid? That's sort of why I'm actually here."

"Umm…" I replied non-committally, searching for the right way to say '*no, of course not*'.

"Come on Ad, please?" Josh whinged, clearly anticipating the impending rejection. "What would Professor Shetty do in this situation? He'd lend me the money!"

"Well, I'll ask him then," I snapped back.

"No," said Josh firmly. "You can't ask him for money *and* mention the blindfold thing. He'll think you're taking the piss."

PART SEVEN

"Hello, is that Mr Chaudhary?" I said, my voice nervously shaking and rattling like a rickety old steam train. I took a deep breath and composed myself.

"Hello, is that Mr Chaudhary? My name is Adam Carroll-Smith." My voice was bolder and steadier than before.

"Hello," I began for a third time. "May I *please* speak with Mr Chaudhary, immediately?" My voice sounded urgent, almost angry.

"Yo Chaudhary, listen," I yelled arrogantly. "It's LL Cool A!" I pulled the imaginary phone away from my ear, looked at myself in the mirror and scowled.

Mr Chaudhary, it transpired, was a difficult man to get hold of. It had been seven days since Professor Shetty had sent me his mobile number, but in that time, a succession of calls to him had gone unanswered. Even a slightly worried email to Professor Shetty had failed to elicit a response. I had been reduced to practising what I would eventually say to Mr Chaudhary in front of my bedroom mirror, like Travis Bickle if he'd swapped New York for Hampshire and semi-automatic weapons taped to his body for a nice cardigan.

The Indians' first tour match was still more than a week away, but Mr Chaudhary's silence was deafening and more than a little unsettling. Professor Shetty's email had almost suggested that he would be expecting my call – so why wasn't he answering? My mind swam with the grim possibilities. What if Professor Shetty had spoken to Mr Chaudhary and they'd changed their minds? What if they'd run the idea by Sachin and he'd given it the thumbs down? Worse still, what if they'd googled me, found my Facebook page and seen those disturbing pictures of me with long, straightened hair and wearing guyliner back in 2006? I looked like Hazel Irvine! That would almost certainly have made them change their minds.

I picked up my phone and stared at Mr Chaudhary's number. I had already called him three times that day, and it was barely past lunchtime. A fourth call today might nudge me into 'nuisance caller' territory.

Ah, bugger it, I told myself. Faint heart never won fair cricket administrator. I pressed call and held the phone to my ear and waited for the familiar dulling trill of the dial tone.

For the past few months, my whole life had been geared towards this moment, towards achieving this goal. The words of Robert Louis Stevenson stuck in my head: '*To travel hopefully is better than to arrive*'. I had daydreamed away hours thinking about bowling at Sachin since I was eleven. I had enjoyed fantasising about it. But as it inched closer to becoming a reality, I was both excited and petrified at the thought of actually getting what I wanted. It was like I was about to lose my virginity all over again. I just hoped Mr Chaudhary and Sachin would be gentle with me.

I took a deep breath. This phone call was *it* – the very point at which my dream of bowling to Sachin would become a reality. And dreams, despite what eyepatch-wearing 90s popstar Gabrielle may claim, very rarely came true.

But now one of the biggest and longest-held of mine was about to make that great leap from fantasy to reality. I felt a nervous bead of sweat tickle down my forehead.

"Hello?"

Gulp. I should have been expecting him to answer. It

was, after all, a fairly ordinary thing to happen whenever you called someone. But on some level, I had just assumed Mr Chaudhary would never pick up the phone. Now he had, and I was utterly unprepared. Maybe deep down, I thought all this was too good to be true. I still half-suspected the whole thing might be a carefully constructed practical joke organised by Rosh and my brother. But no: here he was, at the other end of the phoneline – the Indian team manager, Mr Chaudhary.

"Hello, is that Mr Chaudhary?" I stammered, utterly petrified. (I decided against the 'Yo Chaudhary' intro.) "My name is Adam Carroll-Smith." (I'd also ditched 'LL Cool A', at least until we knew each other better.)

"Hello," he said disinterestedly. A beat passed. I expected him to say something else, but he was clearly a man of few words. But that was alright – as long as his few words included the phrase *'yes you can bowl at Sachin Tendulkar; when is convenient for you?'*

"Yes, well," I spluttered nervously, "I got your number from a mutual friend of ours, Professor Shetty at the BCCI."

Alright; I was over-selling my friendship with Professor Shetty. I didn't know if he had a cat or who his favourite member of Girls Aloud was (my money was on Nicola – she's really blossomed recently), but he was a nice man. He wouldn't mind me hyping the closeness of our relationship.

"OK," monotoned Mr Chaudhary.

"He gave me your number and I believe he forwarded you an email I sent him, too," I continued, trying not to let Mr Chaudhary's distracted tone put me off my stride. "Have you seen that email at all?"

"No," he deadpanned. "I have not checked my emails for a little while so I may have missed it."

Alarm bells immediately began to ring. This wasn't a *great* sign.

"Oh right," I ploughed on, my heart rate rising. "Well basically, I wrote to him saying that this summer, I am on a bit of a mission to try and track down Mr Sachin Tendulkar and with one ball, try and bowl him out, and…"

"Ah, that would be impossible," he chimed, matter-of-factly. Another non-believer.

"Well, yes, nearly impossible," I began to explain. "But I've been practising a lot and doing a lot of research and I've got Roger Whelan in my corner now, too. I believe if the stars align…"

"No, no, no," he said quickly, cutting me off mid-sentence. "I do not mean bowling him would be impossible for you." I appreciated the vote of confidence, but I could tell the conversation was about to take a turn for the disappointing. "I mean bowling *to* him would be impossible at this moment."

My heart sank.

"Hello?" Mr Chaudhary said, impatiently. I had been stunned into silence; Tasered into quiet submission by the swift shock of his direct and unsympathetic rejection.

"But Professor Shetty said he would advise you to 'do the needful' to help me achieve this little dream of mine," I whined. "Is there really nothing you can do at all? It would only need to be one ball. I would be in and out of your way within a minute or two…"

"We are *very* busy with the tour."

His voice was sterner than before. I immediately panicked.

"How about a quick game of French cricket with Sachin? It's like normal cricket, but more, sort of, *French*."

What the hell was I saying? French cricket was '*cricket, but more, sort of, French?*' What did that mean? Batting with a baguette and bowling with an onion? Fielders at silly mid-*oeuf*? (Sorry. I know).

But my pleas fell on deaf ears. I contemplated suggesting Sach and I might play a quick game of Swingball or Mousetrap or Pictionary, but the jig was up. Mr Chaudhary was not going to budge.

I felt like someone had booted me in the guts, stolen my

wallet, used the cash to bid on 'An Intimate Evening With Geoffrey Boycott' on eBay and then returned to hand back my empty wallet and tell me I was expected for dinner at Boycs' in half-an-hour. And that there would be no booze. And that Ravi Shastri would be joining us. And there would be a slideshow of Geoffrey's *1000 Greatest Forward Defences*. And the dress code was 'ball gowns for all guests not called Geoffrey or Ravi'. I'd not felt lower since I heard the rumour that Muse had split up was false.

What about Professor Shetty's promise? No one was going to 'do the needful' for me anymore. I slumped onto the sofa, deflated and dejected. It was back to the drawing board, and I didn't even own a drawing board. I didn't even know what a drawing board was.

It's better to travel hopefully than arrive, eh, Robert Louis Stevenson? I had expected better advice from the man responsible for Muppet Treasure Island (arguably Kermit's finest ever role). Mr Chaudhary had gone from being my potential savour to my nemesis.

****

It was finally the opening day of the Indians' tour. A week had passed since Mr Chaudhary had metaphorically pissed on my chips and turned my green light from the BCCI into a bloody great 'stop' sign. I had sulked for two days straight after the rejection. Actually, it was more like two-and-a-half days, but on the third morning I remembered I had some Pop Tarts and suddenly, things didn't seem quite so bad.

As I crunched through breakfast that morning, I realised I had two options. I could either take the rejection from Mr Chaudhary as proof the challenge was impossible – or steadfastly and stubbornly refuse to give in. Jono's plan – signed (almost) in blood – committed me to doing the latter. The taunts I would inevitably receive from Rosh if I packed it all in now were also undeniably a motivating factor, too. No one ever admits it, but I reckon at least a few notable victories by elite sportsmen and women can be attributed to a desire to stop their mates taking the mickey out of them for being a bit rubbish. I can only assume Mitchell Johnson is a bit of a Billy-no-mates or has particularly nice friends.

But more than that, getting so close had only served to motivate me all the more. The initial reply from Professor Shetty was still a massive step in the right direction. He hadn't ignored me, or laughed at my request. He had seen fit to refer me to the one person who he knew for certain could make a net session with Sach happen. Perhaps Mr Chaudhary was just playing hard to get. Thankfully, I knew all about how to deal with people playing hard to get. You don't get to fifteen (15) snogs without knowing a thing or two about charm. My duel with Mr Chaudhary wasn't over yet.

It was an overcast morning when I set off from Brighton for my first sighting of Sach in the flesh. As I pulled out of the city centre, I stopped to fill my car with petrol, and after topping up, checked my emails on my phone as I walked into the shop. A voice boomed over the tannoy that *'the use of mobile phones on the forecourt was not permitted'*. I manfully jumped out of my skin and flushed bright red with embarrassment. I don't do well with being told off. I got a rollicking at primary school for forgetting my pencil case and responded by immediately wetting myself, and having to spend the rest of the afternoon in the tiniest pair of black nylon Umbro football shorts ever made. I wasn't far off repeating the trick when the disembodied voice ticked me off as I scanned my phone.

"Sorry mate," I said, holding my right hand up in apology as I strode into the station shop, putting my phone into my pocket theatrically, like some sort of bad drama school mime artist.

"That's OK," the man behind the counter replied, wearily. But like the rebel I so surely am (turkey sandwiches with hot cross buns as the bread! Think about it! It's madness!) I immediately turned down the crisps and snacks aisle and got my phone out again.

I had a new email from a familiar source – Professor Shetty. Flanked by Wheat Crunchies and flapjacks, I felt an excitement bubbling up inside me – a giddy sense of anticipation I would ordinarily have put down to my proximity to so many bacon-flavoured snacks, but not this time. This time, I had Shetty fever. I clicked the mail open with my thumb, crossing my forefinger and middle finger for luck as they rested on the back of my phone. He didn't disappoint.

Dear Mr Carroll-Smith,

Maybe you can send a mail to Sachin Tendulkar directly and seek his consent for this? His email is [Sachin's personal email address].

Regards,
Prof. R S Shetty

I stared at the message, dumbstruck. What the hell was going on? Had the wonderful Professor Shetty really just sent me the email address of the greatest batsman to have ever played the game? Was that what had happened? SACHIN'S PERSONAL BLOODY EMAIL? This was incredible! I felt a surge of absolute joy rush through my body. I wanted to grab fistfuls of snacks and fling them into the air in happiness. I wanted to scream 'I've got Sachin Tendulkar's email address!' and kiss a stranger. I wanted to high-five the cashier through the little hole in his bullet-proof glass. I did none of those things. They probably would have made me pay for the discarded snacks, I'm not much of a public shouter, there was no one close enough for me to grab and kiss, and the hole was too small to do a high-five through. But still – I was *excited!*

But I know what you're thinking. *Pull the other one, Adam; Professor Shetty didn't just email you out of the blue to give you Sachin's personal email address.* And no, he didn't. You were right to think that, you shrewd thing, you. Well done. And can I say, that's a fetching outfit you've got on today. Maybe top it off with a fez, just to complete the look? Think about it, eh? But no, as you so rightly surmised, it didn't come from out of the blue. This was the reason why he sent that wonderful, joyous email:

Dear Professor Shetty, I had written, days previously.

*I have spoken with Mr Chaudhary who has told me that he will **not** be able to help with my request to bowl at Sachin Tendulkar.*

Yours sincerely,
Adam Carroll-Smith

Yup, that's right. I dobbed Mr Chaudhary in. I tattled on him. He had rejected me and so I, like a toddler telling his mum about the naughty bigger boy who keeps pushing him off the swings, had told Professor Shetty all about it.

I had expected a polite *'I am sorry, but Mr Chaudhary's word is final'* sort of reply; but Professor Shetty obviously really, *really* wanted to help me out. What next? Sachin's pin number?

I slowly made my way to the tills to pay for my petrol, my phone in hand and a gormless, dumbstruck look on my face.

"Pump four?" came a sighing, bored voice from opposite me. The attendant was either doing a terrific impression of the gormless, dumbstruck face I'd been pulling or he was just gormless and dumbstruck. I gave him the benefit of the doubt. "Please remember there are no phones to be used in the petrol station, sir," he added, spying the phone in my hand.

"Yep, no problem," I beamed. "It *was* only an email though."

"Whatever it is," he huffed, "I'm sure it's not more important than the safety of the cars and customers on site."

Hmmm. Sachin's email, or the safety of cars and

customers? Sachin's email, or the safety of cars and customers? Sachin's email; the safety of cars and…on balance, I could just about see where he was coming from. Just. If it had been an email from Sachin himself, I'd have borrowed one of Josh's inventive swears and told him where to stick it.

I skipped merrily back onto the forecourt. I looked around at the other people filling up. The man in the Ford Escort – he didn't have Tendulkar's email. The woman in the Mini definitely didn't. She looked like the sort who thought computers were the work of the devil. The rich old boy topping up his Mercedes had more money than me, but he didn't have the email address of one of cricket's all-time legends. I bloody well did.

I leapt into my car and punched 'Northampton' into my satnav and pulled away with an enormous smile on my face. I was on my way to watch India's first game of the tour, armed with a little nugget of information that took me closer to Sachin than I had ever been. It felt like Christmas Day, my birthday and getting laid all rolled into one. I kept my fingers crossed the inevitable anti-climax (and cramp – from too much turkey, cake or physical exercise, respectively – and not always on the occasions you'd expect) that followed all three wasn't right around the corner.

As I raced along the M25 (at legal speeds, of course, officer) I wondered what I would write to Sachin in my email. Chances are he didn't check his emails all that regularly, so I would have to give the email a catchy subject to really grab his attention. Maybe I could play on his ego – something like *'Hey Sachin, I'm going to bowl you out'* – or perhaps I should go with something a bit more cryptic – *'I have a challenge for you, Sachin…'*. I imagined opening my mailbox and seeing the name 'Sachin Tendulkar' in the inbox. It was an exhilarating thought.

Maybe this would be the start of regular correspondence between us? We might become email pen pals; I would update him with stuff about my life (additions to the snogs list/more reasons why Matt Bellamy, lead singer of Muse is annoying/ the man in the library who uses a knife to decapitate his Jelly Babies and then only eats the bodies/a new pen) and he'd give me all the gossip from the world of international cricket; choice little nuggets about tough guy Dale Steyn's pre-match routine involving a facial, a pedicure and a 'Songs of the Whales' album, or the news that Michael Clarke had two pictures of his own face – one smiling, one sad – tattooed on his bum cheeks (not technically true, if any lawyers are reading. Well, probably not).

After daydreaming my way onto the M1 (not literally, officer) I decided to pull over at Newport Pagnall services. I desperately needed a wee, but more importantly, I had to tell someone about this latest development. I had to do some bragging. I called Rosh.

"Hey Ad, what's up?" He sounded chipper. Or drunk.

"Oh, just checking in really," I lied. "Although I *do* have a bit of news."

"Oh yeah? What's that?" he asked politely.

"Guess what I've just got," I giggled.

"An over-inflated opinion of how interesting this piece of news will be, for one thing…"

"Come on," I hectored him, "be serious – guess what I've got?"

"A new girlfriend?" We both laughed.

"Don't be ridiculous," I chuckled. "*Sachin Tendulkar's* email address."

"I'd have believed you more if you'd said it was a girlfriend," Rosh scoffed.

"I'm being totally serious. But hey," I shrugged, "it's no big deal…it's just the greatest batsman of all time's personal email address. One of the big cheeses at the BCCI just sort of gave it to me. I didn't even ask for it. He just…volunteered it."

"Bollocks…" Rosh snapped back instinctively.

"I swear," I swore. "He just emailed and basically said: *'Sorry you had no luck with Mr Chaudhary, but hey, why don't you drop Sachin an email directly'.*"

"So what is it?" Rosh asked, conspiratorially. "Go on, tell me."

"No way," I howled. "You'll go and send him an email saying that I'm some crazed stalker who dresses up as Sachin or tell him I have a life-size blow-up model of him that I feed spaghetti hoops to."

Rosh laughed. He knew I was right.

"Anyway, I'd better go," I sighed. "I'm still about an hour away from Northampton."

"Northampton?" Rosh sneered. "What the hell are you going there for?"

"The cricket. It's the Indians' first match of the tour."

"Yeah," Rosh laughed, "against *Somerset*. In *Somerset*."

I said nothing. This was a new low in the annals of my greatest organisational snafus. What the flip was I doing? Nobody's radar had failed this spectacularly since Steve Harmison's first ball in the 2006 Ashes series, or Gazza ended up playing for that Chinese second division team a few years ago.

I'd got so swept up in the euphoria of getting Sachin's email address that I had completely ballsed this whole thing up. I *knew* the Indians were playing Somerset. So why the hell had I punched Northampton into my satnav? I'd been staring at the Indian's fixture list for months now. I knew it like the back of my hand – and yet somehow I had managed to get my wires more crossed than a drunken electrician.

Rosh howled with laughter down the phone.

"That has got to be a record for the most pointless journey anyone has ever taken, ever," he guffawed. "You should give the *World Book of Guinness Records* a call."

"The what?" I barked. I was readying myself for a spot of Olympic-level pedantry. Rosh's laughter at my directional cock-up had cut like a knife. I wasn't about to let him depart a conversation thinking he was smarter than me.

"You know, the *World Book of Guinness Records*," he replied.

"I've never heard of it."

"What?" he giggled. "How haven't you heard of it? It's full of all the weird records people set. Like, for example, did you know that the record number of Jaffa Cakes anyone has eaten in a minute is only seven, which I think seems quite low…"

"I think you mean the *Guinness Book of World Records*," I sniped, pedantically.

"That's what I said," he replied.

"No," I sneered, "you said the *World Book of Guinness Records*."

"Yeh, exactly," Rosh agreed. "The *Guinness World Book of Records*."

"That was wrong, too," I tutted, mockingly. "The *Guinness Book of World Records* is a book, sponsored by Guinness, which contains all the feats of speed, weight, height, endurance and all that stuff. The *World Book of Guinness Records* sounds like a book, published globally, that lists how many pints of Guinness are sold each year. The *Guinness World Book of Records* sounds like a book of records set on a planet owned by Guinness. Get it?"

"Nah," Rosh replied.

"It's easy to remember. Just think," I told him, "it's a book, made by Guinness, featuring world records. So that makes it…?"

Rosh thought for a moment.

"A good stocking filler."

Bugger. I laughed. He'd won. I shouted a hurried goodbye over his continued giggling and put the phone down.

It was already 12:30. I tapped 'Taunton' into the sat nav. It would take me at least three-and-a-half hours to get there. I scanned the route. The quickest route took me past Northampton on the M5. Even if I wanted to get where I should have been going in the first place, I would still have to drive all the way to the shitting place I had stupidly set off for. It was too much. Sometimes you have to accept defeat and move on. It was definitely not my day. I turned around and drove back to Brighton. Tomorrow was a new start – I would set off early, get to the ground in time for the beginning of play and start my Tendulkar quest in earnest tomorrow.

At least, that was the plan. In reality, I slept through my alarm. It probably had something to do with the entirely pointless five-hour road trip I had taken to see the sights of a service station on the M1.

****

Fruitless email correspondence #2

TO: ANOTHER OF SACHIN'S SPONSORS (names have been withheld to protect the unhelpful/unresponsive)

```
Dear Sir/Madam,

My name is Adam Carroll-Smith. This
summer, I aim to bowl just one ball to
the great Sachin Tendulkar and in doing
so, fulfil a childhood dream.

I see you are one of Sachin's sponsors
- that's a very wise choice. Sach is
certainly a man of great repute.

But did you know he never learned
to swim? The next time you see him,
feel free to gently tease him with that
little nugget of info. I'm sure he will
laugh, as his lack of swimming ability
certainly hasn't held him back on the
cricket pitch. And why should it? The
players leave the field the moment it
starts raining.

Anyhoo - as one of Sachin's sponsors,
```

I wondered if you might be able to help inch me closer to achieving my goal. As I mentioned above, I would only need to bowl one little delivery at him, and then I would have succeeded in my quest. It's that simple.

I must confess I do not fully understand what it is you do (I assure you I'm not stupid – I have a 2.1 in Business Administration from The University of Bath; I could send you a facsimile of my degree certificate if necessary) but whatever it is, it seems you are certainly (one of the) leaders in your field.

As a show of gratitude for any help you could offer me, I shall promise to mention your name to three* of my friends and give them a glowing endorsement of what a fine institution you are.

Looking forward to hearing from you.
Adam

*I could go to five, at a push.

RESPONSE: None. As a result, I bad-mouthed them to three friends instead.

****

PART EIGHT

Somerset vs. The Indians, Taunton, July 15 - July 17
Day Two
S. R. Tendulkar – c. Buttler b. Meschede
– 26 (50 balls, five fours)

Tired and frustrated, I anxiously plodded along through winding country roads and busier-than-I-would-have-liked motorways towards Taunton, intermittently punching myself in the leg in frustration. How the hell had I managed to be so stupid? I'd driven halfway (and the rest) to the wrong ground one day and then overslept the next. What sort of an idiot does that?

I thought back to the time I was pulled over by the police because I had driven off with a pair of shoes, my mobile phone and my wallet on the roof of my car. I recalled the times (yep, *plural*) I had walked away from ATM machines without taking my money and the 'sleeping bag' incident at the Glastonbury festival in 2007 (in short, I didn't bring one and had to wear almost every item of clothing I had brought with me in order to keep warm at night, including a pair of boxer shorts – *clean, thankfully* – pulled tight over my head to keep my ears warm). Ah yes, I thought, *that* was how I had managed to be so stupid. I had form.

Wearily, I finally entered Taunton and managed to find the cricket ground, tucked away next to a huge Morrisons supermarket. It was rather beautiful (the ground, not the Morrisons – although that did have a special offer on Mars milk which I found particularly easy on the eye and one of the cashiers was a bit of a fox, especially for a 62-year-old grandmother of six); a tall church spire dominating the skyline to one side of the ground, while the other backed onto the quietly trickling River Tone. The smell of a barbecue wafted gently around, and that familiar low hum of a cricket crowd – hushed, beer-pickled conversation punctuated with the odd clang of raucous laughter – bobbed through the humid summer air. The ground looked nearly full, with Indian fans seemingly outnumbering the locals. A few children, armed with miniature bats and a tennis ball, had organised an impromptu cricket match in the shade of the stand in front of the ticket office. It was all terribly genteel and English, like Stephen Fry eating a scone. A pleading, throaty roar suddenly shattered the quiet ambience.

"Sachiiiiiiiiiin!"

I looked up to see four Indian fans sat on the very back row of one of the stands, all waving a giant Indian flag and whirling their arms around maniacally in the air.

"You are number one, Sachiiiiiiiiiiin!" they all bellowed in unison.

But why were they shouting for Sachin? What was he doing? Was he batting already? Was he already out? Had I driven all this way only to miss seeing him – for the first time – in the flesh entirely? I would be so bloody furious with myself for stopping for that terrible coffee and soggy sandwich if I had. And why had I stood flicking through the new copy of *Private Eye*? (I thought it might have told me which 'wing' was the nice one that all the actors and musicians and Eddie Izzard supported. It didn't.) And why – why, why, why, why, why, why, *why* – had I almost driven to an empty cricket ground in the wrong bloody county yesterday? Don't get me wrong: the M1 was lovely this time of year, but I had places to be and people – legends of cricket, in fact – to see.

I charged behind the back of the stand, and through a narrow hallway, my face growing redder by the second as I tumbled, arms flailing, through the crowds at the steeply-priced bar, my bag shunting and jostling through the thirsty punters and causing approximately £14,000 worth of spillage (it was really quite steeply-priced) en route. Finally, I burst through the passageway and back out into the brilliant sunshine – and straight into another loud, but decidedly more shrill cheer, the force of which nearly knocked me off my feet.

"We love you Sachiiiiiiiiiin!" the high-pitched voice yelped.

I winced as the full force of the shriek juddered against my eardrum, but the bellowing woman was too excited to notice.

"Oh, Sachin…" the small woman said, her voice tight and weak with nerves. She was fretfully wringing an Indian flag, occasionally bringing it up to her face and covering her mouth with it. I had managed to navigate myself to a spot by the sightscreen, almost perfectly behind the bowler's arm, and if the small lady beside me was an barometer, this was undoubtedly a prime spot for bonkers Tendulkar fans. This was my patch. I was among like-minded lunatics. We'd probably start reminiscing about our favourite Sachin clips on YouTube at any moment.

"Excuse me," I said, inching my way slowly towards her, wary of her screaming into my other ear. "Have I missed Sachin? Has he batted yet?"

"Oh no," she replied quietly, before flashing me a wide smile. "It has been raining all morning. Somerset are still batting." She was in her mid-20s, I guessed, with enormous, welcoming brown eyes.

"Oh good," I smiled. "That's a stroke of luck. I made a few wrong turns in the car on my way here," I said, with staggering understatement. "I was worried I might have missed him."

The woman smiled politely, before quickly turning to her

left, craning her neck and standing on her tiptoes. Whatever she was searching for, she looked dissatisfied that she hadn't found it. She went back to anxiously twisting and turning the flag in her hands.

"Are you looking for Sachin?" I asked. She said nothing, before craning her neck again. She seemed agitated and on edge. Perhaps it was me. I had this sort of effect on women, although generally after a few weeks rather than a few minutes.

"Whereabouts is he?" I asked again. "I heard you cheering…"

Suddenly, the woman let out a sharp, exhilarated squawk and sprinted away out of sight.

It was the end of the over and the Indian players were slowly moving into their new positions. It was hardly scream-inducing, edge-of-your-seat sporting action. It was, to the untrained and trained eye alike, just a load of men wandering about in cream clothes (which, to be frank, is all cricket is for a large part of the time anyway). From the far corner of the ground, another, deeper cry of 'Sachiiiiiiiiiin' rang out. I scanned the field for his familiar sunhat and squat little frame, but there was no sign of him.

"It's funny watching the Indian fans, isn't it?" A steward, with a small, neat grey beard and glasses perched on his long, thin nose, had silently shuffled up beside me. He was the sort of man who started and finished conversations on his own. He didn't need me there, I was a wall and he was a squash ball. He was just bouncing ideas off me and batting them back to himself. "Yeah," he continued, before I could reply, "they're obsessed with that Tendulkar aren't they? They can't get enough of him."

I heard the low purr of a group of people mumbling beside me. The woman had returned with a gaggle of friends, each as excitable as she was. They were tightly huddled, animatedly whispering to each other in urgent tones, like gossiping schoolgirls sharing secrets. I had never seen a reaction like this at a sporting event before. It was hard to imagine a group of laddish Chelsea fans all huddling together and getting flustered at the prospect of seeing John Terry. Unless they were with their girlfriends, of course, in which the huddling might have been more of a protective measure.

"It's funny isn't it – just look at how excited they are," I said, pointing over my shoulder at the Indian fans. "You wouldn't see a group of Chelsea fans…"

"Here we go again," said the steward, cutting me off. "Here he comes."

I had spent hours watching him on television, seen thousands of photographs of him and read just about all there was to read about Sachin Ramesh Tendulkar. His statistical records were indelibly scored on my mind. The tiniest details about his life – his likes and dislikes, his hopes and fears, even his questionable taste in music – were as familiar to me as the minutiae of my own life. I was the proud custodian of an almost obsessive collection of anecdotes and titbits of information that explained exactly who Sachin Tendulkar, the man and the cricketer, was.

But suddenly, all that feverish accumulation of knowledge was irrelevant. I realised that every image of him I had in my mind was posed and static, or soundtracked by excited commentators. Sachin did not exist in the real world – his life, as far as I was concerned, began and ended on my laptop screen. He lived – panned and scanned, in high definition and low – within the rectangular borders of my television.

The Sachin I knew was just a cobbled together collection of numbers and snatched fragments of video footage, a Frankenstein's monster of data and spurious details, not real flesh and bones. The narrow eyes glaring out with intense concentration from under his helmet, the broad smile that greeted every landmark score; they were not real to me, they were just the bookends of highlights packages; part of the familiar visual vocabulary of a recorded Tendulkar innings.

The supposed personal details I knew of his life away from the cricket pitch meant nothing either; they simply did not belong to the Sachin Tendulkar I knew.

I mean, come on: Sachin didn't really watch *Coming to America*, surely? He didn't really listen to The Eagles! Those were things ordinary mortals did. Sachin wasn't a man who ambled around the house in his slippers eating biscuits and scratching himself like the rest of us normal chaps – he was a mythical cricketing creature, a ruthless dispatcher of bowlers fighting to defend India's honour. How could someone like that not be able to swim? It was like suggesting Peter Pan was an expert trombonist whose favourite film was *Flubber* or that Robin Hood had a phobia of moths and was a big Pink Floyd fan. It was preposterous.

But now here he was.

In the flesh.

Crikey.

He was only twenty yards away.

And walking slowly towards me.

Double-crikey.

He was looking me straight in the eye.

The shrieking around me was deafening.

Triple-crikey.

Now he was only ten yards away.

My knees went weak.

My mind went blank.

I lost count of 'crikeys'.

My hero was *right there*.

I was like a menopausal divorcee at a Take That reunion concert.

Hot, flustered and surrounded by screaming fans.

(Although happily not sporting a 'Mark, will you marry me?' t-shirt).

"Sachiiiiiiiiiin! We love you!" The chorus line of Indian fans crescendoed with their loudest shout yet, bringing me out of my Tendulkar-induced trance.

"See what I mean?" added the steward. "He's like a god to them. I think it's almost a spiritual experience for them to see him in person. But he's just a man; he's just flesh and blood like the rest of us. There's nothing special about him."

"Yeah," I replied, my eyes still fixed on Sachin, as he paced around aimlessly, like a bored teenager traipsing around the shops with his mum. "Nothing special."

The steward was right, in a sense. This was an outpouring of emotion unlike anything I had ever seen. Sachin's every move was cheered and his attention sought by all corners of the ground, each as desperate as the next for as little as a wave of recognition from their hero. Just seeing him in person for the first time had moved me. It was almost cult-like and I was a fully-fledged, card-carrying member. I had drunk the spiked punch. I was a Tendulkarite and a Sachinist. I could not believe he was here. I could not believe he was even real. It was like seeing the Loch Ness Monster. The Sach Ness Monster.

But *nothing special?* Rubbish. Just making eye contact had knocked me near senseless. I was sweating, too. Either that soggy sandwich at the service station was disagreeing with me, or Sachin Tendulkar had reduced me to a quivering emotional wreck. So much for being cool, calm and collected under pressure. If I even got the chance to bowl at him today, I was in no fit state to do so. I'd have probably just asked him for a hug and burst into tears.

But what was it that Roj had said; 'every dream is just a succession of choices one makes?' I had a dream, and now I had a choice to make. I needed to go and seize the initiative. Sachin was within spitting distance. I had to do it. Not spit at him, obviously, that would get our relationship off to a bad start. Not many lasting friendships have sprung from one person spitting at the other. But what was the worst that could happen if I just asked him if he fancied having a quick net session after the close of play? He was, after all, a famously polite man (I read an interview where he said one of his biggest pet peeves was impolite people – yet another reason why I discounted the idea of spitting at him) so I'm sure he wouldn't be overtly rude to me. If I didn't ask, I would never know. The next time he jogged over, I would ask him. I closed my eyes and visualised how the conversation would go:

"Sachin! Sachin! Fancy a net after the close of play tonight?" I would bellow.

"Erm…Sorry, who are you?" he would ask.

"My name is Adam. Big fan of your work," I'd joke, playfully. "Listen, I've been practising my bowling a lot recently, because I reckon I could bowl you out with one ball – even though I'm not very good and you are a legendary batsman."

"Hmm. Tell me more," he would say, stroking his chin, ponderously.

"Oh! Certainly. Right, well basically," I would say, a self-confident smirk spreading across my lips, "I believe that anyone who is able to bowl a half-decent delivery could, on a one-off basis and if luck was on their side, bowl you out. Or any of the greatest batsmen of all time for that matter, like Sunil Gavaskar, Ricky Ponting or Dermot Reeve. If I bowl a straight delivery, you might miss it and then I would have bowled you. It's a statistical possibility – admittedly a very slim one – but why be put off by the odds being against you? It's worth trying, I think. It's a philosophical journey, in a funny sort of way – an attempt to prove that it's better to try and fail at something, even if it's a bit silly, than not try at all."

"That's a very interesting theory, and I admire your 'can do' attitude," Sach would reply. "And your hair is very nicely styled, too. I accept your challenge. Are you free at about 8?"

"Actually, 8:30 would be better for me."

"Excellent."

We would exchange warm, friend-for-life type smiles.

"That is fantastic news, Sachy," I would chuckle. "Hey, can I call you Sachy?"

"Of course you may," he would beam.

"Marvellous – oh watch out Sachy, ball headed your way."

"Thank you Ad," he would say. "May I call you Ad?"

"No," I would reply firmly. "I prefer Adam."

"I apologise."

"That's alright."

It was a done deal. How could he refuse such an erudite and charming explanation? I would have to speak quite quickly to get all that out between balls, but hopefully the adrenaline rush I was certain to get would sort me out. I took a deep breath, relaxed my shoulders and began to psych myself up. I was ready for him.

"Well batted lads," shouted the steward, clapping vigorously, snapping me out of my very important mental preparations.

"What's happened? Is someone out?" I asked in a semi-daze.

"No," he responded. "Somerset have declared."

"Oh, bollocks," I cursed.

"Yeah I know. I'd have given Hildreth a bit more time at the crease, too," he moaned.

The Indian players – including a familiar looking wee man in a wide-brimmed hat – were jogging off. My window of opportunity was slowing closing. I hadn't come all this way to pass up my first real opportunity to proposition (not like *that*) Sachin.

I sprinted around the back of the stands and headed towards the pavilion where the players were headed. I bobbed and weaved through the crowds until I had made my way to the front of the stand directly beside the pavilion. A groaning throng was already in position, bellowing loudly at the Indian players as they trudged off. There was no way I could get to the front. But I had no choice. This *had* to happen. I took a deep breath and hoped my voice would be louder than the squabble of voices in front of me.

"Sachin!" I bellowed. "Can I bowl at you? I'm trying to prove I could bowl you out!"

It wasn't working. The racket of the Indian fans was too much. The Indian players were almost all off the pitch. The noise reached an almost hysterical level. Sachin was obviously close. I wriggled my head into a small gap for a better view at the pitch.

There he was. Bats, posters and shirts and a thousand pens were thrust his way, but the little man just walked on by.

"SACHIN!" I roared with desperation as he disappeared from view. "LET ME BOWL AT YOU! I CAN GET YOU OUT!"

The people around me chuckled derisively, taking my very earnest request as some sort of joke. An Indian man beside me turned to stare at me.

"Oh my word, you are very loud," he said. "You have a voice like *floghorn*."

I smiled back politely. I assumed he meant foghorn. A floghorn sounded like someone who sold saxophones for a living.

"Sorry about that," I grimaced with embarrassment. "I was just trying to shout at Sachin." The man smiled at me sympathetically.

But then: *Whack.*

Something floppy slapped comically into the back of my head. (Stop sniggering, you at the back. Get your mind out of the gutter. It wasn't what you're imagining it was.)

And again: *Whack.* It was ostensibly playful, but annoying all the same, like a game of Buckaroo or Damon Albarn. I shuffled nervously around to see what the hell was happening. In front of me stood a middle-aged Indian man in a blue jumper. I looked at him and cracked an unsure smile. He smiled back.

Whack.

He had what looked like a rolled-up poster in his bony wee hands.

"Sorry, can you stop that please?" I said. He laughed.

"Don't be so disrespectful to Sachin!" he giggled. You know what came next.

Whack.

"I heard you," he smiled. "You think you will bowl out Sachin Tendulkar – you couldn't bowl him in a million years!" he cackled.

"Oh, I see," I smiled. "Well, you're probably right, but there is a slim chance…"

Whack.

The man turned quickly and began whispering to the man to his right. They both laughed.

Whack.

This man was clearly a crazy Sachin fan. Maybe I could pick his brains for some help? Perhaps he knew of a way for me to get closer to the great man?

Whack.

"Actually, I wonder if I could talk to you, sir…" I began.

Whack.

"I don't talk to people who disrespect Sachin Tendulkar!" he laughed.

"But I'm not…" I began to protest.

Whack.

"OK, I'm actually…" We were both laughing now.

Whack.

I turned around and tried to fidget my way out of the scrum of people.

"…Going to go," I finished, tittering crazily to myself.

Whack.

This was life in Sachin's world. No wonder he didn't stop to sign autographs.

India's innings got off to a steady if unspectacular start, but I was willing a wicket to fall with every delivery, in the hope of getting Sachin out to the crease as soon as possible. With the score on 51, the tourists' second wicket finally fell, bringing their number four batsman out to the crease, one SR Tendulkar. For the first time in my life, I would see him bat at close quarters.

My pen was poised over my notepad. Had he picked up any technical faults after weeks playing the frenetic bish-bash-bosh brand of cricket of the IPL? Was age finally starting to catch up with the Little Master as he crept closer and closer to the big four-oh? Was he, at last, perhaps showing signs of imperfection?

The short answer, was 'no'. The longer answer was 'no, not at all'. The longest answer was 'no, not all, he's Sachin Tendulkar, you idiot. Why do you persist in asking such asinine questions? And have a shave, you look scruffy'. My grandmother supplied the last one. Or at least the last bit of it.

All the trademark Tendulkar shots were on display; the wristy flick off his pads, the textbook push down the ground and of course; the elegant back-foot cover drive, where tiny Tendulkar somehow rocked his weight back, climbed up onto his tiptoes and with incredible balance and timing, punched the ball away to the boundary.

He made just 26 runs, but it was a masterclass. Like seeing the Mona Lisa in person, something I already knew to be magnificent was rendered more so by the fact it was right in front of my eyes. My notebook remained empty of pointers, besides hastily-scribbled notes to reinvestigate Josh's ideas of blindfolding Sachin or distracting him with a streaker. I caught the bloke next to me in the stand peering over my shoulder. Goodness knows what he thought I was planning when he saw the words 'blindfold' and 'streaker' written under Sachin's name, but when I added the phrases 'get someone to tickle him?' and 'custard pie to the face?' to the list, he soon moved away. The suggestive wink I gave him probably didn't help matters either.

After Sachin was dismissed, my interest in the game evaporated. This was what he had done to me. I finally understood why Indian fans just got up and left matches once Sachin had batted. Once you've experienced a little slice of *great*, it's hard to stomach a diet of plain, common-or-garden *good*. A fleeting glimpse of the great man was enough to turn me into the cricketing equivalent of a fat, spoiled Roman emperor.

Stumps were finally drawn as the baking sun dipped below the horizon and I sleepily made my way towards the exit. As I weaved through jabbering huddles of Indian fans lamenting their side's performance (a decidedly shoddy 138-8 in reply to Somerset's mammoth 425-3), I saw a scrum of activity by the pavilion; a scrum of bodies had formed and more tiny bats were swishing eagerly in the air.

Something big and exciting was happening. A Somerset fan, clearly as eager as me to find out what was happening – but also strangely keen that he found out before I did – blocked me off as I tried to lean right over the advertising hoardings at the foot of one of the stands.

He was a big lad, with big sunglasses and a bushy great 'tache. I am very much not a big lad. Stand me in front of Chris Tremlett and I'd probably come up to his crotch (in which case, if I am ever forced to compare sizes with him – not *those* sizes; although I'd certainly lose that competition too – I'd insist on it being side-by-side).

I shuffled with irritation as I craned my neck to see what was happening. The shouting of the kids at the front cut through me uncomfortably. This, I thought to myself, must have been exactly how Ringo Starr felt throughout all his years in The Beatles – largely oblivious of what is happening in front of him, bored of the sound of hundreds of constantly screaming fans and stuck behind a tall man with a moustache and glasses.

As quickly as the commotion had started, so it died down again. The crowd dispersed, leaving just a mass of crumpled litter and debris in its wake. On the pitch, a few stewards in jackets roamed around aimlessly.

"What about Tendulkar then?" one shouted over. It was the chap from earlier with the neat little beard. "Only got 20-odd, didn't he? See, he's not that special is he?"

"Yeah – I reckon he's past it," I replied with a chuckle. "If you gave me the chance I reckon I could get him out."

"Yeah, you probably could," the steward laughed.

Word was clearly spreading. The Little Master was absent from the field for the whole of the next day. It can't have been a coincidence. The bloke with the rolled up poster was probably a plant put there by Sachin to try and put me off my quest. One opportunity to collar Sachin had passed, but oh yes – he was running scared.

PART NINE

England vs. India, 1ˢᵗ NPower Test Match,
Lord's, July 21 – 25
Day One

There is nothing quite like a Lord's Test match. Just as you cannot claim to be a tennis fan without having visited Wimbledon or a serious drinker until you've woken up in Paddington station with your trousers on your head and a ticket to Edinburgh tucked in the waistband of your boxer shorts, so it is with Lord's and cricket.

Other grounds may be newer or bigger, but all lie in the shadow of Lord's. (Not literally, thankfully, as that would make parking nearby pretty much impossible.) It is the sport's founding stone, upon which all else bat and ball is built; the lush green centre of the cricketing universe around which everything else orbits. From the famous Long Room, its walls lined with portraits of the game's most enduring talents, to the plumby-accented, seemingly permanently snoozing MCC members in their famous 'bacon and egg' coloured ties – Lord's truly remains a one-off. And not in the way that Darren Pattinson's England debut or the night I spent with that Icelandic barmaid were 'one-offs', you understand. Slightly different than that. Not better, necessarily (she was *Icelandic*, for goodness sake) but certainly different.

Tucked away in a leafy corner of North London, the

modern world has changed and evolved around Lord's. Hotels, hospitals, petrol stations – masses of dull grey concrete now flank and tower with dreary uniformity over the ground. But inside its gates, just yards from the din of hoodied youngsters blaring tinny music from their mobile phones (it's always Tinie Tempah. Why is it always Tinie Tempah? It's never any Fleetwood Mac), the minutiae of cricketing history is still preserved, made and recorded, just as it has been since the ground hosted it's first Test match in 1884 (when youths listening to Tinie Tempah on their phones was presumably less of a problem).

With the Indians next to showcase their talents at the Home of Cricket, there was only one place to be on the morning of Thursday, July 21st – and that was sat among 28,000 fellow cricket lovers, a 'refreshing little something' in hand, eagerly anticipating seeing the great Sachin Tendulkar try to score his 100th international century.

But unfortunately for me, as play got under way, I was sat on my own, in an uncomfortably stuffy and entirely stationary car on the outskirts of London, listening to instructions on how to make the perfect carrot cake on *Woman's Hour* on BBC Radio 4. My 'refreshing little somethings' were a bottle of tepid water and a half-eaten packet of Hula-Hoops on my dashboard. It's always good to know how to make a perfect carrot cake, I told myself. Girls like chaps who can bake shit. (And by 'bake shit', I mean 'bake stuff', rather than 'bake not very well'. Chicks don't dig dudes who bake shit *shit*. Or indeed, dudes who bake excrement.)

It was midday and I was still trapped in my car, entirely cut off from events unfolding at Lord's without Radio 4 longwave. For all I knew, I could have been missing Sachin swashbuckling his way to his one-hundredth international century, sending the entire ground into rapturous applause and reducing millions of cricket lovers around the world to tears of joy with the sheer scale of his achievement.

And who knew what else might have been going on? Jimmy Anderson and Graeme Swann might have finally given into the latent and simmering sexual tension between the two of them and started holding hands between balls (I mean balls as in *deliveries*, not holding hands *between* each other's...oh never mind) at second and third slip. Good on them. But if they had, I wanted to see it. At the very least I was missing an opportunity to point out that Andrew Strauss had the exact same facial features as Bungle from 1980s kids TV show *Rainbow*, only transplanted from a bear's face onto a human face.

It had only been four days since my first sighting of Sachin in the flesh but my appetite had been well and truly whetted. Every time I thought back to that fleeting flash when his gaze met mine for the first time, my stomach leapt with a peculiar excitement. I was like a love-struck teenager, re-playing the moment over and over.

But the fact remained that so far, that was as close as I had come to meeting him. It was close enough to have been in contravention of a fairly stringent restraining order, but not close enough to have been accused of committing any form of assault (not that I had either planned, you understand. I'm too disorganised to be a stalker and too lazy to assault anyone). Today, I told myself, was the day all that changed.

As I finally made my way to the ground, I asked a friendly steward where the press entrance was. He looked me up and down suspiciously. I had a brown satchel slung over my shoulder and uneven stubble on my chin. I looked as though I'd slept rough the previous night, and seen in this morning with a bottle of gin and a cigarette. He immediately recognised me as a journalist and pointed me towards the press entrance. There, if all had gone according to plan, a press pass would be waiting for me, courtesy of an old chum from my days as a journo.

A burly but cheerful-looking chap with a shaven head was

manning the small opening, situated just down the road from the famous Grace Gates. I would have called him balding, but not to his face. He was a *big* lad. Bold as brass, I strolled up to him and announced my arrival.

"Hello," I said. "There should be a press pass here for me."

"Have you got your ECB accreditation card?" he replied.

"Erm, no," I said. "A friend of mine said he'd spoken to the press guy here and…" I looked at the bald shaven-headed doorman. He looked distinctly unimpressed. He was mentally marking me down as a blagger.

"My name is Adam Carroll-Smith, if that helps," I said, suddenly more sure of myself. My friend – let's call him A.N. Idiot (not his real name) – had promised it would be sorted. This was probably just normal, stringent procedure. It was Lord's after all.

The doorman turned away and chatted to a colleague briefly, before turning back to me, and crossing his hands in front of his waist, nightclub bouncer-style.

"I'm sorry," he said frankly, "there isn't a press pass for you."

To my ears, that sounded like an opening offer. This felt like a haggling situation, and I was prepared to bargain.

"OK," I said confidently, "but the thing is, I really need to get inside. I'm meeting Sachin Tendulkar." It was a lie, but only an isolated, tiny, mini, micro white lie. I pursed my lips in thought and toyed with the stubble on my chin. The doorman remained impassive. Lord's, it transpired, was essentially very much like any bog-standard Tiger Tiger nightclub. If you're name isn't down, you're not getting in. Somehow I doubted whether Lord's did the same drinks deals though (two orange Bacardi Breezers for £2? Bargain. A sickly, disgusting bargain, but a bargain all the same) or whether I'd find a drunk girl called Tracy in the gents toilets trying to beat her boyfriend up with the heel of her stiletto. Maybe, but probably not.

"I've been let down by someone who promised to sort me a press pass," I explained. The doorman smiled sympathetically. "But the thing is," I said, inching closer to the gate, "I *really* need to get inside." I raised my eyebrows at the doorman. "I *really* do." I felt my hand tighten around my wallet in my pocket.

That was weird, I thought to myself as the words left my lips. *It sounds like I'm trying to bribe my way into Lord's.* I stared at the doorman. He was now gazing into the middle distance somewhere above my head.

"So, I'd better go and find out what's happened with my press pass," I spluttered nervously. The doorman didn't flinch. I lowered my still suggestively raised eyebrows and scarpered back to my car.

I had driven all the way to Lord's with the express aim of speaking to Sachin Tendulkar, but left having achieved nothing more than unsuccessfully attempting to bribe my way into the spiritual home of the most gentlemanly game on the planet.

I checked my wallet. My bribe maximum would have been £11.26. It was lucky we hadn't started talking figures.

Day Two

The second day's play got off to a far better start – I arrived at the ground in time for the start of play and joined the throng of people filing down from St John's Wood tube station in expectation of a great day's cricket. Better yet, I had a ticket.

England had managed to prod and nurdle their way to 127-2 in difficult batting conditions before the rain arrived the previous day, but with the sun streaming down from an almost blemish free sky, hopes were high that they would bat all day and rack up a big score. At least that was the hope of the majority of people pouring into the ground; I could think of nothing worse. For the first time in my life, I was hoping for an England collapse. Don't get me wrong: ordinarily, I would have liked nothing more than to watch Jonathan Trott grind the opposition down with his Heinz 57 varieties of leg glances. I would normally be riveted by one of his doughty, scratchy, longer than a blue whale's broom innings; but not today.

I had not come to Lord's to watch competitive, professional cricket played by dedicated players striving to make the most of their abilities; I had come to watch an effortless exhibition of batting by a once-in-a-generation genius. Trott was in the blinkin' way.

As I passed into Lord's, it seemed I was not alone in thinking like that. Conversations in the short queue for the gents and the considerably longer queue for a pint all centred on whether Tendulkar might get a bat today. Most seemed resigned to the fact he wouldn't. England were, after all, a fine side. They wouldn't just roll over.

But it seemed perverse of the England players to let Sachin Tendulkar run around in the field all day when he could have been putting on a batting masterclass – like inviting Roger Federer to the opening of your tennis club and then asking him to umpire an over 55s mixed doubles match.

Secretly I longed for the days when an England innings could be guaranteed to collapse quicker and messier than an ice cream sundae in a microwave. Come back, Graeme Hick; come back Mark Ramprakash! Return at once, Gavin Hamilton! (Remember him? One Test match. Two ducks. One direct ticket to international oblivion. Or 'Scotland' as it's more commonly known.) All is forgiven!

Life was simpler a little more than a decade ago, when the England cricket team was full of talented but fragile batsmen like Hicky and Ramps, a succession of hastily-selected and quickly-ditched county seamers (Chris Silverwood, Mike Smith, Jimmy Ormond...the list is endless), doughy, honest triers (I'm looking at you, Mark Ealham) and wide-eyed, under-prepared spinners whose stock delivery was a long hop and their change-up a full-toss (take a bow Ian Salisbury, Chris Schofield, Richard Dawson, et al). England might not have been very good, but at least you knew they wouldn't hold you up if you had an important social function to get to. The old England would have kindly cleared out of the way before tea and allowed Sachin to get some runs under his belt before the close.

But this new England proved to be as ruthlessly bloody efficient as always (I blame the amount of time most of them spent in the South African school system), playing with the same calm, measured composure that had characterised their batting on the previous tour of Australia. Trott and KP were both obdurate and immovable after Andrew Strauss and Alastair Cook had been removed early on, and a long day beckoned for the Little Master in the field.

Don't for a moment think I am complaining about a day's cricket at Lord's. It was a glorious day for cricket. But somehow it was hard to get quite as excited watching Sachin performing a long barrier at mid-off as it was to see him playing a rasping back-foot cover drive. I wasn't bored, but I was restless and agitated, like KP at the non-striker's end when a left-arm spinner comes on or Shane Warne after three hours without a little lie down on a sunbed or some artful plucking of his eyebrows. Allegedly.

Lunch came and went – I'd brought my own rolls, but they'd gone all minging in my bag. The fillings had all gathered in the middle and the bread had started to sag at the sides; they looked a bit like Angus Fraser at the end (or indeed, the beginning) of a long spell. After the interval, England moved serenely on, with Pietersen edging ever nearer to another Test match hundred after tea.

But as the day drew nearer to a close, I had decided enough was enough. It was wonderful to watch England acquit themselves so ably against the world's number one Test team, but that wasn't why I was here. Watching Sachin mooch around half-heartedly in the field was starting to annoy me.

In fact, the whole Indian team looked about as eager to succeed in the field as Freddie Flintoff and Robert Key sat in front of plates of sausages in a 'first one to eat loses' contest. I scooped up my bag and decided to take a little stroll.

As I weaved through loitering crowds by the bar and watched still dozens of fans milling around outside Lord's gates, I overheard two Indian lads – both in their late twenties – arguing furiously but in hushed, semi-whispered tones. I plonked myself next to them for a spot of eavesdropping.

A roar from the crowd signalling another Pietersen boundary temporarily threatened to drown them out, but the smaller of the two raised his voice above the din.

"We are here for one day only," he half-shouted, angrily.

"I don't care," hissed his friend, as the crowd's applause died down.

"We should at least try. We will regret it if we don't."

They stood in silence for a moment. What were they talking about? Maybe one of them wanted to ditch the Test match and head to Oxford Street for some shopping? Perhaps the taller of the two wanted to pad around the gift shop rather than watch as England's batters piled up the runs.

"I was hoping to get to see Sachin bat today," I blurted out as I shuffled closer to them.

"Us too," replied the taller of the pair, "but I think England will bat all day now."

"It's a shame isn't it?" I said despondently. "I've only really come here to watch Sachin bat. It's nice to see England doing well, but it's all about the Little Master for me."

"Well we are Indian fans so we have come to see India do well – but if they are not doing well, like today, then we just want to see Sachin Tendulkar bat too," the smaller one said.

"I see," I chuckled. "Well, we might get lucky. We might

get to see him before the end of the day. Have you ever seen him bat live before?"

"No," they replied in unison.

"We are both from Indian families but we have lived near Solihull our whole lives," the smaller one added.

"Oh nice. I've never been to Solihull," I replied, somewhat predictably. The pair of them shot me a look that suggested '*I've never been to Solihull*' was a response they had heard many times before. We stood for a moment in awkward silence.

"We heard that Sachin has a house right near Lord's," the taller one exclaimed suddenly. His chum looked miffed, but tried his best to look as passive as possible. His slowly-building fury began to bubble ever closer to the surface once he saw my face light up with excitement.

"Sachin *lives* near here?" I squealed.

"Yes! Within a stone's throw from Lord's," the taller one replied, his voice working up an octave or two as he spoke.

"…Apparently," the smaller one added, with a note of pessimism in his voice.

"No, he does. *Definitely*." The taller chap turned to his friend as he spoke, before shooting me with a grin.

"Probably slightly more than a stone's throw away, the way I throw," I butted in, attempting to lighten the mood. "I've not got much of a throwing arm." I did a very poor mime of me throwing a cricket ball. It looked like I was doing an impression of Alan Carr fending off a wasp, or trying to effeminately stroke the fur of a tiger. I knew Sachin had a house in London, but until now, I had no idea where. Now I knew it was somewhere in this tiny pocket of North London. How many houses fit for a megastar like Sachin could be within walking distance of Lord's?

It was a lot to take the word of two random blokes I had only just met, but these were the type of openings, the little nuggets of information I needed to collect if I was going to succeed. I would go door-to-door if I had to. I might stumble upon Sachin popping back home to feed the cats or to put the recycling out.

"I'm Adam," I said boldly, offering my hand.

"Rav," said the taller of the two.

"RB," added the other.

"Pleasure to meet you both," I grinned. "Do you have any idea where his house is?"

"Yes," said Rav. "It's around here somewhere."

"Definitely?" I asked.

"Definitely," he replied, with a smile.

It was enough for me.

Day Three
S.R. Tendulkar – c. Swann b. Broad – 34
(58 balls, six fours)

I got to Lord's early, but did not join the chattering masses making their way into the ground. I didn't have a ticket, but that didn't matter. Today, I had an altogether different plan.

I would not get the access to Sachin I needed by sitting passively in the crowd. If Tendulkar would not come to me, I would have to go to him. I would find his house and ask whoever was in if the next time Sach was home, he could come out to play.

I'd typed out a little letter and everything. With any luck, his wife would read it and demand that he stop upsetting me by being so bloody difficult to pin down, and come and have a net. Either that or she would hand the note over to the police and I'd be arrested for posting a nuisance letter. They could add it to the one I sent to Matt Bellamy, the lead singer of Muse, asking him very politely if he would stop writing and recording shit records and move to the Moon.

The roads around Lord's, so it turned out, were jam-packed with some of the most expensive houses in London; huge, sprawling buildings with luxury cars – complete with obligatory personalised number plates – locked away behind wrought iron security gates. Some thorough research the night before (i.e. some not very thorough googling) had revealed one road in particular – the picturesque Cavendish Avenue – was well known as a celebrity hotspot. Not only that, but it was situated just a few hundred yards around the corner from the North Gate entrance to Lord's. And so, as thousands streamed into the ground that morning, I kept walking.

As I turned into the street, I spotted a group of fans – maybe half-a-dozen, predominantly English – all huddled around the entrance to a house with an enormous wooden gate, painted a bold blue. They took it in turns to take photos of each other posing in front of the gate, their fingers flicked into V-signs (happily, with their palms facing out, as opposed to the rather more aggressive alternative). When they weren't queuing up for snaps, they would dash across the road and try to take pictures of the house itself, peeping as it was between overhanging branches of large trees planted in its garden. I noticed one of the group was with her son, who was swinging a miniature cricket bat. This must be the place. They must be cricket fans. Another man had an uncomfortable and unwieldy-looking backpack on. Threaded through the straps was a cagoule; a big, horrible, shiny cagoule.

He was *definitely* a cricket fan. Only a cricket fan could even spell 'cagoule'. Ask anyone who hasn't sat in a near empty county ground on a damp Saturday morning what a cagoule is, and they'll probably tell you it's either some kind of Welsh stew or the name of a rare sexually transmitted infection (depending on whether or not they're Welsh, I suppose).

I walked as casually as I could towards them, eventually stopping on the very edge of the group. I tried to catch a snippet of what they were talking about, but the whispering was utterly inaudible. They were either very excited and overawed or planning on forming a human battering ram and smashing the gate down.

"Come on gang, we should get going, the cricket is about to get started," the chap with the backpack on said forcefully. I spied my opportunity.

"Are you chaps off to the cricket as well?" I asked, in my politest and most polished public schoolboy tones. I was, after all, a strange man hanging around ominously, so I thought it best to try and disarm him with my poshest accent. In the end it sounded a bit like I was doing an impression of Eoin Morgan trying to do an impression of Stephen Fry, but it got the job done.

"Oh, absolutely. Yourself?"

"Oh yes. Hoping to see Sachin bat today, of course, as I'm sure you all are." I nodded towards the rest of the group and smiled.

"Quite right. It certainly would be wonderful to see him get his one-hundredth hundred."

I liked this guy. He had a friendly, rosy-cheeked face, a bit like the sort of chap I imagine used to manage the MCC touring team on foreign tours. I could picture him giving strict pre-tour guides about the country they were about to visit ("...*avoid the water in India, gentlemen, and the women in Australia...*"). In another life, I could see him patronising the natives and refusing to take off his official blazer and tie even as the temperature hit 40 degrees in Sydney.

"I noticed you all taking photographs earlier in front of the house," I said boldly. "Is this the great man's house?"

"It is indeed," he smiled back. "It has been for a great many years apparently. Are you a fan?"

"Oh absolutely. I have been since I was a kid," I enthused. "I don't think we'll ever see anyone like him ever again. He's just such an icon, isn't he? Young or old, he just transcends generational divides."

"Absolutely," the man nodded in agreement. "And he's been through so much, too. So many ups and downs, but he's still going strong. Most people have retired by his age, but he's still as influential now as he ever was."

"Exactly," I replied.

Unexpectedly, the conversation dried up. I could see him starting to shift uncomfortably on the spot. I was holding him up.

"Sorry to do this," I blurted. "But before you go, would you mind taking a very quick picture of me, in front of the house?"

"Oh of course, no problem at all."

I handed over my camera, before settling into position. One quick click and the deed was done.

"Thanks so much," I said, as I took the camera back. "Sachin's been a hero of mine for a great many years. I can't believe he lives so close to Lord's, although I suppose it makes sense."

"Sachin?" he interrupted.

"Yes, Sachin," I smiled.

"Oh," he replied, with a note of confusion in his voice.

"I just assumed with all the talk of icons and…is this not his house then?" I burbled.

"No," the man chuckled.

"Whose is it then?" I asked.

"Sir Paul McCartney," he announced proudly. "From The Beatles," he added, really bloody helpfully.

This was a cocking nightmare. I looked at the picture on my camera. There I was, grinning inanely. I'd just posed for a picture in front of Paul flippin' McCartney's house, for no reason. Not only was this definitely not Sachin's gaff, but I'd also given complete strangers the impression that I *liked* Paul McCartney. I thanked my lucky stars that it wasn't Ringo's house. I might have had to flee the country in embarrassment.

For the rest of the day, I sat in Regent's Park listening to *Test Match Special*. I called Mr Chaudhary a few more times, but with no luck. I sent Professor Shetty another email, just to say hi. Nothing came back.

Sachin, meanwhile, batted exhilaratingly to get to 34 – his trademark back-foot cover drive getting an unfurling, sandwiched between sweetly-timed straight drives and deft, wristy leg-side clips.

Even with just the familiar hum of *TMS*, I could picture each stroke so clearly, his balletic and pinpoint footwork as clear in my mind's eye as it was to any of the spectators inside the ground. Even the sound of his bat on ball was cleaner and purer than the sound made by anyone else. A tangible magic seemed to be returning to the Little Master and it was coursing out of my tinny radio speakers, just as it had cut through the static on Rosh's old tape.

But just as it looked as though he might finally pouch that long-awaited and most special century, wee Stuey Broad stopped bickering with umpires and shouting at Kevin Pietersen for conceding overthrows (seriously, it's always KP) long enough to get Sachin to edge a drive to Graeme Swann at second slip. With Sachin back in the pavilion, I pulled out the letter I had been intending to post to his house and read it again:

Dear Mr Tendulkar,

My name is Adam Carroll-Smith and this summer, I have been attempting to fulfil a boyhood ambition by bowling just one ball at you. However, thus far, you have proven a difficult man to pin down. Therefore, I am dropping you this little message to see if anything could be done to arrange for me to come to a net session and bowl just one delivery at you. I have no discernible cricketing ability, but that's not stood in Luke Wright's way, so why should it for me? You could even think of facing one ball from me as preparation in case Jonathan Trott bowls at you during this series. I'm about as good a bowler as he is; only I don't look exactly like Zippy from Rainbow like he does.

But jokes aside, this really would mean an incredible amount to me and I can assure you I am absolutely serious. I am a former tabloid sports reporter and as such, have had the opportunity to watch a lot of top-level sport, but nothing to compare to watching you bat, sir. I would be happy to make a donation to any of the charities you support if we could make this happen. If you can help at all, please do get in touch.

Many thanks,
Adam

P.S. Great shout on Coming To America *– it's a brilliant film.*

I rooted around in my backpack, and pulled out a plastic bag. In it were some envelopes and a book of stamps. I folded the letter neatly, fixed a stamp in position and wrote 'Sachin Tendulkar, London' on the front of the envelope. I got all the way to a post box before I realised what an odd thing it was that I was about to do. But then I did it anyway. There was, as Polonius said in *Hamlet* (see Mum, Dad – I didn't waste my education, I'm quoting Shakespeare!) some method in my madness. Not much, but some.

PART TEN

I was woken up by the sound of my phone ringing beside my bed. It was Josh. It was just after eleven o'clock in the morning, and the Test match had just resumed.

I had stayed the previous night with my old friend Ed in North London. I was going to watch the day's play at his house before travelling down to Lord's later to try and grab Sachin as he boarded the team bus. I yawned deeply and ignored Josh's call. If it was urgent, he would call back. Fifteen seconds later, he did.

"Morning," I said, winching myself out of bed, like some enormous beached whale in Homer Simpson boxer shorts.

"Sachin is ill!" Josh shrieked down the phone, his voice taut and strained like KP whinging at wee Stuey Broad for hogging the changing room mirror to blow kisses at his own cherubic and totally hairless face.

"He has a virus," he continued, breathlessly. "Apparently he's gone to hospital and he might be out for the rest of the tour! What are you going to do?"

My mind was racing. If Sachin really was out of the tour, that was it. Done. Finished. Kaput. What the hell could I do? My summer started and ended with Sach. This was a nightmare! I could find out which hospital he was in, dress up as a nurse, sneak in, take a set of stumps and a ball and bowl at him while he was feeling under the weather, but that felt like crossing a line. I shook my head and scowled at my own stupidity. It was a terrible idea. I didn't have the legs for a nurse's uniform. The bum? Oh yeah. But the legs? No way.

I sprinted into Ed's living room and switched the television on. Almost immediately, David Lloyd began reading a statement from a man I knew very well – my nemesis, Mr Chaudhary.

"Mr Sachin Tendulkar," began Bumble, "is suffering from a viral infection and will not field until he has had a medical assessment."

And that was it. How brilliantly bloody vague. I called Josh back.

"What do I do?" I whined.

"Nothing you can do," he replied, bluntly.

"Ah bollocks to this, I can't sit and watch the cricket just waiting for news about Sachin. I'll go mad. I'm going. To the pub," I ranted. "I'm going to get drunk."

It wasn't the most mature reaction to a setback in the history of the world, but the thought of Sachin scarpering back to India so soon after he had arrived was almost too much to bear.

"Day in the pub sounds sensible," said Josh sympathetically, "but one bit of advice…"

"No," I snapped moodily, "I don't need any advice. This summer has been about one thing – bowling to Sachin, and now that might be about to go up in smoke. So bollocks to . it all. We've had months of build-up to him getting here, I've been in the nets and spent what feels like days trying to get *anyone* to help me get in touch with him – and now he might be about to piss off home. I don't need any advice. I need to get drunk."

"I know, I was just…"

"No. I've realised that I'm not in control of this," I squalled petulantly, "so I'm off to the pub. He's ill today and with any luck, he'll be well enough so that on another day, I'll be able to bowl at him. But for today – that's it, I'm done. Alright?"

"Yeah," Josh said calmly. "All I was going to say was that you should take some ID with you, because if you've had a shave recently, the bar staff will think you're about 12 years old and you probably won't get served."

Thankfully, I did have some ID and I did get into a pub. I turned my phone off for the afternoon and sat drinking pint after pint, alone. I lost track of the time. I lost count of the number of pints. I forgot about Sachin and cricket in general. I did well not to forget my wallet, keys and phone when I finally left the pub. As I stumbled out onto the street to find the sun slowly setting, I finally turned my phone on, and a flurry of messages and missed calls hurried onto my screen. I ignored them all. It was that sort of day.

Day Five
S.R. Tendulkar – lbw b. Anderson – 12
(68 balls, one four)

I woke up in a strange bedroom to the piercing sound of an electric drill juddering through a nearby wall. Where the hell was I? I scanned the small, scarcely decorated room for clues. There was a broken record player and a pair of sparkly silver platform boots. Either I had managed to befriend David Bowie or I'd been kidnapped by an eccentric but accommodating vintage shoe collector. I wasn't sure which was worse. One meant I might have to sit through *Labyrinth* and…actually the other probably meant I'd have to sit through *Labyrinth* too. And I hate *Labyrinth*. Goblins? Mazes? David Bowie looking like Axl Rose's mum? No thanks.

"Alright you massive idiot?" boomed a voice from the other side of the bedroom door suddenly. Violently, the door flew open, clattering noisily against the wall. It was Rosh. I was in his flat. The boots belonged to his flatmate's sister's boyfriend's sister, or something. I cheered quietly to myself. No *Labyrinth*.

As I rubbed the sleep from my eyes, Rosh slowly pieced together my movements from the previous night. Apparently, I'd taken a bus across London to Dalston and just shown up on his doorstep, blathering wildly about Sachin being ill and having to leave the tour and my dream laying in tatters, or some such melodramatic nonsense. Then I'd waltzed (probably not literally – I could scarcely walk in a straight line so I would imagine 16th century Germanic folk dance was probably beyond me) into his spare room and fallen asleep straight away, wearing all my clothes. And probably a few stray items I'd found at bus stops and in public toilets on the way home too.

It couldn't have been much later than 9.30pm when I'd flopped onto this alien bed in a drunken stupor. I looked down at my feet. I hadn't even managed to take my shoes off. On my wrist was a bracelet with the words 'What Would Oliver Reed Do?' written on it. My mind boggled at the thought of where I'd found it, not to mention what I'd done to earn it. I've read *Hellraisers*. I just hoped it didn't involve arm-wrestling any sailors.

"What's the time?" I asked Rosh, huskily.

"Half eight."

"Oh, gross. Too early," I burbled, composing myself briefly.

"You missed a good day of cricket yesterday, by the way," Rosh said. "England are going for the win today but India could still do something. They're 80 for one, chasing 458 to win."

I sat upright in bed. This was a big hangover. Bigger than the hangover of Samit Patel's belly over the elasticated waistband of his whites or the size of the innuendo-fuelled laughs my brother got when he walked into my room and brazenly demanded that I *feel this, it's well stiff* (he was talking about his quiff; he was using some new hairspray).

I was about as close to snapping as big Samit's trousers too. Why the hell had Rosh woken me up at 8:30am? I was livid. Or as livid as I could be with a hangover like this.

"Did you get my text last night?" Rosh asked.

"No, I was off my phone yesterday, I was…erm…well I can't remember, really."

"Yeah, well whatever – did you hear the news about Sachin?" he asked eagerly.

"Yeah, Josh told me. He's ill. His tour is over. Rubbish."

"Yeah, it was *utter* rubbish," Rosh sighed. "Sach is *still here*. It was just a bit of a bug. I think he's still under the weather but he came back to Lord's yesterday to field. He'll be batting today…"

"What?" I yelped.

"…And there are 20,000 tickets on sale for the day's play, so I thought…"

"Let's get down there!" I bellowed.

"Well, yeah, exactly. But they have just gone on sale *right now*." Rosh glanced at his watch. "So we had better get going or there will be a massive queue."

I threw some clothes on and felt my hangover instantly keel over in the face of a rush of endorphins and happy adrenaline. It wasn't all over. Sach was **back**.

****

"Is that him?" asked Geno, innocently. "In the shades?"

"No. That looks like the bus driver. And he's about sixty years old and about three stone overweight, for fuck's sake," Roshan snapped impatiently. More bodies – some in Team India tracksuits, some in blazers, one in a boobtube that really didn't flatter the wobbly, hairy belly of the bloke wearing it – filed past.

Rosh's friend Geno had been staying at his flat the previous night too. I had managed not to notice him as I toppled inside, despite the fact he is an enormous, rake-thin Italian man who looks a bit like Jesus if he played bass in Razorlight, smoked menthols and pouted a lot. Geno had slept on Rosh's sofa the previous night, and was already awake when we began busily getting ready to race across London for the start of play.

When he heard we were dashing off to a place called 'Lord's', he may have been expecting something rather different (more Catholic pilgrims, healing water, and miracles of a different kind than KP holding onto a catch or Rahul Dravid scoring 200* to help India chase down 458 – that sort of thing) but he had insisted on joining us. Rosh was keen for him to tag along too, although on reflection, he may have just been nervous about leaving him alone in his home. He looked the sort to take a piss in the sink and drink your milk straight from the bottle. Or worse, invite his mate with a bongo over for a 'jam'. (Give me a sink-pisser and a milk-swigger any day over a man who fraternises with bongo players. Bongos are for balancing drinks on or hiding specialist interest magazines inside and NOTHING else. And 'jam' is something you put on crumpets. It's not a verb.)

The three of us had managed to get to Lord's for just after 9.30am, but the moment we arrived it became clear we were already way too late. The queues for tickets had long since snaked off out of sight around the side of the ground. Stewards were even turning away eager punters as they stepped off the tube at St John's Wood station, telling them their Lord's pilgrimage had been in vain.

We at least managed to make it as far as the ticket booths before all hope of getting inside was extinguished. Rumours flew around that people had been camping out since 2am the previous night to guarantee their seat. That was dedication on a level which defied sense, alienated normal members of society and probably meant returning home later that day to a note reading: '*Derek, I've left you. I thought you were joking about camping outside that cricket ground last night. My lawyer will be in touch about the divorce proceedings. Rosie.*' Poor Rosie.

After being denied our opportunity to watch some cricket – and potentially Sachin's century of centuries – we had, rather predictably, gone to the pub. I began explaining cricket to Geno, but his eyes glazed over and he – like all Italians – reverted back to dreaming of espressos, scooters and Paolo Maldini's ageless and thunderously powerful thighs.

Against that, my explanations of the art of reverse swing stood no chance. I did at least manage to explain why I had been so keen to come to the cricket – and in particular my mission with Sachin. He nodded in the appropriate gaps in conversation. He even managed a 'cool' at the end of my little speech. Geno was definitely on board with the idea. By the end of the day he'd be a member of the cult of Tendulkar too.

I doubted it would be the first cult he had joined in his life, though maybe the only one where no-one made him take a strong hallucinogen by way of an initiation. Judging by his general demeanour, it seemed he might have taken one anyway, out of force of habit.

We spent most of the day talking about music (Talking Heads – good; everything else – not as good), films (anything with Colin Farrell – shite) and booze (all of it great, except Malibu). I checked the score in the cricket every half an hour or so, until England began to turn the screw and inch closer to victory after tea. Swept up in the excitement, we bundled back down towards Lord's, *Test Match Special* blaring from the tinny speaker on the back of my phone as England wrapped up the game.

We stopped and cheered and high-fived each other as Billy Bowden gave last man Ishant Sharma out lbw. The weather was beautiful. The game had been beautiful. I had enough booze in my belly that even if Kerry Katona had walked past, I'd have sworn she was as beautiful as the lovechild of

Sienna Miller, Gemma Arterton, Natalie Portman and KP's missus (I'm not sure how they'd be able to actually conceive a lovechild, but in the interest of scientific endeavour I'm sure they'd at least give it a go. I know a few chaps who'd chuck in a bit of research money).

And so as thousands of jubilant, pink-cheeked England fans gambolled out of Lord's, pink petals from the flower boxes on the back of the Tavern stand fluttering to the ground around them like victory confetti, Rosh, Geno and I stood and drank in the atmosphere. It was bloody lovely. To start with, anyway. But that seemed a long time ago now.

"What does he look like again?" I showed Geno the picture of Sachin on my phone once more. He stared at it intently then nodded. He had seen enough. This time, he would remember his face.

Well, he would remember it for about fifteen minutes, at which point he would point excitedly at a seven-foot tall ginger-haired security guard and ask if he was Sachin Tendulkar. Then he'd ask to look at the picture again, nod solemnly after a quick look at it, and proceed to point at a pregnant woman in a comedy fez and a t-shirt with 'Who's the Daddy?' emblazoned on the front and ask if she might be the small, distinctly Indian *man* whose picture he'd just seen.

'Nope,' I would reply, calmly, before mentally adding 'a long and sustained campaign of kicking him in the bollocks' to the ever-growing list of 'ways to hurt Geno' I was compiling in my head.

Another hour ticked by. It was absolutely ages since the game had finished. By now, all but the most die-hard of fans had left the ground. Many were still milling around outside, hoping to catch a glimpse of the Indian team as it left the ground. We stood there for what seemed like weeks. I needed a wee. Rosh was hungry. Geno had given up trying to spot Sachin and was back in a state of espresso/scooter/Maldini-induced reverie.

"Shall we just go?" Rosh volunteered.

"No. Sachin **will** come out," I barked, while doing the 'I need a pee jig', bouncing from one foot to the other and trying my damnedest not to openly grab my crotch in public.

"Yeah, but you're drunk and they've just lost. And he's not well. And you need a piss. He won't want to speak now," Rosh reasoned, impatiently.

"He might."

"He won't," Rosh moaned. "And even if he does, he won't agree to have a net with a clearly inebriated bloke with an enormous wet patch down the front of his jeans. I don't care how nice he supposedly is."

"I can hold it in," I said, my hopping increasing in intensity. "Let's just give it a bit longer."

"Whatever. He won't want to talk, Ad." Rosh folded his arms in a huff.

"Who won't?"

Oh excellent. Now Geno had waded in. Brilliant.

"Tendulkar," I replied, before turning back to argue with Rosh.

"*Who?*" I thrust the picture of Sachin on my phone under Geno's nose **again**. He took the phone from me and held the screen closer to his face. I piss-jigged my way back to face Rosh. He should have been acting more supportively. He knew what I was trying to achieve here. I told him I needed to hang around for as long as possible, just in case.

"In case what?" Rosh queried impatiently.

"I don't know," I whinged, childishly, "literally anything could happen. Mr Chaudhary might come outside and I might be able to grab a quick word with him, I might be able to speak to one of the other players and get them to pass a message onto Sachin, I might…"

"Didn't we see this guy already?" Geno slurred, suddenly collapsing once more into the conversation. "Wasn't he the guy in the shades?" I snatched the phone back from Geno.

We decided to call it a day, seconds later.

We trekked back to Rosh's flat, discussing who had the best haircut in the England team (KP, by a distance; he looks like a rebellious WWII fighter pilot called Buster or something) and stocking up on booze en route, before getting home and popping some Talking Heads on his shockingly clichéd and painfully East London vintage record player.

Rosh fell asleep almost instantly. Within minutes, his sloppy, drunken snoring was all but drowning out 'Once In A Lifetime'. It was hard to blame him. The room was warm and a day of drinking had taken its toll on me, too. I closed my eyes and began to drift off. The music faded into near silence.

"I've been thinking about your plan to play cricket with that guy." Geno's voice suddenly shattered my fuzzy head, like an ear-piercing Monday morning alarm.

"Oh yeh?" I spluttered.

This was weird. Geno had been thinking about me trying to bowl Sachin Tendulkar? I was literally astounded that he had. How had that snuck between Paolo Maldini's thighs (so to speak) and wormed its way into Geno's brainbox?

"Yeah man, I read about this great thing called Cosmic Ordering. You should check it out. I think it might be just what you need to get the job done."

Oh boy. I had heard of Cosmic Ordering. Noel Edmonds had claimed it had helped him to get back on the telly with that stupid bloody game with the boxes. I'd had a natural suspicion of it ever since.

"Come on man, give it a try. Let me just try and explain it to you," he begged.

I made a non-committal noise. Sort of a '*hmmnffffppph*'.

"Come on dude," he pleaded, "didn't Jesus say: *Try everything once, my child?*"

I'm pretty sure the answer to that was no.

"Seriously man," Geno implored me, "it will be good for you. You never know, you might find it interesting. I've only just started reading about it myself, man. I was the same as you to start with. I was like: 'hmm, this stuff sounds crazy, man!' But I'm serious – it's really something."

"I'm not sure," I replied hesitantly, shrugging my shoulders. At the very best, I felt certain a crystal skull or Ouija board was about to make an appearance. At worst, I could feel the ritual sacrifice of a goat coming (actually, probably more likely to be a rat; this was East London after all).

"Come on, dude; trust me." Geno shot me a wide grin.

I didn't trust him. No offence Geno, but I didn't. And I still don't. (I should be on safe ground though, I think Geno only reads Kerouac and Hunter S. Thompson. And *Nuts* magazine). But I was desperate. I had to at least give it a try.

"OK," I said, my right knee jiggling up and down nervously. "What do I have to do?"

"Well first," he said with a grin, "we need to get naked."

Bugger. Off. Suddenly the slaughter of an innocent rat didn't look so bad. I'd rather eat one than have to get my kit off with a strange and impossibly hairy half-Italian man. He started taking his jacket off.

"No, no, Geno. This really isn't for me," I stuttered. I could feel myself shaking with pretty genuine fear. I wanted to run and shake Rosh awake for safety. Geno stared back at me. Then he laughed.

"No, I joke, I joke," Geno chuckled. It didn't feel like a joke.

"No, listen," he continued. "Cosmic Ordering works like this: a person just has to write down a list of six things…" He mimed writing a list on an imaginary sheet of paper and looked at me, his huge bushy eyebrows raised high. "And that list is then submitted to 'the cosmos'…"

"The cosmos?" I interrupted. Geno ignored me.

"…and then you wait for it to become a reality."

Geno reached down beside the sofa he had plonked himself down on, and pulled out a sheet of paper and a pen.

"It seems a bit…" I wasn't even sure *what* it seemed like. But it certainly didn't feel like a nice mug of tea and a slice of Marks and Spencer flapjack.

"I know, I know…" said Geno, nodding his head sagely and handing me the pen and paper. "Now write down what it is you want to achieve…this thing about the cricket man and whatever else."

I took the pen and paper and placed them on my lap. Geno stood up suddenly.

"I am going now. You can write your list alone, without me watching," he smiled. "Do it naked if you like…" he laughed. It still didn't feel like a joke.

We said our goodbyes and I waited for the front door of Rosh's flat to creak shut. Immediately, I jumped to my feet and put the pen and pad on Rosh's kitchen table. This just didn't seem right. It wasn't cricket.

Rosh woke with a start. He squinted anxiously around the room.

"Has he gone?" he said immediately and with real panic in his voice.

"Yeah," I said, exhaling noisily, "he just left."

"Oh man, I'm sorry I left you with him, but I just had to have a little sleep." I nodded and smiled politely. I didn't need to tell Rosh about the Cosmic Ordering thing. Or the fact that he almost woke up to a semi-naked Geno. He seemed genuinely sorry for lumbering me with his very nice but slightly mad friend.

Fully restored by his nap, Rosh was ravenous. He plodded into his kitchen and began rifling through the drawers until he found a Chinese takeaway menu.

"Do you want to share something?" he asked.

"Yeah – whatever you get is fine." I closed my eyes and stretched out on his sofa.

"Right, I've written what I like, you add anything you want," said Rosh, thrusting a sheet of paper and a pen under my nose. Both looked *very* familiar. I recoiled, lifting myself upright on the sofa and arching my neck away from the stationery instinctively, like Rosh had just shoved a plate of dog turds under my nose.

"What are you doing? It's only a pen and paper."

I had to tell him. I couldn't react like that to a piece of paper and a spindly biro and not explain myself.

"Well, when you were having a nap, Geno started talking to me about 'Cosmic Ordering'…"

Rosh looked at me as if I was telling him his mother was actually an enormous crystalline substance used to make dog toys squeak when you squeeze them. He was utterly, utterly mystified.

"Basically," I continued, "it's where you write down a list of things you want to achieve and that list is then submitted to 'the cosmos'. Then you just have to wait for the list to become reality."

Rosh stared at the list he had made on the paper, and the words 'chicken chow mein' and 'battered chicken balls'.

"And this was the piece of paper he gave you to make your Cosmic Ordering list?"

I nodded.

"But you didn't…"

I shook my head.

"But now I have…"

I nodded again. Rosh looked a curious mixture of confused and…well, just confused and really bloody confused, actually.

"So…does that mean I've just 'Cosmically Ordered' a chicken chow mein and some battered chicken balls?"

"Yeah," I said, stifling a chuckle, "I think so. Now you're just supposed to sit back and wait for them to become a reality," I said. Rosh looked deep in thought. This was seriously breaking normal takeaway ordering procedure.

"Wouldn't it be quicker if I actually rang the Chinese takeaway and ordered it over the phone?" he surmised rapidly.

"Almost certainly," I said. Rosh played with the corners of his mouth with the thumb and forefinger of his right hand. He said nothing for a few moments.

"Shall we give it ten minutes though?" he said suddenly. "You never know – we might end up getting free food, if that's how this Cosmic Ordering thing works. Maybe I'll just sit back and wait for my chow mein to become a reality."

We both chuckled. Silly Rosh, he does like a joke. He picked up his mobile and dialled the number of the Chinese takeaway. He swiftly placed the order (non-cosmically) and hung up.

"Fifteen minutes," he said. "Although I still think we should have waited for a bit."

Now, if this were a Hollywood film, the doorbell would have rung at this point. Of course, it didn't. Because Rosh doesn't have a doorbell. But he does have a door-knocker. AND IT WAS BLOODY WELL KNOCKING.

We both nearly jumped out of our skins. If this was a man bearing free Chinese food, then goodness knows what would happen. We would either piss ourselves with fear or…nope, it would just be a pant-wetting moment of fear. No matter how nice the food smelt.

"I don't want to answer it," shuddered Rosh. He scrunched up the piece of paper with the takeaway order on and threw it to the floor.

"Me neither. This is weird." The door knocked again. This time, even louder.

"Why didn't you tell me about that piece of paper and the Cosmic Ordering stuff?" Two more hurried knocks echoed around Rosh's flat.

"HELLOOOOOOO!" A ghostly voice fluttered menacingly from the other side of the door. We were stuck in a real-life low budget horror film – but not one of those good ones where there is usually a wholly gratuitous nude scene involving the talentless but attractive female lead. No, more like one starring Danny Dyer. And shot entirely in Essex. Truly horrifying.

Rosh inched over to the door and tentatively eased it open. A shaft of dusky sunlight burst into the room. A tall, skinny silouette lumbered through the doorway. Rosh and I stood motionless in horror.

There stood a hairy Italian man in just a t-shirt, looking somewhat chilly. It was Geno. I was still a bit scared.

"Hey dudes, I forgot my jacket," he said, breezing back into the lounge. He picked up his coat and swung it over his shoulders, pirouetting neatly back towards the door in one fluid, flamboyant motion. He stopped abruptly and leant on the doorframe.

"Hey, Adam," he drawled. "Did you write your Cosmic Ordering list yet?"

"Umm, not really, no." Geno looked genuinely disappointed.

"Ah, come on man, just do it!" he chuckled loudly.

"I know. I will. Rosh wrote one though." Geno turned on his heel and looked at Rosh. He nodded his head, exaggeratedly.

"Nice going Rosh!" he said, nodding his head even more enthusiastically. "What did you write dude?" Rosh looked dumbstruck.

"Actually, that's uncool of me to ask you that. You don't have to say. I hope it was good, man. But whatever they were, you've just got to wait for them to become reality, man. The cosmos will deliver," added Geno as he skipped out of the house cheerily, slamming the door behind him.

A weird tension hung in the air between us. Neither of us wanted to be a part of this Cosmic Ordering thing, but somehow, I'd dragged us into it. I felt like it was my fault and from the look on Rosh's face, he felt like it was, too. We just wanted to listen to music and play X-Box and occasionally play Amy Winehands (look it up). The only Cosmos I was interested in had pictures of Reese Witherspoon on the front and handy articles on hair care inside.

"How about this," I bargained inan attempt to remove the scowl from Rosh's face, "if the Chinese takeaway turns up and we don't have to pay for it because this Cosmic Ordering thing really works, I'll make a list and put the Sachin thing on it. How about that?"

A wild, primal look flashed quickly across Rosh's eyes.

"Bollocks to that. If we manage to prove this ordering thing works tonight, I'll be making a new list and writing '*Emma Watson wearing nothing but a jaunty little hat, please*' and you can see yourself out."

"Can I take the Chinese with me?" I asked.

"No," he barked instantaneously, "I'll need to eat something to build my strength up before she arrives. Tell you what; I'll increase the order on the Cosmic Ordering sheet. I'll add a duck on. Deal?"

Sachin was no closer, but there was the chance I might end up with a free crispy duck*. The way things were going, I was counting that as a win.

* *The duck never turned up. Nor did Emma Watson.*

******

Fruitless email correspondence #3

TO: YET ANOTHER OF SACHIN'S SPONSORS (names have been withheld to protect the unhelpful/ unresponsive)

Dear Sir/Madam,

My name is Adam Carroll-Smith and I am on a quest this summer to bowl one ball at the great Sachin Tendulkar. Good eh?

I am just contacting you to see if

you guys could, at some point while Sachin is over in the UK, help me achieve my goal? It would not be a time-consuming exercise. *

Many thanks,

Adam

*Longer than boiling an egg (3-5 minutes, depending on the size of the egg), but shorter than an episode of *Last of the Summer Wine* (45 minutes).

RESPONSE:

Hi Adam,

You would need to speak to my colleague XXXX XXXXX in the UK PR team. I have forwarded your email onto him.

Thanks, XXXXX

TO: XXXXX

Hello there XXXXX, thank you very much for getting back to me. I look forward to hearing from your colleague.

Adam

P.S. Could you let XXXX know that an episode of *Last of the Summer Wine* is actually only 30 minutes, not 45? It might help sway his decision to help!

RESPONSE: None.

****

PART ELEVEN

***

England vs. India, 2nd NPower Test Match,
Trent Bridge, July 29 – August 1
Day Three

The phone was ringing. I was *absolutely* crapping myself.

"Hello, Mandy speaking, how may I direct your call?"

"Hello there Mandy," I said, as assuredly as possible. "Could you put me through to Mr Tendulkar's room, please?" I lowered my voice as much as I could, in a futile bid to make myself sound more important. And older than 17.

"Certainly sir, do you have a room number?" she replied, cheerfully.

This was unsettling. I had expected to meet a bit more resistance than this. She wasn't supposed to just turn around and start being helpful. Hadn't she completed her customer services training and taken the *shitocratic* oath (first, do nothing helpful for the customer and try as hard as possible to cock everything up)?

"Erm…no I don't, I'm afraid. I did have it, but I appear to have lost it," I said with the same poise and icy calm of loveable posho and future Prime Minister Andrew '*Never call me Andy*' Strauss shooting a pheasant or a polar bear or a Thundercat or whatever it is they shoot on their hunts.

I tacked a hearty, deep laugh on the end of my sentence for good measure. I sounded surprisingly at ease – but this was still a barefaced bit of blagging. Surely she would see through it.

"No problem sir, let me just have a look for you," Mandy trilled merrily.

Flippin' heck. I listened closely to the sound of her fingers click-clacking over the keys of her computer.

"How do you spell the guest's name, sir?"

"T-E-N-D-U-L-K-A-R."

"Sorry, was that 'B-E-N-'..."

"No, 'T' for tango," I corrected her.

I chuckled at the thought of a bloke called Ben Dulkar. He sounded like he worked in sales, loved Jager-Bombs and called everyone 'chief'. I bet he listened to Snow Patrol, wore flip-flops in winter and thought Boris Johnson was *'a total fucking joker'*. He sounded like an idiot.

"Ah yes, here he is," chirped Mandy. "Bear with me one moment." I really hoped she meant Sachin and not this odious Ben Dulkar character. We'd have nothing to talk about. I hadn't even been to Peru on my gap year and didn't even know what 'chang' was. It sounded a bit like a small oriental gong. Maybe that's what it was.

The phone line suddenly went completely dead. Mandy had obviously popped me on hold while she frantically searched for her manager. *There is another of those nuisance callers for Mr Tendulkar on the phone*, she was probably shouting while I sat in stony silence. After a minute or so, the line clicked back into life.

"Sorry about the wait sir," she said, with customary breeziness.

"That's quite alright."

"Can I take your name, sir?"

It had been a long couple of days. England were dominating the Test match after a topsy-turvy opening to the game, and the Little Master had failed with the bat again. Whispers were starting to circulate that he might – just *might*

– be past it. I didn't add my voice to the conspirators. I was half-expecting that if I did, I'd feel the *whack* of a rolled-up poster on my head again.

I had lurked dutifully outside Trent Bridge after each day's play in the hope of seeing Sachin, but succeeded only in taking a picture of the back of an Indian fan's head. Even the bloke asking the players to sign his forearm with a board marker was doing better than me.

As the players filed onto the team bus, it struck me how much easier this task would be if I was trying to bowl Abhinav Mukund. For a start, it'd be much easier to get in touch with him. Judging from the reaction (or lack of it) of the Indian fans when he boarded the team bus, he'd be glad of the attention.

And bowling him would be easier, too. Jimmy Anderson had dismissed him for a first-baller in this Test – a dismissal which added further weight to my conspiracy theory that poor old Abhinav's surname has been mis-spelled and he actually had some Scottish heritage. *Abi McKund.* It had a ring to it. It explained his dismal batting, at least. He could expect a call from Gavin Hamilton any minute.

Back in my hotel room after the day's play with too many pints of ale swilling in my belly, I slumped onto my bed and fired up my laptop. Bored, I searched through the thousands of tweets posted by fans throughout the day's play at Trent Bridge.

One tweet caught my eye, from a user called Rohit Kakar. One of his tweets, with a picture attached, read: *'Still can't believe I met the Little Master and took this pic with him!'* I clicked on the tweet and loaded up the picture. Sure enough, there was Sachin, surrounded by a group of clearly elated Indian fans.

Immediately, my Sherlock Holmes-like investigative skills kicked into overdrive. Where had the picture been taken? It looked like a busy road, and in the corner of the picture was an official-looking clipboard with the emblem of the Indian team. This was definitely a photograph of Sachin signing into the team hotel.

Within seconds, thanks to some intense Chloe O'Brien-style cross-referencing and frantic, brow-furrowed googling, I had the number for Team India's hotel. Bingo. What better way to arrange a net session with Sachin than by sorting it with the man himself in the comfort of his hotel room? And that was *exactly* what I was about to do.

"Can I take your name, sir?" Mandy repeated. I had been stunned into silence. I'd not only got past the first hurdle of the hotel receptionist, I'd galloped all the way to the finish line. I was just about to speak to Sachin Tendulkar in his bloody hotel room!

"It's, erm...Patrick," I spluttered. (My middle name, FYI.)

"OK," she squeaked. "I'll just connect you to Mr Tendulkar's room."

Poor Sachin. The whispers about his form were growing louder, and now he had to face the prospect of me brazenly calling up his hotel and demanding to be put through to his room. The phone line began gently ringing in my ear.

Suddenly, it all started to feel very real indeed. What if I was interrupting him while he was watching *The Weakest Link* or a particularly involving episode of *Morse*? He'd be furious with me.

Or what if the phone had started rattling away on his bedside table just as he was dunking a chocolate digestive in his tea? I'd probably interrupted his concentration and now he was having to fish soggy biscuit (two words which strike fear into the hearts of public schoolboys across Britain. Probably best not to ask why. Don't even google it, actually) from the bottom of his cup – and that was no time to speak to anyone.

And even if he was in a good mood, what the hell was I

going to say to him? Should I just blurt out my reason for calling straight away, or should I play it cool and ease my way into the conversation?

If I did the former, it might immediately alert him to the fact that I was just some idiotic chancer. If I did the latter, I'd just give Sach more time to work out that I was, without question, just an idiotic chancer. I was stymied by the inescapable fact that I was both an idiot and a chancer. Me and my bloody 'personality'.

My mind raced, but still the phone kept ringing. I sat motionless as the line burbled away. My palms were wringing wet with sweat. I hectored the ringing phone under my breath: *Stop bloody ringing. Pick up the phone, Sach,* but the annoyingly inanimate object failed to yield to my demands. There was only one thing left to do. I invoked the classic technique for making someone appear on the other end of a phone line – I started swearing. It was a sure-fire way to get a response. More than once the employees at my local library or at my mobile phone network have answered the phone to the sound of me shouting 'shit cakes!' down the line. I always felt guiltier with the library guys. Sometimes I waited until the mobile network guys answered the phone before swearing at them.

"Shit-hats!" I bellowed.

"Cock-master!" I shouted.

"Fuck-nuggets!" I yelled.

No sooner had the phrase 'fuck-nuggets' left my lips, than the ringing stopped. Someone had picked up the phone.

"Hello, Mr Tendulkar?" I said, my voice wobbling all over the shop like a drunk, newly divorced mum-of-four trying to dance in her new high heels in the Yorkshire Grey, or Monty Panesar trying to steady himself under a high catch.

I felt my stomach doing somersaults of nervous excitement. My boyhood hero was, in a manner of speaking, just inches away from me. RIGHT. NOW. I could hear his breath against the receiver. He was even closer to me than he'd been at Taunton. I had managed to puncture my way through the thick layers of protection around Sachin and get within his inner sanctum. I was on the inside! **Sachin Tendulkar was sat at the other end of the phone line from me**! Admittedly, he was probably nervously wondering what sort of idiot would ring him out of the blue and shout 'fuck nuggets' down the telephone, but that didn't matter. We'd soon put that behind us. It'd soon be an interesting anecdote we would tell about the start of our friendship when we took family holidays to Center Parcs or played air hockey down the arcades on a lads' week to Magaluf. If worst came to worst, I could always blame Mandy. Or Ravi Bopara (again).

But the silence continued. It must have been at least 20 seconds now. Something wasn't right. Immediately, my sense of excitement evaporated. I was no longer elated at the thought of Sachin at the other end of the phone, I was pissing myself more than Freddie Flintoff in the back garden of 10 Downing Street. I heard a crackle at the end of the line. Someone was definitely there. But what was going on?

"Hello, Mr Tendulkar?" I repeated gently. "Are you there?"

"Hello?" came the distant, barely-audible reply.

"Hello, is that Mr Tendulkar?" Adrenaline coursed through me. This must be what it felt like to get a black Nando's cards they give to celebs! Someone had answered. *It was Sachin!* Although, bloody hell, Sachin's voice was very high-pitched. And was that a Nottinghamshire twang I detected?

"Hello there sir, it's Mandy again."

Ah. That would explain the high-pitched thing. And the accent. And the fact I'd found the voice strangely arousing. "I'm sorry sir," she said, "but Mr Tendulkar is not taking any calls at the moment. Would you like to leave him a message?"

Of course I wanted to. I wanted to leave a message that let Sachin know exactly how important it was that I get the chance to bowl at him. At the very least, I wanted to explain why he might possibly have heard me shouting the word *'fuck-nuggets'*.

But if I left my mobile number, I'd probably be put on some sort of blacklist and marked (rightfully) as a nuisance to be avoided at all costs. The wrong move now could blow any chance I had of making this happen. I erred on the side of caution, like Andrew Strauss mulling over a declaration when England are 1,200 runs ahead against Australia under-15s (Girls). I said my goodbyes to Mandy and put the phone down.

I wasn't sure whether to be mildly pleased at how easy it had been to almost get through to Sachin's hotel room, or mildly pissed off to have got so close. I decided to ring Josh for some assistance on how I felt.

"Ring them back immediately," he barked after I had explained what had happened. "Ring them back and pretend to be his wife! I bet you they put you straight through! Just say you're Sachin's wife and you can't get through to him on his mobile and have to ask him something about the…DVD player at home or the boiler or how to turn the car alarm off, or what the dog's name is…just say any old shit."

There were holes all over this plan. It was holier than a block of Swiss cheese that had been used for target practise at a shooting range. For all I knew, Sach's wife could be on tour with him right now. She might be sat in his hotel with him. And even if I did manage to get Sachin to take the call, he'd pretty quickly work out that I wasn't, in fact, his wife. I shared my not unreasonable concerns with Josh.

"Look Ad," he replied, forcefully. "You need to take these risks to get this thing done. It's not going to happen if you shy away from these sort of things. You need to be more like those women who threw themselves under horses back in the day."

"The suffragettes?" I said quizzically.

"Yeah, them," Josh agreed. "You should be more like them."

"Josh," I said dismissively, "wanting to bowl at Sachin Tendulkar is nothing like the struggle of thousands of women to be viewed as equal citizens with men."

"It is a bit," he replied. "For a start, you're a girl…"

"Very good," I groaned.

"And you look a bit like a horse…"

"Very funny," I sighed.

"And you'd love to spend most days letting short men in elaborately-coloured silk clothing sit on your back."

I put the phone down. Then I picked it back up and re-dialled the hotel. I wasn't sure why. Mandy quickly answered the phone again.

"Hello," I said in a high-pitched voice. I sounded more like a pre-pubescent boy than the wife of an international cricketing superstar.

"Hello there, how can I help?" came the slightly bemused reply.

I couldn't do it. It was too ridiculous. I slammed the phone down in a panic. What the hell was I doing? These were the actions of a madman. I had taken advice from Josh. *Josh!* I tossed my phone aside and resumed tense laps of my room, agitatedly running my hands through my hair as I paced. After a few minutes, my phone started ringing again. It was Josh.

"So, what happened?" he asked excitedly. "Did you get through? Did impersonating his wife work?"

"Josh," I said patronisingly, "I'm not willing to break the law to have a bowl at Sachin Tendulkar. I just felt a bit illegal and I don't want to go to bloody jail because of this bloody thing I'm trying to do!" The line went deadly quiet.

"Right, that's it," he said, after a few moments of increasingly angry-sounding breathing. "I'm going to ring the hotel and *I'll* get through to him. If you won't do it, I will."

"No Josh…"

He cut me off mid-sentence. I called him back immediately,

but he didn't pick up the phone. I tried again a few minutes later, but his line was engaged. Oh *bollocks*. My mind reeled at the possibilities of what he was doing. Poor Mandy. This was probably rapidly turning into her worst day at work ever. I doubt the hotel's training procedures included a module on dealing with the likes of Josh. Hostage situations? Probably. Foreign callers? Undoubtedly. But *Josh*? No chance.

For all I knew, he was now practising a dreadful Indian accent and pretending to be the Indian Prime Minister and offering Sachin a position as Minister of Finance if he agreed to have a net session (blindfolded, of course) with a 'close personal friend' of his called Adam Carroll-Smith. He might even have teed up the possibility of a streaker making an appearance during this impromptu practise session.

I frantically searched the internet to see if prank-calling carried any jail time. I wouldn't do well in prison, and nor would Josh. I wasn't worried about dropping the soap (I'm more of an organic body scrub man rather than an old-fashioned soap kinda guy anyway, although the pretty little tub the stuff came in was still pretty slippery); it was the thought of those mandatory exercise sessions out in the yard that made me recoil in horror. And those bunk beds. I *hate* bunk beds. And Josh would hate it because the other prisoners would probably laugh at him when he tried to re-shape his eyebrows with his funny little tweezers in the communal bathrooms. Still, at least he could fend them off with swearing skills. Finally, my phone rang again.

"Didn't work," Josh panted, urgently. "Scrap that idea. Move on." I could hear him swallowing nervously. He coughed, weakly.

"What happened?" I asked fearfully.

"Just chalk it up as another blind alley that you've explored but that didn't work," he wheezed. "But anyway, that's OK – blind alleys can be good sometimes. Sometimes they lead to good things." He sounded delirious.

"How are blind alleys ever a positive thing?" I asked him. "By definition, 'leading someone up a blind alley' is a negative thing to do. Blind alleys *don't* lead to good things – they don't lead anywhere."

"Not true. You know my mate Ade?" Josh asked me, frantically. "He pulled some girl in Envy nightclub in Portsmouth and he took her into this alleyway behind the club and…*you know*…did the deed, so to speak."

"Good for him," I retorted, sarcastically. "What's your point?"

"Well it is pitch black down that little alley," Josh continued. "You can't see a thing, but he still had a *whale* of a time with that girl. So, you know, blind alleys aren't always so bad. Sometimes good things happen down blind alleys. And he saw her a load more times after that, so that meeting down a blind alley *did* lead somewhere. See? Blind alleys *do* lead places. That's philosophy that is. And romantic."

I grunted disinterestedly.

"Actually," Josh mumbled to himself, "it wasn't that romantic in the end. She dumped him after a few weeks because she started going out with a bloke who used to be a wrestler in the WWF. And she only sent him a text to let him know. She didn't even have the decency to ring him. Bit unkind of her, really."

"Surprising, that – you'd expect better of a girl who sleeps with random blokes in a dark alley wouldn't you?" I joked.

Josh chuckled. He sounded tense and tired. "Anyway Josh, what happened with the hotel? Just tell me. Whatever it was, I won't be angry."

Josh sighed deeply.

"Well…" His voice was low, and sounded heavy with guilt. "I called the hotel and asked to be put through to Mr Tendulkar, but the guy on reception said they had no guests by that name staying in the hotel."

"Right," I said calmly, keen to drag the rest of the story out of him and not scare him off like a petrified pigeon.

He paused once more and took another long, soothing breath.

"What does 'lewd' mean?"

I'm still not sure if he was joking or not.

Day Four
S.R. Tendulkar lbw b. Anderson – 56
(86 balls, eight fours)

"Hello? Hello sir, can you hear me? My name is Adam Carroll-Smith!" I barked into my phone. A group of England fans appeared from nowhere and started chanted loudly beside me, cleverly slipping Matt Prior's name into the lyrics of Kings Of Leon's 'Sex on Fire' to create: *'Wooooaaah, it's six from Matt Prior!'*

Ordinarily, I would have applauded the wit of their wordplay (and treated them to the song I always sang to myself whenever Ian Bell looked like running three: *'Bell-o… is it three you're looking for?*). But right now, I needed some peace and quiet.

England had just wrapped up an emphatic and thoroughly pulsating win in the glorious Nottingham sun. Jimmy Anderson, Tim Bresnan and wee Stuey had ripped through the Indian batting line-up with ease to put the Three Lions 2-0 up in the series.

It was so nearly a case of Edgbaston 1996 all over again for Sachin, for while wickets tumbled at the other end, he looked back to his imperious best – driving with grace and power to race to 56, before Anderson trapped him lbw. Until Harbhajan Singh slogged a few late runs, the highest score of any of Sachin's team-mates was a paltry eight.

But that was of secondary importance now, because I was straining to hear Sachin Tendulkar's agent on the other end of the phone line. Yeah, that's right – *Sachin's agent*. After a frustratingly slow first two days of the Test – and the third day's aborted telephone experiment – an email had dropped into my inbox containing the telephone number of the Little Master's closest advisor at almost the exact same time as England romped to victory.

It had taken him nearly more than six weeks to reply, but finally the seeds I had sown so long ago were reaping a rich harvest. If anyone could make this dream of mine come true, it was Sachin's agent.

"Hello? Hello sir, can you hear me at all?" I bawled in to the receiver, my hand cupped like a shell over it. The 'Matt Prior' song was descending into farce. The England fans started play-fighting noisily and ranking the team in order of '*ladocity*'. Yeah, me neither, but whatever it was Ian Bell came last.

The line was painfully quiet. I turned away from the streams of England fans leaving the ground and down a quiet residential side road.

"Hello, is Mr Saidu there please?" I said firmly and confidently.

"Who?" came the faint reply.

"Mr Saidu?" I repeated, my confidence ebbing away by the second.

"No," said the voice at the end of the line, "I'm sorry there is nobody here by that name."

He put the phone down with a clunk. How thoroughly depressing. I had managed to get the number for Sachin's agent, but it was the wrong frigging number. I was back to square one. And I don't mean the early 90s Barbados-based soca band 'Square One', either, however danceable their back catalogue may be.

I was more depressed than a beanbag beneath Shane Watson's enormous, waddling backside. I caught a glimpse of myself in a car window. I looked as miserable as Duncan Fletcher on a bad day. (Though mercifully not *exactly* like big Dunc, whose face resembles a strategically shaved scrotum with tiny eyes and a little sad mouth drawn on in felt tip.) Nothing appeared to be going right.

I stared back at the screen on my mobile. The words 'Mr Naidu (Sachin's agent)' were still on the screen. NAIDU. His bloody name was Naidu. I had managed to get the number of Sachin's agent and then cocked up something as simple as his name. It was like getting a birthday phone call from Barack Obama and calling him 'Brian' the whole way through, only nowhere near as funny as that would be.

Sometimes it really did feel like I was purposefully self-sabotaging this whole thing, like I was willing myself to balls this all up. I called him back immediately, my heart racing as fast as Jonathan Agnew's when Lily Allen started flirting with him that time on *TMS*.

"Hello Mr Naidu," I said fearlessly as he picked up the phone once more, "my name is Adam Carroll-Smith and I am contacting you because I am led to believe you might be a man who can help me with a little project I am working on; a project which involves your client, Mr Sachin Tendulkar."

"Ah, OK," he said calmly. He sounded genuinely interested in what I had to say. It was a bit disconcerting. I'd expected a scoff of derision at best and *'ah, you are the annoying chap who has been bugging Mr Chaudhary all summer, yes?'* at worst.

"Basically," I continued, taking his prompt, "throughout this summer, I have been trying to track down Mr Tendulkar, even if just for a few moments, to interview him. I have already spoken to Professor Shetty at the BCCI and to Mr Chaudhary, the Indian team manager, who have been very helpful, but they mentioned that you would be the best person to speak to..."

Where the hell had that come from? They hadn't mentioned that at all. But bugger it, I thought. All was fair in love and Sachin. If I had to play the BCCI and Sachin's agent off against each other, so be it.

"OK, no problem!" he replied enthusiastically.

"OK?" I squeaked, with probably too much surprise in my voice. *No problem?!*

"I will be speaking to him tonight or tomorrow," Mr Naidu said calmly. "Can you give me a call in a few days?"

"Absolutely Mr Naidu, but as I say, anything you can do to help would be marvellous," I gushed, sycophantically.

"OK, Adam," he chuckled. "Call me in a few days. I am sure we can do something. Goodbye."

I ended the call and threw my phone into the air in celebration, like a fielder celebrating a wicket or the late Michael Jackson showing off one of his children. Sachin's agent was going to help! He was (potentially) going to put me face-to-face with the Little Master! This. Was. *Huge*.

Granted, it wasn't a green light to bowl at him, but once I was alone with Sach, I could just ask him outright for a quick net session. Sachin is famously regarded as one of the must humble and accommodating superstars going. Surely he'd find my request to have a little bowl at him a charming, quirky suggestion that he would be more than happy to fulfil? It wasn't like I was asking him to help me move house or do some grouting in my bathroom. I just wanted to throw a cricket ball at him.

I was essentially offering him free practise time against an English bowler, during a series against England. Sachin was well known as a thorough and dedicated professional who left nothing to chance in his pre-match preparations, so really, it would have been foolhardy of him to turn me down. At the very least, it might have given him a nice nostalgic reminder of the days when English bowlers were a bit rubbish (hello again RC Irani! Oh alright, I promise I'll stop this now).

As I trekked back to my hotel, I totted up Sachin's scores in England so far. He had only scored 132 runs in five innings at a piddling average of 26.40. By the standards of most top batsmen, it was poor. By Sachin's standards, it was unthinkable.

Maybe I would need Josh's blindfold after all. I'd have to wear it to give *him* a chance.

PART TWELVE

Northamptonshire vs. The Indians,
Northampton, August 5 – 6
Day One

Satnavs are genius inventions. No really, they are. Everyone else I know seems to be able to get on with them. But I just can't work them. They mock me. They lead me astray. That's just a fact. Or at least mine – the little-known 'Total Bastard 3000' does.

Northamptonshire, India's next opponents on the tour, play all their home fixtures at the County Ground – a very nice little ground near the centre of Northampton. The County Ground is located on Wantage Road. You may remember I tried to drive there instead of Somerset. Apparently, I flippin' love Northampton.

But did you know there is also a Wantage Road in Didcot? Neither did I. Now I do, because I went there. Well I almost went there. And why? Oh, no reason. Well, no reason other than I selected the wrong 'Wantage Road' on my satnav screen. I don't think I did select the wrong one, but there we are. Apparently I did. Even though I definitely didn't.

But then who are you going to believe? Me, a fallible, chubby-fingered, sweaty human, or the perfect, robotically precise little machine that magically knows its way around the entirety of Europe? My decision-making and actions are clouded by soppy, irrelevant emotions. The satnav isn't burdened with that rubbish. It's dispassionate and clinically efficient. It's as if motor-racing irrelevancy Ralf Schumacher had sex with a road atlas of Europe and produced a mutant, electronic baby. *That* is my satnav. It's a total, boring, know-it-all dickhead. And don't say it can't possibly have a vendetta against me. You haven't met it. I'm half-expecting to wake in the middle of the night soon, to find it hovering over me with a kitchen knife, coolly repeating the phrase '*perform a murder when possible*'. But then we've all been *there*.

Anyway, as a result, I didn't get to Northampton until lunchtime, at which point I was told Sachin had been to the ground and then left to return to the team hotel. He wasn't due to take any part in the game, but would be at the ground tomorrow.

I called Mr Naidu to see if there had been any update in arranging my interview with Sachin. His phone was permanently off. I called Mr Chaudhary too. No dice. This was a dice free zone. This was Pop-up Pirate.

There wasn't much I could do, but enjoy the glorious weather. So I sat in the sunshine, kicked off my shoes and ate a chicken burger. The burger disagreed with me, so I went back to my hotel. I fell asleep with all my clothes on and the title page of the *Coming to America* DVD playing on a loop on my laptop. A successful day, all in all.

Day Two

I got to the ground early in the hope of catching Sachin as he hopped off the enormous red and blue team bus, but by the time I had navigated the early morning traffic to Wantage Road (yes, the one in Northampton, smart arse), the team bus was already parked up.

I took a stroll around the ground and tried to pick Sachin's figure out among the red-shirted Indian players practising on the outfield, but they were all too tall and too slender to be Tendulkar. And call me an obsessive, but none of them had that aura, that presence about them. They were mere mortals. The Indian supporters were more subdued than usual, too – another dead giveaway that the Little Master wasn't on display. That familiar squall of noise and those customary, lolloping chants of '*Sachiiiiiiiiiin, Sach-in!*' were notably absent. I had become accustomed to the devotional din of his fans. All felt quiet and still without them, and without him.

Sachin was obviously avoiding the searing gaze of the thousands of Indian fans packed into the ground – and the blazing hot Northamptonshire sun, to boot – by putting his feet up in the pavilion.

It was hard to blame him. After watching two Indian girls, both at least 21 years of age, almost faint with overexcitement because Suresh Raina looked at them (I'm not even sure he did, he was wearing sunglasses at the time) you could forgive Sachin for staying put. He might have given some of them a heart attack. I'm fairly sure the average Indian cricket fan would turn down the chance to meet alien life from the distant reaches of the solar system (some of which, judging by the locals, might have already arrived and settled in Northampton) to watch little Sach scratch his bum during a fielding drill or spot him buying a pasty at a service station on the M4.

And so with Sachin locked away, I settled in near the boundary edge and waited patiently for him to do his promised walkabout. Granted, a rugby team's worth of minders and elderly, blazered Northants officials would probably be protecting him on all sides, but I could still get close enough to make my pitch. All that was left now, was to wait. At least that's what I should have done. What I actually did was sit still for about ten minutes, then get incredibly fidgety and bored.

This wasn't the way to do things, I told myself. I couldn't just sit there so passively. Sachin wasn't going to come to me, so I would have to get to him. A thought dropped into my head. It was a mad thought, but it was something I had always wanted to try. I bounded over to the entrance to the changing rooms, a huge grin plastered on my face. There stood a man in a smart blazer. Soon, I would be waltzing past him using nought but the power of my own mind. It was time to go *Jedi*.

"Excuse me," I said in my plummiest tones. "I need to get into the pavilion please, to interview Sachin Tendulkar." I smiled a confident, winning smile. My voice was strong and free from any trace of uncertainty. I was a man with an appointment to see Sachin. Asking to enter the pavilion was a mere formality – or at least that was the impression I hoped I would convey. LL Cool A was *back*.

"Do you have a pass?" the man on the gate asked. I knew the drill from here.

"You don't *need* to see my identification," I replied confidently, arching my eyebrows up like Obi Wan Kenobi.

That's right. It was the '*these are not the droids you're looking for*' approach; a cunning little mind-control wheeze that had managed to fool a pair of highly-trained Stormtroopers in *Star Wars*, and if it had worked on them, it had to work for me now. I wasn't trying to smuggle two annoying robots (the first to ever enter into an intergalactic civil partnership, and good for them too) past the remorseless foot soldiers of a totalitarian, intergalactic evil empire, I was just trying to get the better of a middle-aged, slightly podgy man who worked for a county cricket club in a smallish town in England. He wasn't clad head-to-toe in intimidating white fibreglass. He didn't even have one of those blasters that went '*pyew-pyew*' and fired colourful laser beams. He looked like his name was Ian. Or Derek.

"I'm afraid I do," he laughed.

Hmm. The force was clearly strong in this one. He was

no weak-minded Stormtrooper. He probably had a cousin who was a Sith Lord or something. Maybe his name was Ian Sithlord or Derek Vader. Perhaps the Empire upped sticks and colonised Northamptonshire after Luke Skywalker blew the shit out of the Death Star. It's possible. But I was not about to be deterred. I would soon get the better of this crafty old man.

"I'm afraid I really do need to get inside and interview Mr Tendulkar," I insisted calmly, a smile plastered on my face.

"I'm sorry, but you'll have to take that up with someone else," he grinned politely. "I cannot let you inside, sir."

This was strange. It was definitely not even *close* to working. For the first time in my life, I was faced with the awkward truth that *Star Wars* might just be a great big pile of useless old bollocks. Why the flippin' frig wasn't this working?

But wait. OF COURSE! I had forgotten a very important part of the manoeuvre. No wonder it hadn't worked yet.

"Oh. You definitely can't?" I replied, with a wry grin. I ran my hand through the air in front of the steward, in a vaguely mystic-looking motion – just like Obi Wan had done with those troopers. The steward looked at me in a peculiar fashion. Fair enough, I suppose. I looked like I was trying to charm an invisible snake.

"I *definitely* can't," came the staunch reply. He really was not going to budge. Northamptonshire County Cricket Club was obviously more of a totalitarian, intergalactic evil empire than I'd first anticipated. I didn't have *A New Hope* in hell (sorry, I couldn't resist) of blagging my way past this bloke, and not for the first time, George Lucas had made me look like a right idiot. (The other time was when I took one of my first girlfriends to see *The Phantom Menace* and promised her it would be 'brilliant'. It wasn't. Jar Jar Binks? Yeah, nice one; cheers, George.)

"OK," I smiled. "I'll try again later."

"You can try again later, sir," he chimed in abruptly, "but

unless you have permission to enter the building, you won't be able to go inside." His voice was sterner than before. Clearly, he had me down as a time-waster. I contemplated trying to do the Darth Vader thing where he moved his thumb and forefinger together and the person opposite him mysteriously started choking, but it felt like crossing a line. I was 90 percent certain it wouldn't work, but I couldn't be sure. I didn't want a murder charge hanging over me. I'd just bought a Spotify subscription and one of those enormous bottles of Ribena (with the built-in handle) and both would go to waste if I was banged up.

"Oh that's no problem," I grinned. "I'll just go and get that permission sorted."

I retreated to my seat in the stands and twiddled my thumbs while some frankly dire cricket was played out in front of me. A few hours ambled by and the game advanced past tea. India were turning in an appalling performance. The crowd were bored. I was bored. I hoped the steward blocking my path to Sachin was bored too. I headed back.

"Hello again," I chirped. "Here to interview Sachin. I spoke to one of the chaps in reception and they said it would be fine."

It was a bluff, but I said it with conviction and began easing myself towards the gate. I could see the steward's face beginning to soften. He unfurrowed his not insubstantial brow but remained silent while he sized up the situation. I sensed an opportunity. I had one foot in the door. I did my best to maintain a neutral, composed look. The tiniest slip-up now would surely expose the real me as the feckless, irrational blaggard I really was.

"But Sachin Tendulkar isn't at the ground today, sir."

My composed face slumped into a more familiar gormless expression. The steward smiled. It was an insufferably smug smile, but he was entitled to be triumphant. He had beaten me.

I walked away a few steps before turning back. I held my thumb and forefinger in the air and slowly squeezed them together while looking at the steward. Nothing happened. It was probably just as well.

The match ended limply, the Indian fielders slumping off the field in a slow-moving procession, each looking about as enthusiastic and full of beans as a newly neutered puppy. Northampton, it seemed, had had a profoundly negative effect on the tourists. For the Indians, there was no joie de vivre about life in this quiet patch of Middle England. Even though they have a really nice Nando's. Obviously, that wasn't enough.

As I settled down in my hotel room for the night with a takeaway pizza (Tandoori Hot with no onions, if you're interested) I opened up my laptop to check my emails. Sachin might not have been in Northampton, but maybe just by making the effort to get here myself, some piece of good news might have landed in my inbox.

It hadn't, obviously. Instead, I had a little Google search for the latest news about Sachin. I knew he wasn't injured, but there had to be some explanation for his bizarre no-show at Wantage Road. Turns out, there was:

"Indian batting maestro Sachin Tendulkar is expected to attend an event called 'Champions Live' after opting out of the team's practise match at Northamptonshire," read one news report *"Champions Live"*, it continued, *"is an event to felicitate Indian cricket legend Sunil Gavaskar and will see the international launch of a music CD of poems written by Ramesh Tendulkar, Sachin Tendulkar's father. Sachin's elder brother Ajit has confirmed the batting maestro's participation in the event."*

It had to be a wind-up. I called Mr Chaudhary, but got no reply. Ditto with Mr Naidu. This was India's one warm-up game before the next Test at Edgbaston; surely Sachin wouldn't have ducked out of the match to go to an awards ceremony? This was a man in patchy form, chasing his one-hundredth international century – and more than that, a man renowned for his obsessive attention to detail and unflinching dedication to all things cricket. It made no sense. Surely he'd want as much practise time as possible?

I pushed the pizza box from my lap and began pacing my room. I snarled in disgust at the slowly dripping showerhead in the bathroom. I scuffed my feet petulantly on the hideous swirling pattern on the cheap carpet. I looked disdainfully as the reception on the fun-sized television set fizzed and popped erratically.

This was hellish. I didn't *want* to be here, sleeping in a dingy motorway-side hotel, eating pizza on my own and watching a repeat of *Come Dine With Me* (although it was a good episode. One of the contestants described her pudding as 'subliminal' which seemed a bit cheap to me: '*yeah, it might look like I've not made pudding,*' the contestant could whine, *but I have. It's just subliminal. You've already been eating it, in your minds, without realising it.* '); I was only here because I was serious about tracking down my boyhood hero. But Sachin wasn't keeping his end of the bargain. He wasn't playing fair. He didn't give two hoots.

A real chance to edge closer to fulfilling this dream of mine had been snatched away because Sachin had swanned off to some fancy-pants bash in London. I was livid with the situation. I was tired, miles from home and even further from fulfilling this dream.

For once, the man who supposedly always put cricket first had decided something else was more important. It may have been an event to launch a CD of his beloved father's poetry, but it felt like a subtle reminder. Cheap hotels in Northampton were the place for idiots like me; glitzy bashes in London were Sachin's natural home – and never the twain shall meet. Superstars don't rough it with mere mortals. He really did not live in the same world as me. For Sachin, getting his pads on and facing one delivery from me was akin to a trip to Northampton; unnecessary and inconvenient. Even if the Nando's here is *really* good.

I perched myself on the end of my bed, brushing a stray, jet black hair from the sheets. I stared at myself in the mirror opposite. My hair wasn't jet black. That wasn't one of my hairs. I looked at my watch. It was already after eight o'clock. The event was just getting under way. My phone rang quietly beside me. It was a number I didn't recognise.

"Hello Dad," roared the voice at the other end of the line. I was either live on Jeremy Kyle and being introduced to a son I never knew I had (probably from that dalliance with the Icelandic girl. Actually, was she Icelandic? She might just have worked in Iceland) or it was Jono.

"Jono?" I guessed, my fingers tightly crossed in hope.

"Yes mate, how's things?" I breathed a sigh of relief. I don't like cold weather or frozen ready meals. And I still wasn't sure about the 'left-wing' and 'right-wing' politics thing. I definitely still wasn't ready to be a dad.

"So," Jono said eagerly, "what's the latest on the Sachin pursuit? How is Northampton?"

"Northampton," I sighed, "is Sachin-less. He's in Greenwich at a poetry event or something."

"So?" Jono scoffed. "Bloody well get yourself to Greenwich! Immediately!"

So I did. Faster than you can say *'Is that really a good idea?'*

****

My phone rang early the next morning; too bloody early. I had just managed to enjoy (endure, more like) a whole thirty minutes of uninterrupted sleep. My back was sore. The right side of my head felt damp, for some reason. A fearful smell – like someone had draped sweaty jockstraps over both my shoulders – was festering in my nostrils. Tentatively, I checked my shoulders. No jockstraps. That smell (I swear I could hear particles of clean air screaming as its foul funk approached) was me. I tried to stretch but succeeded only in painfully banging my knee. One wrong move and I might have ended up with the handbrake jammed in a place it wasn't supposed to be. My phone continued to buzz annoyingly on the passenger seat. It was Rosh.

"Alright mate," he chirped down the line, "where are you?"

"London…" I replied, hoarsely. "Greenwich, to be precise."

"Greenwich?" Rosh asked, with a note of shock in his voice.

"Yeah. Greenwich," I mumbled, sleepily.

"Oh right," he muttered. "I just got your texts and your voicemail about needing somewhere to stay last night. I was ringing to see if you were alright, but obviously you are." He was wrong. *Very* wrong. "So," he continued, "who did you stay with last night?"

"No one," I grunted. "Nobody was answering their phones and I was really worried I might fall asleep at the wheel if I tried to drive back to Portsmouth or Brighton, so…"

"Shit," Rosh exclaimed. "Did you try Dave?"

I told him I had.

"Jono?" he asked.

"Didn't reply," I snapped with venom in my voice. "Even though he's basically the reason I came here."

"Blake?"

"On holiday."

"Rich?"

Rosh really wasn't getting the message. NO ONE had replied. I even asked a few ex-girlfriends if they had a bed for me for the night, but their responses – that it would be 'weird', 'awkward' and 'impractical' respectively (which is actually a neat summation of the reasons why I split up with them in the first place) – left me in no doubt about how I would be spending my night. Cramped, cold and petrified, wedged in the front seat of my car at a 35 degree angle. It was orthopaedic hell. As I finished telling Rosh about my wondrous evening, I could hear the earliest traces of laughter creeping into his voice.

"Why didn't you stay in a hotel?" he pressed.

"I can't afford a hotel," I scoffed. "Who do you think I am, the little man with the moustache and the top hat from Monopoly?" I wasn't the little man with the moustache and the top hat from the Monopoly box. I can't grow a moustache and top hats make me look like T-Pain's aristocratic whiteboy cousin.

"Well what about a hostel?" Rosh quizzed me.

"Don't be stupid," I barked, "after that incident with the Americans in that German place a few years ago, I swore I'd never set foot in one again." In a nutshell, I woke up to find an odd American couple taking pictures of my ex-girlfriend and I ('awkward', if you're wondering) while we were asleep. They insisted there was nothing weird about it. I begged – no, demanded – to differ with that assessment. Were it not for the fact I was starkers underneath the duvet covers, I would have forcibly wrestled the camera from their grasp. As it was, I had to watch as they shuffled out of the dormitory with a picture of my ex and I sound asleep. They've probably got it hanging in their nutty room back in Backwater, USA, right now, in a novelty '*My Favourite Pets*' picture frame, alongside hundreds of photos of Jennifer Aniston with the eyes scratched out, jars full of dead bees (marked 'some bees - *dead*') and posters of the musical *Avenue Q* smeared in fox shit and signed by the cast. A bit like the interior of a typical Wimpy restaurant, minus some strategically placed kids' menus.

"So what the hell *did* you do?" Rosh asked, with a scarcely-hidden guffaw in his throat.

"There was only one thing to do, wasn't there?" I whinged. "I slept in my car."

Rosh stifled a giggle.

"You just parked your car up and slept inside?" Rosh laughed.

"Yes," I hissed.

"In Greenwich!" His voice rocketed up a couple of octaves. "Good night's kip?"

"Well, Roshan," I spat, "when I was awake, I was shitting myself that someone might smash my window open and steal the car or the police would come round and arrest me for squatting or something, and whenever I *did* manage to drop off to sleep, I kept thinking that someone actually *was* smashing my windows and the police actually *had* turned up. And I'm sure there is a wasp in here. So not great, Rosh, all in all. I've had better nights. And better mornings, to be honest."

"Well come round now," Rosh offered kindly, "and have a kip here if you want. Or some breakfast or something."

Rosh had done well to resist openly laughing in my face up until now. But I didn't hold much hope of him keeping the front up for much longer.

"No…I can't," I mumbled.

"Why not?" asked Rosh.

I sighed deeply.

"Well," I began, wearily, "because I was basically shitting myself last night, I left the radio on to calm me down and relax me a bit (Radio 4, naturally), but that ran my battery down on my car, so when I just tried to get going this morning, the stupid thing wouldn't start. So I'm stranded in Greenwich until someone can fix my car. And I'm sweating like mad because I had to wear every item of clothing I had with me last night because it got quite cold. But now it's warmed up and I need to start shedding layers."

"Why didn't you put the heating on?" asked Rosh, not unreasonably.

I sighed. I knew what was coming.

"I didn't put the heating on," I began monotonously, "because I thought it might run my battery down and mean

I couldn't start the car this morning."

"What, you mean like the radio…"

"Yes," I interrupted him, "*like the radio did.*"

He burst out laughing, his throaty chuckles juddering uncomfortably against my eardrums.

"Sorry mate, I shouldn't laugh." He cleared his throat and composed himself. "Why was Sachin in Greenwich anyway? I thought the tour game was in Northampton?"

"It is, but Sachin wasn't playing in the game, because – as I found out late yesterday – he had agreed to attend this event at the IndigO2 last night."

"Bloody hell. So you drove all the way from Northampton to Greenwich," Rosh tittered, "to see Sachin Tendulkar…"

"Yes," I snapped.

"At some sort of event…"

"It was something to do with his dad's poetry," I groaned.

"At a *poetry event!*" he squealed. "And then you had to sleep in your car, which now won't start…"

"Yes," I rasped. "And I had a hotel booked in Northampton, too."

Roshan started tittering quietly as I began to slip my spare pair of socks off.

"And let me guess," Rosh said suddenly, "you didn't get to see Sachin?"

"No," I whimpered. Pretty soon Rosh would clock the fact that I'd left the warm sanctity of my hotel room to drive 100 miles away in the pitch dark, just to sleep, petrified and shivering, *quite near* to a large venue that Sachin had been in – for a bit – earlier that evening.

Rosh erupted into gales of mocking laughter.

"So essentially," he began, through sharp bursts of the giggles, "you drove almost 100 miles away from your warm hotel room just to sleep, shivering and petrified…"

"Yes," I grunted, by way of an interruption.

"That's got to be even more pointless than your drive up

the M1 when you should have been in Somerset!" he chortled mockingly. "You've broken your own record! I'll call the *World Book of Guinness Records* again, shall I?"

"It's the *Guinness Book of...* never mind." I couldn't do it. I had no purchase in the sarcasm and pedantry world.

Rosh roared with laughter again. I slammed the phone down in frustration. It started ringing again a few minutes later. Only this time, it wasn't Rosh. No, no, this time, it was something – and someone – far worse; someone altogether more terrifying. Some more piss-taking from Rosh suddenly seemed like a leisurely walk in the park with a particularly well-behaved labradoodle, an especially skinny latte and an entirely guilt-free lemon and poppy seed muffin.

"Who is this?" I asked tentatively, as I picked up the call. But I already knew the answer.

"It's *Big Gun*, you fucker," snarled a voice I hadn't heard in a while.

Oh, bollocks. Big Gun. As nicknames go, it was a memorable moniker. It was also a slightly misleading one, too – it makes him sound like some murderous idiot who collects his own belly button fluff, calls his gran 'a silly old slag' and poses a real and present danger to society. And that's unfair. He's not murderous in the least.

Big Gun is an old friend (I use the term loosely) who now works as a freelancer for the British national press. He is one of the best-connected people you could ever wish to meet. Not that you would ever actually wish to meet him, of course.

A larger than average man, he drinks nothing but energy drinks and survives on a diet of pasties, chips, cakes and crisps. And cheese, which he insists improves each of the main foods he spends all day chewing through. He is mildly xenophobic and consistently the loudest person in every room he enters. He's basically the reincarnation of King Henry VIII, minus the ruffs and gout (although with a diet like his, it is probably on the horizon) and less of a hit with women.

He was calling me for the first time in months. A call from Big Gun out of the blue usually spelled trouble. I expected a heated account of his latest run-in with his girlfriend, or a blow-by-blow re-telling of his most recent brawl with his brother. Or a request that I come and pose as his Peruvian uncle to help him win a bet. Again.

"Hello mate," I said, doing my best not to sound utterly unhappy to hear from him.

"Now listen, I've heard you're trying to track down Sachin Tendulkar this summer for something or other." Big Gun didn't muck around. His time was precious. He was probably in the queue for a pasty at Greggs and didn't have time to indulge in niceties with me.

"Erm, yes I am," I replied hesitantly. Big Gun knew none of my friends. He hadn't met *any* of them. How had he managed to find out about my Sachin quest?

"I think," he growled, "I might be able to help you out matey." His voice – a curious mix of a rural Hampshire farmer and dodgy North London geezer – got progressively more *Eastenders* whenever he got excited.

"I could," he continued conspiratorially, "get you his mobile number if you really wanted it…"

I politely informed him that I did. Good old Big Gun; *told* you he was a friend.

PART THIRTEEN

England vs. India, 3rd NPower Test
Match, Edgbaston, Aug 10-13
Day One
S.R. Tendulkar – c. Anderson b. Broad – 1 (8 balls)

After a day's rest to recover from what had become known as the 'Greenwich Incident' and an intense net session back in Portsmouth with Josh, it was swiftly on to the next Test in Birmingham.

England were now just one win away from securing their status as the best Test-playing nation in the (admittedly piddlingly small cricketing) world, but that didn't seem to matter to the scores of looters who were smashing up shops around the country – including, among other places, Birmingham.

Commentators on TV blamed all manner of things for the sudden and destructive rioting: the recession; a lack of discipline in schools; even single-parent families. I think it was probably more likely the angry reaction of England fans appalled by the news that Jonathan Trott had failed to recover from injury and Ravi Bopara had been called up as his replacement.

In keeping with the wave of civil unrest spreading across the nation, the Test started in lively fashion, England winning the toss and opting to bowl. Before long, Jimmy Anderson,

Stu Broad and Tim Bresnan were doing their own smash-and-grab job on the Indian top order.

The returning Virender Sehwag – newly arrived in the UK after injury, but mentally still on the plane journey over, chewing peanuts and watching *Happy Gilmore* or something – gloved his first ball behind before Gautam Gambhir dragged onto his stumps. Indian batsmen were disappearing back to the pavilion quicker than Adidas trainers from the smashed-in windows of *JD Sports*. But happily, that meant the great SRT was soon strolling out to the crease. In what looked like new Adidas trainers. I'm sure it was just a coincidence. I'm not casting aspersions, you understand.

As ever, the ovation he got was awe-inspiring, the whole ground rising as one to salute him. The hairs on the back of my neck stood on end as he walked to the wicket and took his guard. His dark eyes gleamed out from under his helmet, jagging from England fielder to England fielder, hunting for gaps. It was typical Sachin. I had watched him bat on so many occasions over the years, and his demeanour very rarely changed. He might fiddle and fuss a bit between balls, but a familiar calm would always descend when the bowler began charging in.

But something felt different today. Was there an extra tap of the bat on the ground before the bowler released the ball? Was there the tiniest twitch of his toes where once there was only rock-solid stillness? He looked uncomfortable, like a nervous debutant rather than a man who had spent most of his life with bat in hand. Somehow, he no longer looked at home. His bat somehow looked less an extension of his arms, and more a clunking, alien object swishing harmlessly at thin air. After just eight balls, he was gone, edging a swinging ball from Broad to Anderson at third slip. For once, it was no surprise.

A peculiarly melancholic feeling swept over me. Sachin had made the game look difficult. He had played and missed and scratched around the crease nervously like normal mortals tended to do. From a distance, I could have sworn it was just Rosh at the crease doing a ropey, hungover impression of Sach.

The England boys celebrated his wicket with the same enthusiasm they always did (Sachin's, I mean, not Rosh's – they were never that fussed about Rosh), but their smiles weren't ones of relief, but wry, knowing ones; grins that signalled the textbook execution of a carefully devised plan to get rid of the Little Master. England fans over the years had become accustomed to seeing Tendulkar's wicket celebrated with a primal fervour, or more likely, with all the weary resignation of a 43-year-old divorcee necking a glass of Tesco Value Cava to celebrate her first annivorcery (the anniversary of a divorce, natch). But no more. It seemed he was no longer the great unsolvable riddle, the immovable, undismissable tormentor of a confused bowling attack. Sach, perhaps, was now just another high-class performer in the sights of a well-drilled, world-beating pack of bowlers who feared no one and respected no reputations.

England had kept Sachin down all series and their confidence against him was sky-high. They had made him look eminently fallible. The aura was fading. It may have only paled slightly, but it was fading nonetheless.

Or maybe that was just rubbish. An Indian fan sat a few rows behind me had a different take on events.

"Booooooo!" he roared at the huddled England fielders, still celebrating while Sachin walked off to yet another standing ovation that he politely acknowledged and did his best to ignore at the same time. "Bloody cheaters! Bloody English cheaters!"

It was unclear exactly how England had cheated. Perhaps it was something to do with England's diligent preparation and practise before matches. The Indian team certainly seemed to view such organisation as something not in keeping with the spirit of the game.

In fact, the only way the Indians' practise sessions could

have been any more louche and relaxed was if MS Dhoni strolled everywhere in just a towel, sipping on a pina colada and whistling *The Girl from Ipanema*. (Mercifully, he did none of those things – although I'm fairly sure the reason he didn't was more due to the mild temperatures and the fact he didn't know the tune to *The Girl from Ipanema*, than anything else).

England swiftly skittled the Indians'for an under-par 224, boosted only by some lusty late slogging from Dhoni (in standard cricket whites, not just a towel). Alastair Cook and Andrew Strauss were just coming out to begin England's reply when I got a call.

"I've got it!" an excited voice panted down the line. It was Big Gun.

"What?" I squealed.

"I've got it!" he said again. "And I *know* it's the right number!"

This was **insane**. I hadn't dreamed he would *actually* be able to help. This was a man who once ate a cigarette 'to see what it would taste like' and gave himself a nosebleed at school by sticking his nostril on a gas tap and turning the gas on. You don't expect people like that to actually deliver on what they promise. You expect them to live in a caravan on their parents' driveway, eat cold baked beans from the tin with the back of a hairbrush, and spend hours discussing their favourite Page 3 girl with their Subbuteo figures.

"How the hell did you get that?" I screeched.

"Don't ask questions mate," he said sternly. It was hard to tell if he was joking or being serious. Things were all going a bit *Godfather.*

"What do you mean '*don't ask questions?*' I said mockingly. "You're not a gangster – you think Sicily is just a funny nickname for your effeminate mate Lee and Don Corleone is Arsenal's new left-back. You didn't have to 'whack' anybody to get this number."

"Didn't I?" Big Gun replied gruffly.

"No. You didn't." I really hoped he didn't at any rate.

"Yeah, fair enough, I didn't," he chuckled. "But I did have to put a horse's penis in someone's bed," he added, in a terrible faux-Sicilian accent.

"A horse's *penis*?" I laughed. "Wasn't it a horse's head in that *Godfather* film?"

The line went temporarily silent.

"It wasn't in the one I saw," said Big Gun. He sounded perplexed. "How much nudity was there in *The Godfather*?"

"None at all," I replied. "Certainly not very much."

The line went silent again.

"Maybe I watched an X-rated version then," Big Gun shrugged.

An X-rated version of *The Godfather*? Starring Marlon *Gland*-o and Andy *Arse*-cia? It was possible.

"You know," Big Gun continued. "The rude parody. Like *Shaving Ryan's Privates*…"

Somehow I doubted that would be a suitable film for World War II veterans. I certainly doubted whether it would be historically accurate, or particularly respectful. I had a horrible feeling D-Day would end up as DD-Day.

"Or *Moulin Splooge…*" Big Gun continued.

Moulin Rouge is one of my Mum's favourite films. Big Gun's version probably didn't star Ewan McGregor.

"…*School of Cock* was another one…" he chuckled.

"Hold on," I spluttered. "That was a kids' film!"

"Well in the porno version, they're *all grown up*," Big Gun said, lasciviously. "Then there's *Edward Penishands…*"

"Oh stop it," I said with a derisive laugh. "That last one is made up."

"Nope," Big Gun insisted, "it's entirely real. Well, obviously not *entirely* real, the things on his hands weren't real…"

My mind boggled with terrible images. I composed myself briefly and shook the thought of poor Edward trying to type a letter or return an overdue library book from my mind.

"It was quite a good film actually," continued Big Gun. "Although do you know what I kept thinking during the whole thing?"

"Was it '*why the hell am I watching a film called Edward Penishands*?" The person in the seat next to me squirmed uncomfortably.

"No. *Imagine* sharing a bag of crisps with him," he said, quietly. "Even if you started with cheese and onion they'd all end up tasting like prawn cockta…"

I cut him off before he could finish the punchline. It was a typical Big Gun gag. But I couldn't sneer too much. I had sent Sachin a letter, called him in his hotel room, tried to visit him at home (or what I thought was his home), pestered countless people who knew and worked with him, and followed him for hundreds of miles around the country – but now, thanks to BG, I had his mobile number. These seemingly insignificant eleven digits could hold the key to finally meeting – and bowling to – my hero.

I called the number. According to a robotic-voiced woman who clearly did not understand the magnitude of this phone call – it was 'unavailable'. The image of Big Gun eating a cigarette came immediately to mind. I thought of him flicking through his collection of inventively-named DVDs. Maybe I'd been right to be sceptical after all.

Day Two

I tried the number a few more times early the next morning with no success, but Big Gun insisted I would just have to be patient and keep trying. It was, according to him, *definitely* the right number. Eventually, he promised, I would get through and Sachin would pick up. The tide was about to turn. If not today, then tomorrow, he promised.

The same couldn't be said for India's fortunes. The only way they could have allowed England to progress more serenely was if their bowlers had escorted the English batters between the wickets on exquisite red velvet sedan chairs, while gently fanning them and feeding them grapes.

Again, I think it was only the fact that red sedan chairs are quite expensive that stopped them doing it. The Indians really did seem intent on making things as easy for the England lads as possible. Rumours that Rahul Dravid had bought himself a replica England training top and tried to get on the England bus in the hope of getting some proper coaching remain unsubstantiated. But not wholly implausible.

The game was rapidly becoming a more one-sided contest than the battle between Shane Watson's deep-seated adoration for himself and his sense of humility. There was even talk that the BCCI were investigating a rumour that Mitchell Johnson had some Indian heritage, in a bid to inject some much-needed consistency into their bowling attack. As it was, it turned out he just had a cousin who worked in Delhi. Well, a cousin who worked in *a* deli.

India were showing no signs of upping their game beyond 'hungover Sunday League side' any time soon. Metaphorically, the whole team were in towels, sipping pina coladas and whistling *The Girl from Ipanema*.

Well, all except the wonderful Sreesanth, who – in addition to being one of my favourite characters in the game – is undoubtedly the most intense, manly cricketer in the world. I imagine he refers to himself in the third person, stands in front of a mirror and punches himself in the face before matches, charges around the dressing room beating his chest like Tarzan and shouting '*Sreesanth! Sreesanth! Sreesanth!*' before curling up in the foetal position – completely naked – and resting for a few moments (dreaming of bowling beamers at KP's grinning face), before bursting upright and doing the whole show again. Because in his own (entirely fictional) words: '*Sreesanth never sleeps! Sreesanth waits for no man! Sreesanth! Sreesanth! Sreesanth!*'

I contemplated trying to catch the Indian team after the game and even managed to find out where the team were staying, but armed with Sachin's number, my whole approach had changed. I wasn't going to get Sachin to agree to anything surrounded by hundreds of other screaming fans. The days of hanging around for him were over. Because – to paraphrase (my entirely fictional) Sreesanth – *Adam Carroll-Smith waits for no man. Not even Sachin! Adam! Adam! Adam!*

Day Three

The Test match was gone as a contest. The only battle I cared about now was between Sachin and I, and that was where my energies had to be directed. England could take care of themselves. They didn't need my support right now.

Now back at home in Brighton, I checked back in with Roj Whelan. He reminded me to practise my celebration (I was still ballsing up the Soulja Boy dance after the *Superman* bit) and told me to keep pushing away and I'd get there. He sent me the video of his dismissal of Sachin. I stuck it on my laptop, blasted 'Eye of the Tiger' and did some bicep curls with a set of batting pads. I wasn't sure why; it just seemed appropriate to break out the Rocky Balboa moves.

I updated Jono and Dave on my progress too, and both were suitably excited that I had Sachin's mobile number. Rosh was less enthused. If I was getting somewhere close to bowling at Sachin, that meant he had nothing to take the piss out of me about.

Well, I say nothing: he still had the old classics to fall back on (my height; my fear of moths; the fact I pronounce tragedy as *tradegy* – the list was more or less endless) but he could only rely on them for so long. He needed new material and this Sachin thing was perfect. If I succeeded, he might begrudgingly have to congratulate me on something. That simply wouldn't do.

I tried Sachin's number again, but it was still steadfastly refusing to connect. Sach felt so near and yet so far away, like I was looking at him through my Grandma's varifocals, or he was trapped like a performing tiger behind a thin sheet of glass.

In a quiet moment, I trawled back through dozens of emails I had sent over the past few months, most of which had fallen on deaf ears (or more probably, fallen directly into spam folders or trash bins). I re-sent them all – to sponsors, fan clubs, ex-pros, charity foundations and everyone in between. It wasn't that I was starting to lose faith in Big Gun; I was just being thorough.

A flurry of the re-sent emails immediately bounced back with error messages or automated replies. *Ho hum*, I thought, *so much for that*. Big Gun had promised it was the right number and told me to be patient. He had told me to stop stressing out about the whole thing. So for possibly the first time ever, I took his advice. I stretched out in my back garden and had a little kip in the sun, with *TMS* for company. It was lovely. The only way I could have been more satisfied with my lot was if I was at a private event with the words 'free bar', 'Lily Allen' and 'erotic massage' in the title.

I woke up hours later to find I had slept through the remainder of the day's play. It was now half past seven and the sun was slowing dipping below the rows of houses behind my flat. I picked up my phone and dialled Sachin's number again. I yawned and waited for the now familiar drone of the robo-lady telling me to try again later.

Only this time, robo-lady didn't appear. Perhaps she'd buggered off on robo-holiday. The phone had started ringing – and ringing with an English dial tone, to boot. *Maybe this is the right number*, I thought to myself. *Maybe this is it? Maybe this is the moment! Maybe, maybe, maybe…*

"Hello?" came the uncertain voice at the other end of the line.

Oh. My. Word. An actual person had answered the phone. They sounded nervous, I thought to myself.

"Oh, hello, is Mr Tendulkar there, please?" I spluttered, my tongue flailing about and suddenly feeling too big for my mouth. I was a camper van and a pair of flip-flops away from being Jamie Oliver, which was too close for comfort.

"No," came the blunt reply. The voice was still tentative and weak.

"Oh, sorry," I said breathlessly, "someone gave me this number and I…"

"Sorry, who is this speaking?" the voice asked.

"My name is Adam," I stuttered, "but…"

"What is your surname?" the voice whispered with curiosity.

"Carroll-Smith," I said calmly.

"Camelsmith!?" the voice replied, with a squawky chuckle.

"No, Carroll-Smith. It's double-barrelled," I explained. "But seriously don't worry…"

"Sorry, I don't know who the bloody hell you are," the voice shrieked suddenly.

"No, that's OK," I sighed.

"I think you've got the fookin' wrong number, pet!"

If I had to describe Sachin Tendulkar's accent, I would use words like '*lilting*', '*gentle*' and '*Indian*'. But if I had to describe the voice at the other end of this phone call, I would be forced to use words like '*Cheryl*', '*Cole*', '*after*', '*ten*' and '*pints*' (which I think is roughly the same as Paul Collingwood after twenty pints, or Ant and Dec after two pints. Between them.)

Bloody Big Gun. *It's definitely his number*, he had insisted. *I've tried it myself.* What a blagger. What a chancer. What a let-down. I called him immediately and told him what had happened – about how his supposed mobile number for Sachin had actually turned out to be for a pissed-up Cheryl Cole sound-alike who laughed at my surname.

"Oh really? A Geordie bird? Interesting, very interesting," was all he could manage by way of a distracted response. He was probably showing some more Page 3 pictures to his raptly attentive Subbuteo men.

"Well, no, actually," I protested, "it's not *that* interesting. It's clearly the wrong number and you insisted it was the right one. Obviously whoever you got the number from is an idiot," I thundered, like a much shitter Zeus.

"He's usually very reliable," murmured Big Gun, suddenly sounding suitably chastised.

"Yeah well," I stropped adolescently, "he's ballsed up here, hasn't he?"

"No, no – he can't have done," Big Gun boomed, suddenly rediscovering his conviction. "He promised it was the right number. In fact, he swore blind it was Sachin's and he's never let me down before. It must be the right number." It sounded like he was trying to convince himself as much as he was me.

"Ring it now and see for yourself," I protested. "It is definitely **not** the right number. I triple-checked the number, so it's nothing I've done wrong. It's your idiot contact."

Big Gun thought for a moment.

"Was it definitely a Geordie accent?" he enquired. "It's just that sometimes it is very easy to get accents confused."

"I can tell the difference between Newcastle and New Delhi," I sniped back. "She was definitely a Geordie, and a woman, for goodness sake! I can tell the difference between a 38-year-old Indian **man** and a British **woman** in her 20s, thanks."

"That's not what I've heard!" he joked.

"Whatever," I huffed, "I've kissed…"

"Oh don't start with this 'fourteen' different snogs thing again," Big Gun interrupted, erroneously. It's *fifteen*. (I do hope you're keeping up.) "Listen," he chuntered, "I'll ring the number now and find out what's going on."

I sat twiddling my thumbs until five minutes later, he

called me back.

"Did you get through to the number?" I asked, eager to be proved right that it wasn't, in fact, Sachin Tendulkar at the other end of the line, but more probably a very confused girl from the North-East who thinks my surname was of Egyptian origin.

"You're right. It's not him," Big Gun sighed.

"What did she say?" I chuckled.

"Nothing – I didn't speak to her. But I really doubt Sachin would have a tone-deaf Geordie girl singing along to 'Everybody in Love' by JLS as his voicemail message."

"Aye, you're probably right, pet," I snapped back in my best Geordie accent. "He's more of an *Eagles* fan."

Big Gun's failure had left me stymied. I didn't have any more avenues to explore. The BCCI had slammed the door shut in my face. Mr Chaudhary had bigger fish to fry than me. Attempted bribery at Lord's hadn't worked. Jedi mind tricks in Northampton had failed. I was even contemplating calling Geno and asking him to run me through Cosmic Ordering again.

My last port of call was Mr Naidu, Sachin's agent. He had appeared from nowhere at the end of the second Test, but just as quickly, he had vanished. He simply wasn't answering my calls anymore. He'd sent me his email so we could liaise electronically, but my messages were going unanswered. I tried calling him again, unsuccessfully.

I called Josh and Rosh and updated them on what had happened with Big Gun and the telephone number, and my communication problems with Mr Naidu. Josh was still enthusiastic about my chances (he'd made a blindfold and had an all-over spray tan in preparation – and that's not even a joke). Rosh, by contrast, was simply relieved he could mock me again.

I sat in stony silence in my front room contemplating my next moves. Maybe I could make an enormous banner and take it to a Test match and hope Sachin saw it? Knowing my luck, I'd have it confiscated by the stewards on my way into the ground. Or maybe I could do a David Gower and hire a plane and fly it over a ground while Sach was batting. That could do the trick, although I'd have to learn to fly a plane, and I got vertigo at the top of a flight of stairs. At the very least, I'd need to hire a plane and pay someone else to fly it. I looked in my wallet. I had £8.11. That was probably not even enough to hire a plane captain's *hat* for an hour. Bollocks. As I sat contemplating reconstructive facial surgery to make myself look like VVS Laxman (it might help me gain access to the Indian dressing room, and help me add a few hotties to the snogs list) my phone buzzed with a text from my brother.

Are you busy? Josh asked.

No. Why? I replied.

Minutes later, my phone began ringing with an incoming call from a mobile number I didn't recognise. I picked it up.

"Is that Mr Carroll-Smith?" A crackly voice at the other end of the line, a strange mix of deepest India and grimiest South London, asked.

"Yes, speaking," I said hesitantly. "Who's calling?"

"Hello there," the comforting voice replied, "My name is Mr Chopra…"

He tailed off at the end of his sentence, as if waiting for me to react at the mention of his name. But I had *no* idea who the hell he was.

"Now Adam," he continued, "I believe you have been trying to track down Mr Sachin Tendulkar for a while. Is this true?"

This sounded ominous. He sounded like he was gearing up to accuse me of something. I was half-expecting the next words out of Mr Chopra's mouth to be '*if you continue to try and contact Mr Tendulkar you will be hearing from the police,*' or '*please stop googling plastic surgeons, you are too short to pass for VVS Laxman*'. I composed myself long enough to confirm that, *yes; I had been trying to track down Sachin* and braced myself for a stern telling off.

"OK, excellent," Mr Chopra said cheerily, immediately putting me at ease. "And I believe you have requested time for an interview of some description with Mr Tendulkar? Are you still wishing to do this?"

Mr Naidu. This had to be his work. Only Mr Chaudhary, Professor Shetty and he knew about my Tendulkar plan and the first two members of that list worked for the BCCI. It had to be Mr Naidu. He must have something to do with this.

"Oh fantastic," I said. "Well yes, I am still hoping to do that. I spoke to Mr Saidu already…" I said.

"Yes," chuckled Mr Chopra. "I am aware of this." Bingo. It **was** Mr Naidu's doing. What a guy. Mr Chopra was one of his minions.

"Mr Naidu mentioned he might be able to help," I continued, "but I've had a bit of trouble getting hold of him recently and thought you might have forgotten about me, but I'm sure everyone is very busy and has better things to do than speak to silly people like me and…"

I was babbling. Mr Chopra chuckled slightly at just how over-excited I was.

"So Adam," he warbled melodically, "what is it you were looking to achieve with this interview?"

Maybe it was the months of never-ending rejections. Maybe it was the irate Geordie girl. Maybe it was because I was bored of inching closer to bowling at Sachin and wanted to start taking some giants leaps towards it. Whatever it was, I didn't mince my words this time. I didn't dress myself up as a journalist humbly wanting just a few minutes of Sachin's time, or pussyfoot around. I told the truth. Like an assassin trying to bring down a circus, I went for the jugular.

"Well Mr Chopra," I boomed, "this summer I am trying to fulfil a childhood dream of bowling just one ball at Sachin Tendulkar."

"You want to bowl at Mr Tendulkar?" he laughed. I couldn't tell if it was a mocking laugh, or a kind-hearted one.

"Yes," I continued brazenly. "I want to bowl just one ball at him. I know it's a grand dream, but those are the ones we should pursue, I think."

"Yes," he said, quietly and thoughtfully. I could almost hear him trying to work out whether I was a loveable charmer or dangerous rouge.

"I think I might even be able to bowl him," I added with certainty. "If it's my lucky day, of course…which it might be."

Mr Chopra seemed to take a moment to digest what I had just said. I could feel myself sliding into 'dangerous rouge' territory, which given my dedicated listening to *Woman's Hour* and fine collection of cardigans, was unfamiliar territory. Finally he took a deep breath and began speaking.

"Well, Mr Carroll-Smith," he chortled, "I do believe we will be able to find you a few moments with Mr Tendulkar soon."

This was incredible news. At the very least, I was now almost guaranteed to at least get some face time with Sachin. I'd asked for an audience with the great man, and an audience was (seemingly) about to be granted.

But I still hadn't received the news I *really* wanted. Mr Chopra seemed to have skirted around the issue of me bowling at Sachin, probably in the hope that I was just joking. But I wasn't. You've read this far, you know I don't do jokes.

"That is brilliant news," I said with genuine cheer in my voice, "but what about the prospect of me bowling one ball at Mr Tendulkar, too?"

"We shall speak again during the next Test match," he said warmly but curtly. "I will hopefully know more by then."

"I understand he has a very fine sense of humour," I replied quickly, anticipating that he was about to brush me aside and end the call.

"Yes he does," he replied. "And you must do too to think

you can bowl him. I am sure he would be most amused that you think you can bowl him."

"Most people are," I admitted.

I was almost welling up. I choked back the tears long enough to splutter out a word of thanks and hung up. After months of fruitless work, fruitless journeys and (quite literally) fruitless motorway service station grub, the end was in sight. Maybe.

But this news brought problems of its own. All of a sudden, there was something I urgently needed to do. My phone was flashing with a new text message.

No reason. Just bored, it read. Josh had texted back.

Fair enough, I replied. *Speaking of being free though Joshy, are you around tomorrow? And are your cricket whites clean?*

Day Four
S.R. Tendulkar – run out (Swann) – 40
(60 balls, eight fours)

England romped to a comprehensive and stunning victory at Edgbaston, securing their status as the world's number one Test team. Sachin, once again, briefly looked as though he was finally going to notch his 100th hundred, only to be unluckily run out when Graeme Swann deflected a drive off his own bowling onto the stumps at the non-striker's end. Tendulkar was left inches short as the ball cannoned into the wickets, drawing a confused noise from the crowd – half celebratory cheer that England had moved one wicket closer to becoming world number 1, and half a disappointed groan from punters who had hoped to be there when Sach finally grabbed his ton of tons. The wait, however, would simply have to go on.

But it was exhilarating all the same. He looked like the old Sachin again. The ball seemed to be magnetically drawn to the middle of his bat once more – his unflinching, balletic poise and dancer's movement at the crease were all on display and for the first time since the beginning of the summer, I was convinced his ton of tons was just around the corner.

But while England and Sachin were battling it out in Birmingham, I was miles south, in sunny Sussex. I had more important things to do. Mr Chopra was taking up my cause. I had to be ready to bowl at Sachin when I finally got the green light. Practise time was over.

****

"Come on lads, let's get started," I bellowed, clapping my hands together and jogging gingerly out of the changing room. The familiar sound of disinterested cricketers – a sort of collective, sighed 'yeah-alright-come-on-then-lets-go' and the weary scuffing of trainers and spikes on nobbly concrete – followed behind me as I jumped from the bottom step of the pavilion ('pavilion' might be a bit of an over-exaggeration – it was more of a rudimentary sort of hut) onto the soft, freshly mown grass.

It was a beautiful, pleasantly hot summer's day. The sun was shining, the flowers blooming and the birds tweeting (in the old-fashioned, non-social networking sense of the word) gloriously. All in all, it was a perfect day for cricket on England's green and pleasant south coast.

"Shall we have a bit of a warm-up?" I asked, enthusiastically.

"Nah," replied Tim.

"Yeah, bollocks to that," added my brother. Both of them clearly adhered to the Indian team's approach to training. It was over-rated.

And with that, we were off. The first competitive (-*ish*) cricket match most of us had played in quite some time. A game had been hastily arranged the previous evening with a rag-tag bunch of friends and acquaintances and now we were underway. The stumps were in, the bails fixed (at one end only) and everyone was resplendent in their finest cricket whites. It was a fine sight.

Well, some people were wearing shorts and what-not, and

others were perilously squeezed into the same 'large boys'-sized shirts they wore at school more than a decade ago, but it was wondrous all the same.

As we all jockeyed into position – with me, a former Portsmouth Grammar School under-16s captain, no less (we won once all season and got bowled out for 17 in one game against Bryanston. I top-scored with 7 and the highlight of the day came when we zipped my friend Mark into a cricket bag and threw him onto the outfield. It was that sort of season, and we were that sort of team. We played another game that season during which we defaced the opposing school's scorebook with pictures of penises and on at least one page, the cod-French phrase 'encoulez le poulet', which sort-of-but-not-really translates as *fuck the chicken*. It didn't come as a shock when I didn't retain the captaincy the following year) – setting the field, everything looked terribly idyllic.

If you ignored the fact that Tim, stood in his whites at first slip, was singing 'Gangster's Paradise' by Coolio, this was the picture you would have seen on village cricket pitches across England at any time in the last 200 years.

Since my competitive playing days had ended, I had watched cricket religiously and I had similarly relished the excitement of getting back to bowling in the nets with Josh, but with the fresh, warm summer air in my nostrils, I was like a caged animal finally released back into the wild.

The meandering, tree-lined country roads leading to the ground, the lovingly-maintained pitch, the rickety old pavilion – these were my plains of the Serengeti and I was a cricketing lion (in reality, I'd be more of a sort of feral stoat or pesky badger, but go with it) who was now back roaming gloriously (i.e. walking, slowly) in his natural habitat.

And before long, I was even back in a role I had filled with aplomb in my school days – leading the familiar shouts of encouragement to my bowlers and heckles of derision at the incumbent batters.

All the old classics made an appearance; from the none-too-subtle 'watch the quick singles', directed at any batsman with even the merest suggestion of a paunch to the ridiculous practise of rubbing my fingers on the pitch between overs, sniffing them, and then warning the batsman that I could 'smell a wicket'. It was reassuring to know I could still lower the tone of such a gentlemanly, honourable game.

After the opening bowlers had charged in – with Josh particularly impressive, and far quicker than I had ever remembered him being – it was time for me to have a bowl. For a few overs beforehand, and at the cost of my concentration in the field (dropped one catch, mis-fielded two ground balls, spent most of the time trying to forget about the 'four sixes in an over' debacle of my youth), I had been psyching myself up in preparation for turning my arm over. But now the moment had arrived. This was it.

The batsman, a friend of Tim's called Rob, was a very leg-sided player – a strong lad with powerful wrists who looked to flick away anything bowled at his stumps, but who he *really* was didn't matter. In my mind, as soon as the ball was in my hand, he *was* the great Tendulkar.

Granted, he was a lot taller (his pads were probably about as tall as Sachin) and a bit bulkier, but that was unimportant. This really was, I told myself, my one ball at the great man. It had to feel like that. I had to up the pressure on myself. I stood at the top of my run-up and spun the ball nervously from one hand to the other to loosen my fingers up.

My mind shot back to my younger days. As a teenager, doubts and worries would surge through my head as I prepared to deliver my first ball in a match. *Just make sure it lands on the square*, I would tell myself. *Don't make yourself look shit*, I would think, my shoulders and arms tensing up with nerves, my stomach bubbling away with anxiety. *Remember the time you got hit for all those sixes...*

But this was different. I knew what I wanted to do and

I *knew* I could do it. This was what I had practised for – to be able to deliver an arrow-straight ball that *might* hit the stumps. I was excited. I was almost certain I was going to get him out with my first ball. I was definitely sure I *could* get him out.

As I stood at the top of my mark, I took one final look at Rob, his bat hoisted high in wait at the striker's end. I felt a light wind tug at the back of my cricket shirt as I jogged in. My mind was totally focused on just one thing; the set of stumps lying 22 yards away.

I leapt into my delivery stride, allowing muscle memory to take over. The ball left my hand perfectly, my fingers cutting across the seam in the hope of extracting some grip from the pitch.

All other sound around me had hushed to complete silence; all I could hear was the ball slicing through the air in a teasing arc, before pitching with a dull thud on middle-and-off on a near flawless length. It was the ball I had visualised so many times; the ball I imagined would somehow sneak between Sachin's bat and pad and zero in on his off stump.

Rob swung, and swung hard, the luminous stickers on the back of his bat flashing wildly across my eyeline, dazzling me for an instant as the sunlight bounced off them. The ball gripped on the dry surface, deviating slightly and hurrying towards him. Everything seemed to be in slow motion as I watched the ball skid on, homing in on the stumps. Soon the stumps would be splayed, the bails twirling to the ground and…

Oh wait, no. He walloped it.

Later that night, I chatted to Roj on Facebook and told him about the match. I told him how I'd psyched myself up to believe that first ball really was the ball I was going to bowl to Sach – and how hard the batsman had then thumped the ball away past me.

"It just wasn't your day mate," he said reassuringly. "And

besides – the only thing that matters is what happens if you're ever in front of Sachin. What this bloke did today is irrelevant. Just remember: before I bowled Sachin, I hadn't even thought about it. I just ran in like I was playing cricket with my mates at home. You've just got to think about it that way – just imagine it's you and your best mate when you come face-to-face with Sachin. Keep believing mate. You can still do it."

Good old Roj. I could rely on him to keep the faith. He still thought I was in with a shot. One way or the other, I'd soon find out for sure.

PART FOURTEEN

England vs. India, 4th NPower Test
Match, The Oval, Aug 18-22
Day Two

"It's bloody ridiculous," I bellowed down the phone to Rosh. "Why is it that these people keep building my hopes up by being so polite and seemingly helpful, only to then ignore me?"

"Well, maybe…"

I cut him off immediately. I was on a roll.

"I'm not going to take it anymore," I growled, like a slightly more mental Howard Beale in *Network*. I just about stopped myself from opening my window and shouting 'I'm as mad as hell!' but the thought did occur. "They can't treat me like I'm a bloody idiot!" I bawled. Rosh went silent for a moment.

"No," he agreed. "But can the rest of us? Treat you like an idiot, I mean. It's just I've got used to it over the years. It's just easier. I quite like treating you like an errant puppy."

"If you're about to tell me you've bought me a dog collar and a lead," I said, "I'm putting the phone down right now. We don't have that sort of friendship."

"No," he continued. "I mean you're like a puppy because I know you mean well most of the time, but you can't help but run into the traffic, piss on the carpet, and dry hump people's legs."

That was unfair, I told him. I've never tried to run out into the traffic.

I didn't have tickets for the first two days of the Test match, but that didn't matter. One thing I certainly did have was Mr Chopra's telephone number. He had told me to call him once the final Test had started. Dutifully, I did as I was told.

I called him twice during the morning session of the first day's play, and then once more during the lunch break. On no occasion did he answer his bloody-flipping-sodding-arsing phone. I left him a polite, controlled voicemail and waited patiently for him to call me back.

But he didn't. I called him twice more between lunch and tea, for good measure. The game had stopped for rain with England stuck on 75-0, but the man who represented my best hope of bowling to Sachin was obviously still working hard. His phone was off.

Undeterred, I sent him a polite, measured text message, stressing my keenness to confirm when I would be able to sit down with Sachin – and just as importantly, whether he had spoken to Sach about my plan to bowl at him. But it – like that morning's phone calls – went unanswered. Play was finally called off in the late afternoon and I gave Mr Chopra one more call shortly after the close of play. You can guess what happened.

I had twiddled my thumbs for long enough. I'd been a picture of composure all day, but now I needed to blow my top. I needed a bit of an old shout. And now Rosh – bizarre comparisons of me to a pissing puppy aside – was patiently bearing the brunt of my bad mood.

"It's ridiculous," I whined at him down the telephone line. "If I hadn't watched him batting and fielding so much on this tour, I'd be seriously starting to doubt that Sachin Tendulkar was even a real bloke, and not just some genetically-engineered creation of the BCCI. He is more elusive than Bigfoot, the Invisible Man and the Loch Ness Monster rolled into one…"

"*The Big Invisible Foot Monster*..." Rosh suggested.

"Why is he so hard to get close to?" I moaned.

"Or the *Loch Ness Big Man*..." Rosh continued. "Actually that just sounds like a big Scottish bloke with ginger hair who drinks in the pubs up in Loch Ness..."

"I mean, where the hell does he go between games?" I pondered.

"The *Loch Ness Big Man*? I don't know. Maybe the offie?"

I ignored Rosh and pressed on with my rant.

"How can he possibly not have the time to let me bowl *one ball* at him? It's like Sachin is this little cricketing robot who the Indian management pack away into a little bag between matches and only assemble when they arrive at a cricket ground."

"SACHIN *10*-DULKAR," said Rosh in a robotic voice.

"That's the only possible explanation. I'm just fed up." I sighed deeply. "I just don't know what to do anymore."

"You'd have thought they'd have built him taller," Rosh mused.

"What?" I snapped moodily.

"If Sachin really was a robot," Rosh continued. "They'd have built him taller. I mean if you were going to build Sach as a cricketing robot, why not build him seven foot tall? He's only like two foot three inches tall in real life."

"Rosh..."

"Although," he continued, "I suppose there would be more bits to assemble..."

I coughed agitatedly. He didn't stop.

"And the bag they had to carry around would be heavier. *Oh man*," he said urgently, "I wonder who'd win a fight between the *Loch Ness Big Man* and a seven-foot robotic cricketer?"

"Rosh, shut up," I snapped, finally. "I'm not interested in the crap you're talking.* I've been after this Chopra bloke all day and he's just ignored me. I thought he was the big breakthrough. He rang *me*. But now he's gone silent and I just think that's rude and unprofessional."

"Sorry," Rosh sighed. "But just keep your chin up mate. This Chopra bloke is going to call. He said he would. Keep the faith." His voice was full of sympathy and compassion. It was disconcerting. He hadn't even called me 'thundering shit-bobble' or anything insulting for the whole conversation.

After I'd briefly contemplated ringing Mr Naidu and dobbing Mr Chopra in to him, Rosh and I said our goodbyes and I made myself a cup of tea. I felt the hot, cloying fog of anger that I'd been under gently lift. Rosh was right; I just had to remain patient. Twenty minutes later, my phone rang. It was Mr Chopra. I *knew* he'd call. Didn't I say just a few paragraphs ago that he'd call? Course I did.

"Hello," I replied coldly, as he cheerfully introduced himself down the line. I waited for him to explain why he'd been ignoring me all day, but no explanation was forthcoming. He was like that Tony Blairs; steadfastly refusing to apologise for that war he started with Greg Bush, the President of Americans, out in Iraq. (I am available for incisive political satire if any of the producers of *Mock the Week* or *Have I Got News For You* are reading.)

"Adam," Mr Chopra continued, unapologetically, "this is very last minute, but would you be available to meet me tomorrow to discuss your project?" he asked firmly, finally breaking my frosty silence.

Was I available to meet him to discuss my project? Is Shane Watson's name an anagram of *He Owns Satan*? Yes! (Which might explain why he's so unpopular and also why he's been promoted to vice-captain; although if Shane is Satan's owner and is still only VC, quite what that makes Michael Clarke is anyone's guess).

"I am most certainly available whenever is convenient for you, Mr Chopra," I replied self-assuredly.

"OK," he laughed. "Is 8.30am outside The Oval cricket

ground tomorrow morning too early for you?" Technically, 8.30am was way too early for me. But for Sachin, I was prepared to make such sacrifices.

Day Three
S.R. Tendulkar – c. Anderson b. Swann – 23
(34 balls, four fours)

I was up early and racing on my way from Brighton to London at 6.45am. I got to Clapham just after eight, and quickly made my way the short distance to The Oval.

I *hate* mornings. Everyone who knows me knows this to be a fact. It is my solemn belief that 'morning people' are just plain weird and not to be trusted. You can't do anything in the mornings. The pubs are closed, the telly is rubbish and Chris Moyles is on the radio. Say no more.

I don't get over-excited easily (I could probably find a few people who would refute that claim, but trust me, I don't normally), but as I turned the corner and walked down past Oval tube station towards the ground, I was absolutely euphoric. The weather was lovely, I was at one of my favourite cricket grounds in the world, and I was about to sit down and discuss Sachin Tendulkar with a man who would be able to make my childhood dream come true. I had even managed to avoid catching a single minute of Moyles' show on the radio on the drive up. Actually, that was a lie – I listened to it for a minute or two to find out the text number, and then I sent a message in which read: '*Hi Chris, you're a total flippin' shit-hammer who seems to have mistaken 'shouting a lot' for 'being funny'! Big fan! (not really)*'. As mornings go, this one felt *good*.

As the clock ticked over to 8.30am I nervously paced up and down outside the ground. Mr Chopra said he would call the moment he arrived. Stupidly, I hadn't asked what he looked like when we'd spoken previously, and nor had he enquired about my physical characteristics. That was probably just as well as, if he had, he'd now be strolling about looking for a man of 'around six foot' (5ft 9in is *around* six foot) with 'the looks of a movie star' (not technically a lie – Frodo from *Lord of the Rings* is technically a movie star). But still, he might have been looking for a while before he noticed the real me. For some reason, I pictured Mr Chopra as a man in his mid to late 30s, wearing a suit and carrying a briefcase. Maybe with a little moustache too.

I yawned deeply as the clock ticked over to 8.45am. No one in a suit had walked past me so far, and the only man with a moustache looked like he might have slept rough the previous night. Mr Chopra, I'm fairly certain, didn't get up to that sort of thing. I left him a polite little voicemail and paced up and down some more, trying to shed the abundance of nervous energy coursing through me.

I grabbed a quick coffee and sipped it slowly. As I crushed the cup and slam-dunked it in a nearby bin, I looked at the clock on my phone. It was now 9.15am.

By 9.30am, I was leaving my second voicemail of the morning. I tried to pitch it somewhere between concerned, furious, desperate and relaxed. I'm fairly certain I'd failed, but as my mood darkened I was also fairly sure Mr Chopra probably wouldn't ever listen to the bloody thing anyway.

As 10.00am approached and more and more spectators began funnelling down to the ground from the station, I found myself debating whether or not to send an angry and fairly expletive-ridden text message to Mr Chopra.

Eventually, I decided against it. What if his car had broken down on the way to the ground? Or his train had been cancelled? Both were plausible explanations for his tardiness, and if either of them had actually occurred, I wouldn't be able to get our thus far cordial relationship back on track if poor Mr Chopra had received a text message from me with the phrase '*you are a useless cockwallet*' in it. Even if he *was* currently partaking in some fairly 'cockwallet-ish' behaviour by leaving me on my lonesome.

· I sat in silence and groped for more plausible reasons why he might be so late. Maybe his phone had run out of battery and he'd walked straight past me that morning? I should have worn a pink carnation so he'd known who I was. Granted, I might have ended up having coffee with a man who referred to himself as 'randyguy4321' and insisted I was *definitely* the man he had been talking to in a *very* niche interest online chat room, but it was a risk worth taking and one I probably should have grasped. Instead, I'd just have to keep my eyes peeled for people I thought looked a bit like a Mr Chopra. It wasn't the best of plans.

My stomach growled with hunger pangs as I cradled another cardboard cup of coffee – long since past being even lukewarm – in my hands. A group of England fans in matching ODI shirts barrelled past me, already half-cut and with arms slung around each other's shoulders. They boomed out 'Jerusalem' (it must have been an updated version, as it seemed to contain a somewhat slanderous theory about Ian Bell. The general hypothesis seemed to be that he was a bit like Action Man, and didn't need to wear a box, because rather than male sex organs, he just had a smooth flat area. How they knew that for certain, I didn't ascertain) before staggering out of sight. I checked the time again. It was almost 11 o'clock. My patience was gone, and by teatime, so was I, back home to Brighton in a huff.

I left Mr Chopra one final voicemail, expressing my concern that some terrible fate had befallen him, while also subtly hinting that if he had simply forgotten about me, then I would be liable to *inflict* a terrible fate on him – or at the very least, send the useless cockwallet the text I had nearly sent him earlier in that day.

While I stropped my way home, England were busy racking up yet another mammoth first innings total (591-6dec, with Ian Bell – he of the potentially smooth, flat area –

top-scoring with 235 of the most attractive runs ever scored. If he'd got to 300 I think I'd have had to burn off a DVD of the innings and elope to Las Vegas with it). England even managed to nip out five Indian wickets before the close – Sachin, unfortunately, being one of them.

But I didn't care about that. I'd been stood up. Who the hell gets stood up? Even girls I went to school with – girls who knew I had form for turning up to dates in a cowboy hat – had never stood me up. I was a bar of chocolate, a bottle of Jacob's Creek and a pair of oversized women's knickers away from being Bridget Jones.

Worryingly, I already had two of those three items at home. *Bugger it,* I thought. *Why not go the whole hog, buy that missing third item and just become Bridget Jones for the night?* So I did.

I've always loved a Flake. Even if I did manage to drop quite a lot of it on the over-sized knickers.

Day Four

I was still fuming at Mr Chopra when I got to The Oval the next morning. I was hot and bothered, and already at the end of my tether as I hopped off the tube at 10.30am. But it would be unfair to pin all the blame on Mr Chopra. The rubber chicken mask and over-sized chicken's feet certainly weren't helping my mood.

I walked – well, waddled – down to the front of the ground to find Amy Winehouse, a few members of the Jackson Five and the cowboy from the Village People (among a myriad of strange characters) waving at me. Either my coffee had been spiked or these idiots knew me. After briefly mistaking the rag-tag bunch for India's bowling attack (you're excused, Praveen Kumar), I quickly realised they were my friends.

It was the day of my friend Chris' stag do, and fancy dress was the order of the day. And it truly was an order in the 'must not be disobeyed' sense of the word. My usual fancy-dress get-out of not shaving, wearing cricket whites and getting plastered (aka The Flintoff or The Botham – or if I could find a comedy handlebar 'tache, The Boon or The Lillee) was not an option. I was a chicken, whether I liked it or not (I didn't). For the day, I would be as hot and uncomfortable as a real battery hen (and by 'battery hen', I mean a chicken in a cage. My brother had never heard of the phrase before; according to him, a 'battery hen' sounded like a low-budget sexual aid).

The rules of the stag were simple. No matter the weather, the costumes had to stay on. No wigs or waistcoats could be removed. Chicken masks could be lifted slightly to facilitate the pouring of booze into one's face but otherwise must remain clamped firmly over one's head.

I bemoaned my fancy dress luck (it had been a blind draw to determine who came as what) and silently wondered what would happen if I met snog number sixteen this evening. I didn't bother to ask if the rules stretched to such eventualities. Besides, not many women's 'type' is a sweaty man in a chicken costume. And any that were into that sort of thing probably weren't the sort I wanted on the list with the other fifteen. It was a high-class list, after all.

We filed into the ground and took our seats. Drinks were soon flowing. I lost count at five just after lunch. My hair was matted to my head with sweat. My feet ached. I'd forgotten all about Mr Chopra. It was *brilliant.*

A text from Josh buzzed onto my phone.

Having a good time? It read.

Bloody great. I'm a poissed chicken I replied, with uncharacteristic lack of concern for my spelling mistake.

Good lad. What's a poissed chicken? Sounds French, replied Josh. On such high-intellect exchanges are the greatest of brotherly bonds built.

I popped my phone back in my pocket and as the hot sun poured down, I felt a boozy snooze coming on. I cracked open the beak of my chicken mask to allow a bit of air inside and began to drift off.

I don't know how long I was dozing for, but my drunken kip was ended with a shock. It was Chris' mate Phil jabbing me in the ribs.

"Your phone is vibrating mate," he slurred. "And I should warn you – if it does it for much longer against my leg, I'm liable to get a bit over-excited." Phil winked.

Phil is six foot six inches tall. And he was dressed as an effeminate cowboy. I felt like I was perilously close to becoming part of a sordid sort of show that would be illegal even in Amsterdam. A cowboy and a *chicken?* Even the red light district would frown at that sort of thing. And imagine the offspring! Actually, probably best not to. I quickly fished my phone from my pocket and picked up the call.

"Adam?" a familiar voice at the end of the line asked. "It's Mr Chopra here."

He sounded his normal chipper and upbeat self. Obviously he wasn't a man easily burdened by guilt. I huffed the briefest of hellos back and waited for him to apologise for standing me up the previous day.

"Listen, Adam, I am so sorry about yesterday – something came up and I tried to let you know I would not be able to make it but…"

Hmmm. He sounded genuinely apologetic. I wanted to let my fury at him fester for a while but the fact remained I needed him more than he needed me. I grumbled out a semi-enthusiastic 'don't worry, I understand'.

"You are a gracious man, Adam," he said wisely. "Are you at The Oval today as well?"

"Yes I am," I replied, my mood brightening.

"Excellent. In that case, let's get together and discuss Mr Tendulkar," he chirruped. "Are you free now?"

Oh Mr Chopra, I thought to myself. *I can't stay mad at you.* He'd stood me up yesterday but now he was being lovely and wonderful, so I loved him again. I really *was* becoming a bit too much like Bridget Jones. Those oversized knickers were even starting to chaff a bit under my chicken clobber.

"OK, well I am in the bar in the pavilion," he said. "I will tell the guys on the entrance that you are coming and they will let you up as my guest."

This was fantastic news, but all of a sudden, I saw a flaw in this plan. In fact, through a drunken fog, I managed to see a couple.

1. I was drunk
2. I was wearing a chicken mask and chicken feet

"Ah, umm," I hesitated, "actually, could we maybe get together in fifteen minutes?" I asked nervously. "It's just that I'm actually here on a friend's stag party and I need to get changed into my normal clothes. At the moment I'm dressed as a sort of...*chicken*." How exciting, I thought to myself, as I put the phone down. Maybe he'd even get me a gin and tonic by way of recompense for yesterday's almighty fuck up? I day-dreamed about what the inside of the Oval pavilion might look like as I began to slip my chicken feet off. Immediately a clatter of guttural noise – like all the after-dinner speeches at a rugby club dinner being shouted at the same time – erupted from my pals beside me.

"What are you doing?" asked Chris. "You're breaking a stag rule!"

"I know," I protested quietly, "but…"

"Forfeit!" he shouted, his Amy Winehouse beehive wobbling as he spoke.

"No, listen," I said pleadingly. "I *have* to take it off. I need to go and speak to someone about bowling to Sachin."

I glanced around the group looking for a glimmer of compassion from any of them. Surely they would understand? Surely they would grasp the seriousness of the situation and, just this once, bend their Draconian drinking laws for me?

Of course they didn't. At least Phil looked to have calmed down a bit.

"If you have to take it off and leave, we will discuss your forfeit in your absence," said one of the Jackson Five, ominously.

I stuffed my costume into my bag and swung it over my shoulder. I didn't have time to dwell on what horrid punishment the stag party were concocting for me. I had a date with destiny.

"Has nobody come down to tell you about…my name is *Adam Carro*…" I stammered unconvincingly.

"Sorry," the man smiled, cutting me off mid-sentence.

I was stood outside the members' entrance to the Oval pavilion, the exact entrance Mr Chopra had told me to use, but apparently, no one was expecting my arrival.

Maybe there was some sort of mix-up. I called Mr Chopra to see what had happened, but *surprise, surprise;* his phone was just ringing and ringing, before going to voicemail. THIS WAS RIDICULOUS. How unprofessional could one man be? A few more minutes passed. This was beyond a joke now. Either Mr Chopra was a tremendously rude man, a tremendously stupid one, or a mixture of both. But whichever it was, that was it. After ten minutes, I'd had enough.

I pretended to take a phone call and ambled away from the members' entrance, and began putting my costume back on. My friend Ed, who really had lucked out on the fancy dress gear and actually looked quite cool in his farmer outfit, suddenly appeared and perched himself next to me as I began to get changed.

"Is this bloke giving you the run-around?" he asked, sympathetically. I nodded. I'd told him about the previous day's aborted trip to meet Mr Chopra.

"Well don't worry about it mate," Ed said with a smile. "I'm sure he'll ring soon."

I pulled the chicken mask stroppily over my face. "No, he won't," I huffed.

"Anyway," Ed sighed. "As regards your forfeit. After much deliberation…"

"Get on with it," I snapped. "Don't '*X-Factor results night*' me."

Ed looked at me sternly and cleared his throat once more.

"After much deliberation," he continued methodically, his eyes narrowing evilly, "we have decided that you must go and buy everyone a round of drinks."

Was that it? I was shocked at their leniency. I'd been expecting far worse. Something involving nudity or the possibility of arrest at the very least. I thought this was a stag do. It was like they weren't even trying, thankfully. Perhaps my doe-eyed pleadings had made them feel a little bit guilty for even enforcing the punishment, and they'd decided to show some clemency.

"OK," I smiled, standing to my feet, my costume now back in position.

"Well actually, there is one additional caveat," Ed added suddenly. "You have to drink your pint from one of your chicken feet."

Ah. There it was. The 'kicker', as the Americans call it. But still, I'd done worse. I shrugged and continued settling back into my outfit while Ed made a quick phone call. We began slowly ambling the lengthy walk back to our seats, Ed still chuntering away on his mobile, when mine began to ring too.

It was Mr Chopra. He immediately and passionately apologised for dicking me around (I'm paraphrasing). This time, he promised, he really was ready to meet – and he had exciting things to tell me. Ed ended his call and I told him the good news. He looked unsure; almost slightly concerned that I was setting myself up for a fall again, but that didn't matter. I immediately sat myself down again, and began easing my chicken feet off.

"I'm afraid I can't let you do that," Ed smiled, grabbing my wrist to stop me pulling the rubbery clothing off. Now, on a normal day, I love Edward. He is one of my closest friends. But right now, he wasn't acting like one. He was being a bit of a knob.

"I know what you're thinking," he said, his eyes full of sorrow and his voice heavy with regret. "You're thinking '*why is Ed being such a knob?*'"

"I was a bit, yes," I admitted.

"Well," he said, exhaling deeply, "I know what the next forfeit is. That's why."

"Oh, it can't…" I protested.

"Adam; trust me. Keep the suit on." He stared at me intensely.

"Ed, this is important to me! This bloke is going to help me bowl to Sachin. I need to see him right now. You could just lie and say I didn't take it off…"

Ed looked shocked.

"If they found out I'd done that, they'd make me do the second forfeit as well. And I am *not* doing it," he ranted. "Just explain the situation to this bloke. Once you're in the pavilion, you can get changed."

"But he'll think I'm an idiot," I protested. "He'll think I'm unprofessional…"

"*He* will think *you* are unprofessional? Hasn't he stood you up twice already?"

Ed had a point. And I was drunk enough to go along with it.

And so I strolled over to the members' entrance once more and brazenly approached the gents protecting the doors, my chicken mask staring at them unflinchingly, as chicken masks tended to do. Unsurprisingly, they **still** weren't expecting my arrival. And they don't let non-members or giant poultry into the pavilion. Club policy, apparently. The only chickens allowed inside are served on a plate, full of stuffing. I didn't fancy that. I felt like I'd dodged a bullet with Cowboy Phil and I wasn't about to push my luck.

I'd been stood motionless by the entrance for a few minutes, side-by-side with Ed in his farmer's outfit. It must have looked like Ed was the world's most committed and caring free-range farmer – a man so dedicated to his animals that he even took them on day trips to the cricket and held their pints while they went to the toilet. (Although given that I was a chicken with human arms and legs and drinking beer, maybe there would have to be some questions raised about the possibility of Ed's poultry being genetically-modified).

It was clear that Mr Chopra was not going to make any time for me today. Ed slung an arm round my shoulder and suggested we take a stroll back to our seats and watch England move another wicket closer to what would surely be a resounding win. Tired and dejected, I agreed.

Suddenly, a drunken young chap in an England football shirt charged towards us.

"Don't trust him!" he yelled into my mask. Even through the musty rubber I could smell the ten pints he'd drunk that day on his breath.

"Sorry?" I replied.

"He might have his arm round you now, but he's a farmer," he added, as he slowly began walking away. "At some point, he's going to wring your neck."

Ed and I laughed as he stumbled out of sight.

Suddenly, the mask was whisked off my face. Ed held it aloft over my heading, laughing maniacally.

"A headless chicken!" he yelled, pointing at the sort-of severed head in his hand. "You've got to run around for fifteen seconds and then fall over."

"Thanks," I grunted moodily, "I've just broken the stag rule again now."

"Oh yeah," Ed said, ashen-faced with guilt. "Sorry."

"You could always not tell…"

"Sorry. I have to," Ed said sheepishly.

Maybe he wasn't quite such a free-range friend after all. **

By the close of the fourth day's play, Sachin was unbeaten on 35 and I'd just about recovered from my second forfeit by the time the evening rolled around – when the chicken mask finally came off.

But somehow it felt like more humiliation and Sachin-related disasters were afoot. A chicken's foot, to be precise. I had a missed call after play had ended from Mr Chopra, but my race was run. He had messed me around for the last time.

* I was a bit. I'd pay good money to watch a giant Scotsman fight a robotic cricketer. Come on, who wouldn't pay to watch that? And for my money, The Scot would win.

** The second forfeit was pretty bad. Phil was involved. Not like **that**. He kept his waistcoat on throughout though, relievably.

PART FIFTEEN

Sussex vs. The Indians, Hove, Aug 25
S.R. Tendulkar – c. Naved Arif b. Liddle – 21
(17 balls, four fours)

The Test series had ended and now the one-day games were beginning. Sachin had been cruelly denied his 100th hundred on the final day at The Oval when Rod Tucker (who at the time of writing was still an umpire but may have been forced into hiding in the rainforest, walking around with a fake beard on, calling himself Todd Rucker) adjudged him to have been trapped lbw by Tim Bresnan for 91.

The whole ground inhaled audibly with shock as they saw their chance at seeing history being made snatched away. It was the loudest collective gasp heard since Tony Adams walked into the Arsenal players' bar after a match with Caprice on his arm. Personally, I hadn't been so shocked to see something since I'd found Ashley Giles' name on the Lord's honours board, or seen Luke Wright's name in yet another England squad. (Sorry, sorry, sorry Luke, last one I promise.)

But bizarrely, part of me was secretly pleased Sachin had failed. If he'd notched his landmark century that day, the media circus around him would have doubled; tripled, even. My chances of bowling at Sach were likely to be severely hampered if he had succeeded in reaching three figures, and anything that got in the way of me bowling to Tendulkar was bad news in my eyes – even if it was a landmark century.

Was that selfish? Maybe. But Sachin scoring 99 hundreds was pretty selfish when I'd never made more than 55 in a single innings. If he was hogging all the cricketing talent, then the least I deserved was to rake in the lion's share of any good luck going around.

But even so, as I watched him trudge off at The Oval, I was torn – metaphorically, I was wiping a tear of disappointment away from my cheek with one hand, but celebrating, clenched fist, with the other. In reality, I had a gin and tonic in one hand and, well, a gin and tonic in the other hand. The Ian Botham diet, I think it's called.

I had spoken to Mr Chopra again in the days between England's whitewash victory and the Sussex game. He was, I had decided, a peculiar fellow. He had, lest we forget, blown me out three times in less than two days, but yet he unashamedly kept coming back.

I had taken his no-show at The Oval to mean he could no longer help me, but up he popped again, bright and breezy and only too willing to help. He had even called to promise he would call me during the next game against Sussex (happily only four miles from my place in Brighton, so the chances of me getting lost were reduced) and deliver me some '*very good news*'.

He was like the strangest best friend one could ever imagine – someone who seemed to be capable of subjecting me to crushing lows – and would barely apologise for doing so – but who also seemed to be trying his hardest to help me achieve something that was dear and important to me.

He was a puzzle alright, but broadly speaking, he had to be one of two things: either the most heroically polite man, determined not to upset anybody and living in constant fear or ever saying 'no' to any whackjob's crazy request, or he was a slightly muddled, disorganised but well-meaning man who really could make bowling at Sachin happen for me. It was hard to work out which. Both seemed as likely as the other. Not that I spent too long trying to figure it out, because the fact was, after months of trials and tribulations, he was the **only** man left standing. Every other hope I had of success had gone, every other avenue to Sachin emphatically closed. It was Chopra or bust.

Happily, he did at least seem genuinely horrified at how much he had messed me around thus far. Maybe it was a blessing in disguise that he'd been so unprofessional. Perhaps I could guilt-trip him into helping me bowl to Sachin. At this point, any crumb of comfort tasted like a three-course meal. I was getting desperate.

In my quieter moments, it was hard not to just throw the towel in and admit defeat. At such dark times, I just pictured Rosh's smug, mocking face and that got me back on track. He wasn't going to get the better of me. Rosh still had a provisional driving licence, for goodness sake, and occasionally ate biro lids. His biggest claim to fame was being one of the Top 20 junior Real Tennis players in the world as a child – purely by dint of the fact only about 22 children play Real Tennis. But that achievement still trumped anything I'd done. Throwing the towel in was what he would have wanted me to do. It would have maintained his imagined superiority over me – and that simply could not happen. And so off in pursuit of Sachin I went once more. Well, almost.

****

"Are you kidding?" asked Tim quietly.

"No. I'm being absolutely serious," I said, super-seriously. "If you don't come now, I won't be able to get to the cricket. And I *need* to be there. I'm expecting some good news from Mr Chopra today, and for all I know, it might be along the lines of '*Adam, you can bowl at Sachin during the lunch break*'," I gasped anxiously.

"How are you 27-years-old and not able to deal with this

on your own?" Tim asked disbelievingly. "I know girls who would make less of a fuss."

"Yes, Tim," I snivelled aggressively, "but you're from the north of England."

He thought for a moment.

"Even for you, Ad, this is farcical," Tim said. "The cricket ground is only four miles away. It's only a…"

"Don't you dare say it," I moaned. "It's not *only* anything. It's an enormous angry, horrible, potentially-lethal wild animal."

"No," Tim replied condescendingly. "It's just a little wasp."

It was embarrassing to admit, but I'd been turfed out of my own vehicle by a squatting insect that had taken up residence on a half-drunk juice bottle in my drinks holder. But it wasn't some little wasp – it was *enormous*. And there was no way I was going to sit in a cramped, confined space with that evil beast, whether it was for four miles or four hundred miles.

"Just ignore it," Tim suggested. "That wasp is more scared of you than you are of it."

"Tim, if that was the case, I'd be inside the car, and he'd be on the outside! As it is, he's ruling the roost," I said. "I'm just relieved the keys aren't in there because he's so big he could probably drive the bloody thing away."

"Well, it is an automatic. It's designed for old ladies and complete idiots," said Tim dismissively. He really wasn't taking me seriously.

"I'm serious, Tim," I said sternly. "When I say I hate wasps, I don't mean I hate them in the same way that some people *'hate'* chickpeas, I mean I hate wasps enough to want them to disappear entirely – like how normal people feel about *properly* evil things like fascism or Man Utd. Or how you feel about talcum powder."

"Ugh, *talcum powder*," Tim sneered. "What the hell is it? It's just perfumed dust! And who the hell uses it? It's just for newborn babies, old men and adult movie stars. And any product that is only used by those three groups of people should be banned, if you ask me. Those three groups of people should never be together, and even if they were, they couldn't all share the same bottle, could they?"

"Exactly," I nodded. "So come on: if the boot was on the other foot and you were in a talcum powder disaster, I'd come to your aid."

"But I've never called you up at work and said: '*I'm too scared to walk into the changing room at the gym because there is a man in there talcing his genitals*', have I? And I'm never likely to," Tim replied.

"Just because you never have, doesn't mean you never will," I told him, in what I hoped was an authoritative manner. "And if you ever did, Timothy, I would be there for you. I'd stand in the line of fire and make sure that ominous cloud of talc never made it from the old man's bits to your face. Because that's what friends do, yeah?"

"What, prevent an old man's talcum powder cloud from wafting into their friend's faces?"

"Yeah," I said enthusiastically.

"Bollocks. Take a bus," Tim chuckled. "Or walk."

"Fine," I grunted, angrily. "But you can expect to find a big bottle of talc on your bed tonight," I warned Tim. "And an old man in there, applying it liberally."

"Where are you going to find an old man willing to wait in a 25-year-old man's bedroom, talcum powdering himself all day?"

"This is Brighton, Tim," I said coldly.

I had got about 15 paces away from the car before I realised the full extent of my dilemma. I patted the pockets of my shorts expecting to feel the familiar squish of my leather wallet. It wasn't there. But I knew *exactly* where it was. It was probably under attack from the ruthless, rampaging wasp – well, I say wasp, it was more a giant, striped dog with wings, a sting the size of a javelin, and the same cold, evil disregard for human life as Dennis Lillee bowling at an English tailender, or Margaret Thatcher. Bloody Thatcher! Milk snatcher! (Seriously, I'm very much available for topical news quiz shows.)

An hour-and-a-half later and I finally made it to the ground. Sussex posted a competitive total while my stomach growled louder and louder with each passing minute. I was hungry, thirsty and sweaty, and it was all my own fault. Actually, it was the bloody wasp's fault.

By the time India began their reply, and Sachin strode to the crease, I was under a dark cloud. I'd had enough. I had no money, I was an hour-and-a-half walk from home and there was zero chance I was going to bowl at Sachin today. And my jean shorts were very uncomfortably tight, particularly around the crotch area. I was more disheartened than the Tin Man, but even he wasn't wearing these ridiculous sodding shorts.

I had bottomed out (nothing to do with the shorts this time). I'd put up with being given the run-around by Mr Chopra because I could see light at the end of the tunnel. He seemed like a person worth pursuing, but he hadn't called all day, despite yet another of his grandiose but clearly bullshit promises. It really did feel as though this was it – the summer was ebbing away, and I was still no closer to tracking down Sach. If not now then soon, I would have to face the fact that it wasn't going to happen. He was just too untouchable. Everything about the journey so far had been joyous – rejections and cock-ups included. I was meeting new people, seeing new places and chasing something unlikely, just for the fun of it. I had really enjoyed trekking after Sachin around the country, even when I/my satnav (depending on your viewpoint) was heading in the wrong direction, because it was all part of the experience. I had even revelled in the moments when things went awry because I realised I was undertaking a near-impossible task, and that things would inevitably go wrong. But I took each cock-up in the best of spirits because I had hope. Each mishap, I told myself, was still a step (sort of) in the right direction. But that Dunkirk spirit was gone now. Maybe I was just annoyed because I had no cash to buy some chips, but my mood was jet black.

I sat watching Sachin taking his guard and preparing to face his first ball. He was in the same ground as me, but in reality, he was still a million miles away. Why the hell was I still keeping up the pretence that I had a hope in hell of bowling at Sachin Tendulkar? The man was a near-deity, unable to walk in his hometown without a disguise on. His every move was photographed. Every minute of every hour of every day of his life, somebody wanted something. I was just one of hundreds of people trying to get close to him. At best, I was in the middle of a long queue to get to him and there was nothing I could do. There was no guarantee I would ever get to the front of that line. Despite my chipper and positive spin on them, the days of practise, the hours spent talking tactics with Roj Whelan, the attempts to bribe, cheat, lie and Jedi-mind-trick my way to Sachin were in vain.

I was miserable. In fact, I was a bunch of flowers, a slightly bigger quiff and a bigger chin away from being Morrissey. Although even he might have found me a bit gloomy. But could you blame me? A crushing realisation hit me, and hit me harder than a Brett Lee inswinger into my crown jewels – I was not going to be able to bowl at Sachin Tendulkar.

I somehow forced myself to stay at the ground and watch some cricket. Sachin got off to a good start, finding the boundary early with a few well-timed blows. At least, I told myself, I could still appreciate the sheer technical perfection of his batting.

Both openers, in fact, were looking good. I settled in my seat and resolved to try and enjoy myself. Sachin may be out of reach, but that was no reason to turn my back on the game I loved. At the darkest of times, cricket usually perked me up at least a tiny bit – at least enough to brush away those Morrissey comparisons and make me forget about these thoroughly impractical and restrictive shorts.

Another boundary-bound shot crashed with a pleasing clunk into the advertising hoardings lining the edge of the pitch in front of me. It was a lovely, uniquely cricketing sound. As I watched the ball rebound off the thin frontings and back onto the pitch, an idea suddenly belly-flopped untidily into my head.

It was fantastic.

Amazing, actually.

Brilliant, certainly.

Foolproof, by necessity.

It was so good I wondered why I hadn't thought of it before.

It was so simple, and yet absolutely perfect.

And today was the day I was going to do it.

Sachin was out in the middle, batting right now.

He was padded up and ready to go.

I was in the ground.

I was yards – and a wee jump over the fence – from being on the square.

The ball was within arm's reach.

I had to do this.

I settled into a seat right by the boundary edge, on the gently sloped grassy bank that makes up one of the sides of Hove cricket ground. I ran through the consequences of my plan.

Sure, I'd get rugby-tackled to the floor by a steward at some point, but a broken rib would heal. And yes, I would probably be banned from Hove cricket ground for a while, but I hardly ever watched cricket at Hove. And if the worst came to the worst and I got arrested, so what? I read somewhere that some prisons have Sky. I'd be alright as long as the other inmates let me watch *The Simpsons*.

Obviously there were risks and consequences associated with doing it, but the same applied to wearing a 'Muse' t-shirt in public, but plenty of people did that (*risks*: that people know you like Muse, and you are therefore a silly person with terrible music taste. *Consequences*: nobody will talk to you apart from other silly Muse fans, who'll just talk about space and goblins and moon landing conspiracy theories or whatever gubbins Muse fans like).

My mission was clear, I thought to myself; I would snatch the ball from the boundary edge, run onto the pitch and bowl at Sachin while he was out in the middle.

It was that simple. Nothing could possibly go wrong. Alright, it could, but so what? I could bypass the middlemen of the world – Messrs Chaudhary, Chopra, Shetty and the like – and get closer to Sachin than I ever had, or ever was likely to. I didn't need their permission to do this. And best of all, if I did manage to hit the stumps, I would have thousands of witnesses. I might even get talent-spotted. The only people who could stand in my way were wearing luminous yellow jackets. But even they stood no chance. This was it. It was sink or swim. This was my last chance saloon (and countless other clichés). As I bided my time to strike, I called Josh to run my brilliant scheme by him. This was right up his street. He would love this; after all, he was sort of the inspiration behind this amazing plan. In a way, I had taken his streaking idea and tweaked it to come up with the perfect way to succeed in my quest. (I say 'tweaked it': I had removed the most crucial component – that of being completely naked – but the thought was still there.)

"Josh," I said eagerly, almost wheezing into my phone's mouthpiece with exhilaration, "guess what I'm about to do?"

"Ummm…a poo?" he asked, weirdly.

"No," I said bluntly and with a hint of disgust in my voice.

"Oh," he said, sounding suitably reprimanded. "A wee,

then?"

"What?" I squeaked. "No!"

"Some manscaping*?" This was getting silly now.

"Why would I be ringing my little brother if I was about to do some manscaping?" I shuddered in reply.

"I don't know," Josh said disinterestedly. "Tips?"

Tips?! I know for a fact** he tried to shave his own name into his *y'know* hair once, but misjudged it and ended up with 'JO' instead of Josh. Which is weird as Jo is our Mum's name.

"Josh, shut up for a second," I barked, hoping to drag the conversation away from all matters toilet, "I'm at Hove cricket ground watching the Sussex vs. India match. I'm sitting near the edge of the boundary. And I've just had the best idea ever. Today is the day Joshy – in a few minutes, I'm going to bowl at Sachin Tendulkar."

"What? How?" He sounded half-confused and half-excited, like a dog chasing its own tail, or how Matt Hayden and Justin Langer probably felt the first time they did that emphatic, slightly too passionate hug when one of them got a ton.

I ran Josh through my plan breathlessly. Josh fell silent. My face was frozen in a smile of anticipation.

"You're kidding," he replied quietly, once I'd finished my slightly frantic pitch.

"No!" I laughed, maniacally. "He's out there right now! And the best part is, he won't be expecting it. I'll have the element of surprise. All I'll have to do is bowl a straight one and he might be so confused that he just doesn't bother to think about where the ball is going. He might even recoil away from the stumps and think I'm going to throw a beer can or something at him. It's perfect isn't it?"

"No, Natalie Portman is perfect," Josh snapped back. "This plan is definitely not perfect. If this plan were a woman, it would be that old lady who eats things from the bin at Portsmouth Harbour station."

I couldn't believe what I was hearing. Josh had suddenly become *sensible*.

"Rubbish," I shouted. "This plan is it. This is my one little light at the end of the tunnel."

"But it's the light of an oncoming train, bro!" Josh bellowed. "Worse than that, it's not even an oncoming train, it's bloody Ann Widdecombe walking down the tunnel completely naked wearing nothing but one of those miners' helmets with a lamp on! *Don't do it, Adam.*"

But it was too late. My mind was made up. I told Josh there was nothing he could do to change my mind.

"Wait. Just wait for a bit. Please," he begged. "This isn't cricket. You're always banging on about cricket being the best sport in the world because of its honour code, or whatever it is. Do you really want to say '*yes, I bowled Sachin Tendulkar, but only because he didn't protect his stumps because he thought I might have been throwing an empty beer can at him?*"

I thought for a moment.

"*You either succeed fairly, or you fail honourably*, right?" added Josh.

"Sometimes you have to succeed dishonourably," I snarled back.

Images of myself sprinting across the lush green outfield, the tough leather of the ball in my hand and the wind tugging at my jumper immediately leapt into my mind. I could picture myself running in a wide arc up to the wicket, and springing athletically into my action. I could visualise the ball homing in on the stumps, while a bemused Sachin swished aimlessly. It was going to happen, I could feel it. The past few months had all been building up to this one moment. My phone, now back in my pocket, buzzed annoyingly and incessantly.

I remembered what Roj had told me. I wouldn't over-think it. I would just imagine I was playing cricket with one of my mates. And I would try to make sure I celebrated properly. I still hadn't nailed the Soulja Boy dance, but a steward would probably tackle me to the ground before I got all the way through it, anyway. It was all shaping up perfectly.

But my phone was now buzzing almost non-stop in my pocket. I fished it out and tried to turn it off. But before I could, I noticed the number on the screen. It wasn't Josh. It was Mr Chopra. What the hell was I going to do? The chance to get on the pitch was right in front of me, but Mr Chopra was also calling right now. He had promised he would have good news for me today. Maybe this was it, but how could I be sure it wasn't another one of his pointless wild goose chases? There was only one thing for it. I hedged my bets.

"Hello, Mr Chopra," I said urgently.

"Hello Adam, how are you today? Are you well? I've been ringing you for a while, I was worried something was the matter," he said laconically. Clearly he hadn't detected the panic in my voice.

I sprang to my feet suddenly. A ball was heading my way, racing towards the boundary boards away to my left. This was it. This was *the* moment. And I was on the bloody phone.

"Adam," he said quietly, "are you still there?"

I was so focused on the ball bounding towards me that I'd completely ignored Mr Chopra. "Yes, I'm listening," I said monotonously, as I watched the ball thud dully into the advertising panelling to my left. A Sussex fielder began jogging after it as it spun to a standstill on the boundary edge. A steward was also moving ominously into position. I had to go **now**.

My heart chugged with excitement, like a thousand steam engines all heaving back and forth at the same time, or Shane Watson doing a Google images search of his own name.

"Well, Adam," continued Mr Chopra, "I have some good news for you."

I instinctively tried to hoist my leg up and over the top of the boards. A shot of pain coursed through me. *The bloody jean shorts*. They really were **very** tight around the crotch. I let out a small yelp, like a frightened little dog, or Warney having his bikini line waxed. Mr Chopra didn't seem to notice.

It wasn't the first time I had embarrassingly failed to get my leg over during an afternoon out in Hove and nor would it probably be the last. The dark-shirted Sussex player continued to calmly home in on the stationary ball. I made one last gallant effort.

A split-second later, I made a mental note to bin these stupid shorts. It hadn't worked. You wouldn't catch any other serious cricketer (for that is what I am) in such shorts. Mitchell Johnson for a provocative photoshoot maybe, but no serious cricketer. But in an instant, I forgot all about my aborted one-man pitch invasion.

"You'll be pleased to know," said Mr Chopra grandly, ignoring my distracted silence, "that you will be able to bowl at Sachin Tendulkar."

GULP.

Urban Dictionary defines manscaping as 'a man's grooming of his body hair. Like landscaping, but for the body.' Every day's a school day, eh? Rumours that Shane Watson shaves pictures of his own face and the words 'I love Shane Watson' into his body hair are just that – rumours. Wee Stuey Broad, judging by his entirely hairless face, has yet to hit puberty and so doesn't partake. But when he does he'll probably clip Optimus Prime or a T-Rex or the Nottingham Forest club badge into his.

** *Not technically a fact. But don't let that stop you spreading the story around.*

PART SIXTEEN

"Could you repeat that?" I said, my voice wobbling all over the shop. I was completely ruddy-bloody shell-shocked. I was half-certain I'd dreamt what I just thought I'd heard.

"Yes," repeated Mr Chopra calmly. "It appears you will be able to bowl at Mr Sachin Tendulkar." There was just the hint of a cheeky smile in his voice.

Fireworks exploded! Party poppers popped! A fanfare of trumpets blasted a triumphant tune to the highest heavens! Hooray! It wasn't all a dream!

Well, the fireworks, party poppers and trumpeters *were* a dream. There weren't really any of them there. It would have been impractical. There was a cricket match on for a start, and I couldn't afford to have a fireworks display team, a group of people with party poppers poised (all called Peter Piper who picked peppers in their spare time, presumably) and a load of brass players tagging after me on the off-chance I might one day get this particular bit of good news. That would have been pure folly. It would have bankrupted me and made me look like a complete idiot, spending money I didn't have. Who do you think I am? Allen Stanford? Well I'm not. I can't grow a moustache for a kick-off.

"Fuck-er-*flip*ping hell," I said nervously, once the metaphorical trumpets and fireworks had died down. "That is wonderful news, Mr Chopra, thank you so much."

Mr Chopra had stood me up, sent me on wild goose (well, chicken) chases, forced me to get out of bed at 6.30am, ignored dozens of my phone calls and texts and been at least partially responsible for me having to drink lukewarm beer from a sweaty rubber chicken foot. Not to mention his role in me having to complete a second forfeit at The Oval (and I will definitely not mention anything about it). I should have hated him, but here he was, the last shining beacon that could lead me to Sachin, giving me the best news imaginable. I wanted to hug him, or at the very least give him a high five and a cake and a bowler hat full of those chocolate coins or *something*, to show my thanks. Soon, it turned out, I would get the chance. I liked the hat full of coins best.

"Now Adam, I'm afraid we do need to act very quickly," said Mr Chopra, suddenly sounding more professional than he had at any point across our previous conversations. Which admittedly, still wasn't *that* professional.

"OK, no problem," I replied. "*How* quickly?"

I knew the answer before the conversation was even over.

I started running immediately. Actual arm-pumping, legs-pounding, hands-fixed-into-blades-to-cut-through-the-air *running*. Proper bloody running.

But I'm no natural sprinter. Running to me, is a bit like naturism, which sometimes looks like it might be fun (what with all the badminton and picnics), but which always strikes me as being for other people. Much as I wasn't born to play naked racket sports, so I wasn't born to run. My boots weren't even made for walking.

I had to be in London by 6pm to meet Mr Chopra and his colleagues. I checked the time – it was just before 4pm already. I'd been running for under ten minutes and already, almost my entire body was aching.

I realised why you don't see many of the Olympic long-distance runners wearing chunky-knit cricket jumpers and laceless deck shoes. Both are *really* uncomfortable. And don't even get me started on my stupid bloody shorts. I was crossing my fingers that they wouldn't have turned me into a castrato by the end of the fourth mile.

Don't get me wrong, I was probably the most stylish runner ever seen on the streets of Brighton (and that's saying something), but I had somewhere to be. These clothes were impractical. At the very least I needed a pair of those tiny running shorts with the mesh underwear sewn in. But even if I ran at full pelt for the whole four miles back to my car, I still wouldn't make it to London on time.

They say necessity is the mother of all invention and in this case, I suddenly got creative – and brave – when faced with the prospect of actually having to do a concerted period of physical exercise. I flagged down a cab, hopped in and began to explain my predicament. My wallet, I told him, was in my car. I would pay, I promised, once we got back to my house. If the cabbie seemed satisfied enough that I wasn't mental, it was almost certainly because I only gave him the edited version of why my wallet was locked in my car. If I had told him the real reason was because my car had been commandeered by an enormous, possibly talking, probably mutant and arguably kung-fu trained wasp, I'd have probably still been jogging. Within minutes we had pulled up, the cab engine still idling and the meter still running, beside my car.

"I'll only be a minute or two," I told the driver as I eased myself out of the door, my sweaty, nervous palms sliding over the leather back seats. I stood for a moment in the cool summer air, my face close to the passenger side window, trying to spot the wasp inside. I inched closer, pressing my nose against the glass. I couldn't see him.

Suddenly, a yellow and black monster – twice the size of an eagle with lasers for eyes and luminous five-inch-long vampire fangs (possibly, I don't know, I instantly covered my face in shock) zoomed towards me. Instinctively I recoiled, and leapt back from the window. I let out a fairly (very) high-pitched scream and felt my face grow flushed. A bead of sweat trickled down the back of my neck.

The wasp/killer flying beast had been sitting, mockingly, on the driver's seat, like it was king of the fucking castle, and I, the rightful owner of the car, was some dirty rascal. Perhaps he could smell me. Running in a cricket jumper does nothing for a man's personal hygiene. I turned to see the cabbie looking at me with a mixture of contempt and confusion. I'd been single for a stretch, so it was a look I'd not seen for a while. Slowly, I walked back to the cab's passenger-side front window and leant my head inside.

"Sorry about that," I said, with a confident smile, "but there's a wasp in there."

"Oh right," he mumbled. I could see he was already regretting picking me up.

"Yes. It was a big one. Massive. Cheeky shit was sitting on the driver's seat," I explained. "He's probably adjusting my headrest and dicking about with my rear view mirror and…" I paused to catch my breath. "I think his little legs are even long enough to reach the pedals."

"Oh right," sighed the cabbie.

I returned to my car and stared at myself in the reflection of the driver side window. There I stood, with my silly little fringe across my forehead and a cricket jumper on. I looked about 12 years old and I was acting it too. This was ridiculous. It was now quarter past four and I needed to hit the road immediately.

This was undoubtedly a low point in the annals of my 'manliest moments', coming in just behind the time I had a bit of a strop at university because someone had used the last of my hair straightening serum without telling me. I went out with curly hair that night, and came back with a newfound resolve to stop being quite so precious, but that resolve was being sorely tested right now. And the meter in the cab was still running. If I left it much longer, I wouldn't even have enough cash in my wallet to pay the poor bloke.

It was time to man up. I took a deep breath and moved in front of the passenger-side door. I closed my eyes and groped with my right hand until I found the door handle. I opened one eye and peaked inside the car. My wallet was in a little hollow beneath my glove compartment.

I flung the car door open and dived – quite literally – inside. I scrabbled about in the little valley until I felt the reassuringly soft leather squidge of my wallet. I snatched it up and pushed myself backwards towards the open door.

But as I did, a blood-curdling buzz reverberated in my ear. It was the wasp, in all his Kevlar-reinforced glory. I swear I caught a glimpse of miniature machine guns mounted on his wings. He was *huge*.

I screamed and bolted from the car, swishing my arms and legs wildly as I tried to outrun the wasp. But the buzz was following me, the horribly nasal drone darting aggressively towards my face while I ran in a looping arch away from the cab, screaming all the while like a petrified six-year-old girl.

I got about 20 metres away before the cabbie started beeping noisily. The wasp seemed to have gone. I sprinted back to the cab, to find the driver looking at me in shock. Like I said, I really hate wasps.

I handed over the money (checking first that the super-wasp hadn't raided my wallet and stolen all my cards and cash – he hadn't) got into my car and set off.

I had somewhere very important to be.

****

"This is bloody amazing news!" Rosh roared down the phone line as I called him on my hands-free from the motorway.

I had arranged to meet Mr Chopra outside Regent's Park tube station in central London, near where he was having a meeting.

My satnav (which I double and triple-checked to make sure it was directing me to London, England, rather than to the village of London on the Pacific Ocean island of Kiribati. It tried, but I noticed what it was up to, relievably) said I would reach the capital at 5.45pm. I had been driving for 45 minutes already, and I was making good time. But just like being stuck in the back seat of a sports car with Bermudian enormo-spinner and Godzilla-alike Dwayne Leverock, I had no room for manoeuvre.

"Actually," Rosh said smugly as I weaved through some light traffic, "I'm not that surprised. I always knew you'd be able to do it."

"How can you say you always knew I was going to do it?" I asked, perplexed at Rosh's sudden faith in me. "One of the main reasons I'm even on this stupid bloody quest is because of your pig-headed belief that I never even bowled you while you were pretending to be Sachin in your back garden. In fact, in some ways, you're to blame for all the farcical crap I've been put through for the last fuck-knows how many months. If you'd admitted I bowled you all those years ago in your back garden, I wouldn't be in this mess."

"But you never did bowl me," snapped Rosh instinctively.

"Not this again. I *did.*"

"Didn't."

"Did."

"Look, this argument has raged for long enough," said Rosh, bizarrely assuming the role of mature mediator. "Let's just agree to disagree…"

"Fine," I said brusquely.

"Wait," interrupted Rosh, "you didn't let me finish. What I was going to say was: let's agree to *disagree* with you that you *did* bowl me, and agree to *agree* with me that you *didn't.*"

Utter gobbledegook. It probably sounded logical to Rosh, but nobody else. Sometimes he made about as much sense as a Paul Harris 'arm-ball' (seriously, how the hell does a spinner who can't spin the ball, bowl an arm ball? The only time a Paul Harris delivery doesn't '*go on*' with the arm is when one of his pies '*goes on*' to the top of the pavilion off the middle of someone's – no, *anyone's* – bat)

"Whatever," I replied dismissively. "But how come you're so excited that I finally look like I'm going to do this? I was expecting you to be gutted at this bit of news."

"Ah, come off it mate," Rosh said lethargically, "I know we may compete a lot, and constantly take the piss out of each other, but deep down, we are inter racial best buds, aren't we? I've always been rooting for you. I was always – and especially so in the last few weeks – been utterly convinced you would bowl at Tendulkar."

Something was up. None of this sounded right.

"What's wrong with you," I asked him coldly. "You've gone wrong."

"Nothing is wrong. I'm just in a very loving, giving and generous mood," he said lazily. "That's all."

"*Loving, giving and generous?*" I scoffed.

"That's right. Sounds like a three-girl Motown group, doesn't it?"

We were back in gobbledegook territory.

"Poor old *Generous* – that would be no name to call a girl," he continued. "She'd have no chance. Mind you *Loving* and *Giving* aren't much better. You'd expect quite a lot, as a boy, from girls with names like that."

"Erm, yes…" I said uncertainly.

"Because people grow into their names don't they?" he continued, unabatedly. "If you call your son Ian, he'll probably grow up to work in a bank, just like if you call your kid Tom, he'll grow up to be a mono-browed fuck-knuckle. But if you call your kid *Generous,* then she might turn out to be quite *generous*, if you know what I mean."

I did, but Rosh wasn't finished yet.

"It's like with Prince or Madonna. You can't name your

kid something like that and expect they'll end up working in Dixons like a normal person, can you?" he pointed out wisely. "It was obvious what they were both going to grow up to be."

"Pop stars?" I asked.

"No," said Rosh, chuckling wryly. "Fucking *mental*."

He had a point. But I couldn't help but think 'Rosh' should have been added to the 'fucking mental' list. Rosh wished me luck for the rest of my drive but told me he had to go, as he had a date later that night (possibly with *Loving, Giving* or if he was really lucky, *Generous*). I told him if he needed any manscaping tips, pre-date, he should ring my brother. I didn't mention that his speciality was accidentally shaving his own mother's name into his body hair.

I re-checked my estimated arrival time. It had risen slightly, to 5.48pm. Fifteen minutes later, it had risen to 5.51pm. Ten minutes after that, it was 5.55pm. I had hit traffic. Bollocks, bollocks, *bollocks*. Why was nothing ever straightforward? I called Mr Chopra, my hands shaking with fear as I waited for the phone to connect. If I explained I was going to be slightly late because of the traffic, he would have to understand. *Wouldn't he?* Surely he could just push our meeting back a little bit, until 6.30pm. He was a dedicated sort of chap. He wouldn't mind working a bit of overtime.

His phone went straight to answer phone. I left him a message telling him what had happened, but promising to be at Regent's Park as soon as was humanly possible. It was all I could do.

As I ended the call, my radio faded back up, but I was in no mood for music. I slapped my hand on to the power button and sat in silence. The estimated time of arrival on my satnav ticked over to 6.01pm. With the radio off, I had just the gentle shudder of the engine for company. And a faint buzzing noise. Not *again*.

I gripped the steering wheel tight and winced as the buzz – a distinctly menacing, almost mechanical, digitised whirr

– flashed past both ears and round the back of my head. I squirmed in my seat and felt my toes curl.

But there was no way I was stopping. Not even if this flying thing was a wasp; bee; fly, or even a mutant insect with the power to control human minds, made entirely of titanium, with a lightsabre in each of its little legs and broader shoulders than Matt Hayden. Chasing Sachin had changed me as a person in many ways, and this was the final piece in the jigsaw. I didn't have time to fear piddling little insects. I had a date with destiny (she was rejected from the line-up of *Loving, Giving and Generous*).

The clock, or more specifically the digital display in my car, ticked over to 5.55pm. I had spent the last 45 minutes making steady progress and occasionally shouting a variety of obscenities at whatever the little flying insect in my car was. But I was still 15 minutes away from Regent's Park, not far from Notting Hill.

Mr Chopra still hadn't returned my call either, but I took that as a good sign – I wasn't sure why, but it was either that, or I took it as a bad sign. I was in no mood for negativity. Today was *the* day. I just had to keep telling myself that. It was 6.15pm when my phone finally sprang into action; an incoming call from a withheld number. Gone were the days I ignored them. Now I welcomed them.

"Hello?" I shouted, keen to be heard over the rattle of my engine.

"Hello mate!"

Grrr! It was Josh. I growled in frustration and slammed my right fist into the steering wheel, making it shake and wobble dangerously. My hand pulsed painfully from the force of the blow.

"Josh, now is a really bad time," I barked, scarcely-contained panic forcing my voice into a higher register than usual. I cut him off before he could reply.

I was just five minutes from Regent's Park now.

I looked at the clock. It was 6.20pm.

My phone rang again. This time it was Big Gun. *Cancel.*

Then it rang again. Big Gun, *again. Cancel.*

And *again!* What the hell was going on? It was Big Gun again! *Cancel.*

Hold on: this was Regent's Park! Regent's-bloody-flipping-wonderful-Park!

Arriving at destination on the left, sing-songed the robotic satnav lady/bastard love-child of R. Schumacher and a road atlas.

My phone rang *again.*

But this time I didn't cancel. It was Mr Chopra.

He wasn't in Regent's Park anymore.

Bugger-bugger-bollocks-bollocks.

He was in Stoke Newington.

Bugger-bugger-bollocks-bollocks-fuck-fuck-fuck-shit.

But…*oh.*

Did I know where Clissold Park was?

Yes, I said confidently. I did.

Thirty minutes?

Yes, I nodded; **I could**.

It was a beautiful late summer evening, with bright but watery sunlight pouring down as I navigated my way towards Clissold Park. I grinned inanely to myself at the thought of what was to come in just a few moments' time.

I managed to find a parking space almost immediately down a quietish side road and leapt from my car. I did a quick scan of the area around me to see if anyone was watching. Happy that no one was, I did a little skip.

I looked around again and boogied my way through the first few steps of the Soulja Boy dance I'd been practising as my celebration. I messed it up after the 'superman' bit, but I didn't care. I was practically gliding along the street.

As I turned onto Stoke Newington Church Street, there

in front of me was the park, a lush green expanse, humming with gentle activity – a glorious, comforting cacophony of chattering voices, tweeting birds and laughter. A gentle breeze swept regularly and rhythmically through the overhanging branches by one of the park's entrances.

It might sound trite and twee, but after months of slogging around the country, this felt like my reward. Not just that I was about to finally seal the deal to bowl at Sachin, but that it should be in such beautiful surroundings. I thought about what this whole experience thus far had meant to me. Why had I really done it? It felt, somehow, like this was something I'd subconsciously been planning for years.

I sat on a wall opposite the park and waited for Mr Chopra to arrive. I scanned the road ahead, my eyes darting across the horizon in the same way Sachin's dark eyes had peeped for gaps in the field from under his helmet at Edgbaston in 1996.

Mr Chopra said he was wearing a casual suit and sunglasses and that he should be easy to spot. I checked the time on my phone. Then I looked up. Nothing; no one. I picked at a hole in my shorts. And looked up. Still nothing, still no one. I took my sunglasses off and checked them for smears. I looked up.

Something.

Someone.

As if by magic, he had appeared, in the time it had taken me to check my phone and then look back up. He must have materialised from thin air.

I leapt to my feet. It had to be him – how many dapper-looking Asian men in a dark suit jacket, low-brimmed hat and sunglasses were likely to just coincidentally stroll past Clissold Park? Not many, surely.

I crossed the road and made a beeline for him, hoping my cricket jumper would catch his eye, but as I skipped across to the opposite pavement, he turned and began walking away from me, his stylish shoes gently clip-clopping on the pavement.

I was no more than 20 metres from him and closing at a rate

of knots, when he stopped dead in his tracks, put his bag on the floor and took out his phone. Instinctively, I stopped too. I felt like I was a particularly amateur stalker who had just been rumbled. Almost in slow motion, his head turned to meet my gaze. Neither of us said anything.

"Adam?" he said.

"Hello," I said weakly, my feet frozen to the spot.

This. Was. AMAZING. He had actually bloody turned up. After all this time, he had finally shown face. I had privately started to doubt he was even real. I had begun to worry he was a figment of my imagination – the creation of a mind so desperate for some scrap of hope of bowling at Sachin Tendulkar.

It really was all about to happen. This was the moment. There was to be no repeat of the farce of The Oval. After today, I would have to refocus my efforts in the nets with Josh, and get in proper mental shape with Roj, and mercilessly rib Rosh about the fact I was actually going to succeed in my ridiculous plan. The hard work was about to begin, but this moment was still special. I sucked a deep breath into my lungs and savoured it. The sweet smell of the trees floated gently by.

"Lovely to see you," I said, offering my outstretched hand as I moved to within 25 feet of him. He was a cool-looking chap. On first impressions, I liked him. He seemed like my kind of dude. He slowly and dramatically took off his hat and shades, and smiled a broad, welcoming smile.

"A cricket jumper, eh?" he said suddenly, with a mischievous grin. "*Very* nice. Perfect attire for bowling at Tendulkar. Now: are you ready for it?"

Oh shit.

PART SEVENTEEN

Suddenly, I recognised those clip-clopping shoes. And that weird briefcase. And that smug wee grin. *Rosh*. He swept me up into an enormous bearhug and laughed heartily to himself.

"Surprised to see me?" he said, relinquishing me from his beary grip.

"Well, yes, but…I'm…" I was fumbling for a collection of words that made even the slightest scrap of sense, but I was completely tongue-tied. What the hell was going on?

"Ha, I thought you'd be confused," said Rosh, slinging a comforting arm around my shoulder. "But I'll explain everything later. First, you've got something very important to do."

"What?" I said, my brow furrowing.

Rosh chuckled.

"You're joking aren't you? You know why you're here, don't you?" he said, his grin growing wider by the second.

As I'd raced up to London, I thought I knew exactly what was about to happen. I thought I was going to meet Mr Chopra and seal the deal to bowl at Sachin. Now, I had absolutely no idea what was going on. I was like a thinner, less Satan-bearded Mike Gatting staring at that Shane Warne leg-break in the 1993 Ashes series. Utterly clueless.

"Anyway, come on, let's get cracking," he said, grabbing me by the arm and dragging me towards the park entrance.

He was like a man possessed, an almost insane zeal in his eyes and a crazed, immovable smile fixed across his lips. My head was spinning with questions. What the *hell* was going on? I felt like I was in a particularly twee David Lynch film. Was Rosh drunk? Worse, had he been drinking the Kool-Aid left over from one of Geno's cult meetings? Why was I here, and what the frig did all this mean? And where, most importantly, did he get those shoes? They looked like *Office* but were they? *Were they?!* There was so much I needed to know. They looked expensive, too. But how much were they?

"It's this way – not much further," panted Rosh excitedly, as he led me further into the cool air of the park. Gorgeous, cleansing sunlight pulsed rhythmically through the gaps in the trees, sending a stream of comforting warmth onto the side of my face as Rosh dragged me forwards, one giant stride after another. The birds tweeted sweetly overheard. Happy people made happy noises all around me. But no longer could I lazily drink in the sights and sounds of the rolling greenery. I was stunned. I wasn't even sure how I was putting one leg in front of the other. I was wearing the same vacant, glazed expression that spreads across Steven Finn's face whenever he tries to remember how many *n*'s are in his name (three).

My phone vibrated in my pocket, but I couldn't even begin to think about picking it up. That would have involved stopping the Rosh juggernaut. The vibrating subsided. But just as quickly, it started again.

"Rosh, hold on, my phone is ringing," I said, lifting his arm off my shoulder and starting to grope around in my pocket to answer it. (Using my own arm, you understand. I lifted Rosh's arm and gave it back to him.)

"Yes. That'll be Big Gun," Rosh said confidently. And it was.

"Hold on, how did you…" My breathing was shallow and tense. I swallowed nervously, my eyes darting between my phone and Rosh's grinning mug. Where the fuck was Mr

Chopra? WHO THE FUCK WAS HE?

"Answer it then!" squawked Rosh as I gormlessly stood holding my still ringing phone in my hand. I did as I was told and took the call.

"You fucking wanker, I've been ringing you for ages." That was what passed for a 'hello' in the weird world of Big Gun. He probably even called his Mum and Dad wankers, and they were lovely people, against the odds. Maybe they found him in a basket outside a church and raised him as their own.

"Yeah, sorry," I burbled, unsurely. "I've been a bit busy…"

"Don't give me that pile of bollocks, I know exactly what you've been up to, mate. How's Clissold Park looking? All lovely and green?"

This was getting weirder by the second. How did he know where I was? My mouth was agape and my eyes wide with fear and confusion. I looked at Rosh. He chuckled warmly and gave me a reassuring double thumbs up, which unfortunately brought images of Sir Paul McCartney to mind, which frankly, didn't help the situation.

"Now listen. I've got one last number for Tendulkar for you," Big Gun bellowed characteristically. "The last couple were duds. I'll admit that now. But this one is *bona fide*. Alright?"

Bona fide? Where had Big Gun learnt a phrase like that? Maybe he was secretly brushing up on his Latin to break up the hours he spent drinking Carlsberg from his Hulk Hogan mug and giggling maniacally at funny cat videos on YouTube. Somehow I doubted it.

"Oi, are you listening to me?" Big Gun snapped me back to my senses. "Make sure you ring that number – alright?"

"Yes," I mumbled.

"Good. Oh, and say hi to Rosh from me." He gave me the eleven digits, called me a wanker again and put the phone down. How the hell did he know Rosh was here?

Rosh sidled over and slung his arm around my shoulder

once more. A cool breeze swept through the leaves on the trees above, but it wasn't a soothing sound anymore. I felt punch-drunk with bewilderment.

"Good call?" Rosh asked with another cheeky grin.

I was in a complete and utter daze, and not the good sort that Jon Trott gets into either, where he is so focused on scratching his mark, annoying the opposition and working balls through the leg side that if you asked him his mother's name, he'd reply '*85 not out*', ask how many balls were left in the over and then play a couple of dozen more practise on-drives.

This craziness had gone on long enough. I took a deep breath and settled myself down. I'd been confused for long enough now. I shook myself – literally, tossing my head from side to side – out of whatever stupor all this ridiculousness had lulled me into. I wanted some answers.

"Ad – are you alright?" Rosh asked again, still smiling away inanely.

"Well, Big Gun has just given me a number for Tendulkar," I said assertively, "but more importantly than that, he seems to bloody well know I'm here at Clissold Park. And that I'm here with you. *What the shit is going on?*"

Rosh just smiled.

"Why don't you try that number Big Gun just gave you for Tendulkar," he suggested coolly.

"Rosh, can you just explain what is…"

He leant across and eased my phone out of my hand, and began typing the eleven digits I had written on my hand into my phone. He finished typing and offered me my phone back.

"It's ringing."

"Rosh…" I stumbled.

"Ad – it's ringing," he said unemotionally.

I snatched the phone from his hand with a moody sigh and thrust it to my ear. The familiar sound of a phone that was never going to be answered trilled in my ear. But abruptly, the line connected. I waited for a single mum in Dorchester called Tina to answer, tell me she'd never heard of '*Sackin whatever-his-name-is*' and give me a bollocking for interrupting her while she was doing her Kerry Katona 'bingo wings, thighs and arse workout'.

"Hello?" I said, disinterestedly.

"*Surprise!*"

I turned around to see Rosh on his phone too, his hand thrust high in the air in anticipation of a high-five. Unconsciously, I reached up and slapped my palm against his. I had literally *no* idea what we were celebrating. Rosh put his phone back into his pocket, slung his arm around my shoulder again, and started marching the pair of us further into the park. What on earth was that about? Why on earth had Big Gun just sent me Rosh's number under the pretence of it being Sachin Tendulkar's?

"So," Rosh said as we motored along a winding pathway, towards goodness knows where, "are you feeling warmed up? Are you loose? Are you *ready*?"

"Rosh, seriously," I whined. "*Warmed up? Loose? Ready?* Ready for what!?"

Rosh picked up the speed, and led us round a row of trees and out onto one of the park's main open patches of grass, his eyes wide and his tongue lolling out the side of his mouth in concentration. He seemed so happy and excited. It was quite sweet, in a way. Mildly terrifying, but sweet. As we looked out onto the wide expanse, there in front of us were people playing Frisbee, children kicking a football, and a group of teens sitting around sharing a fag.

And a set of stumps, a ball, and a bat.

"For this…" he said, theatrically gesturing with a grand sweep of his arm.

"Go on then, get yourself ready," shouted Rosh, chucking me a rubbery-feeling ball and picking up the tatty-looking Kookaburra bat that had been leaning against a nearby tree.

He rehearsed a few shots – a wristy leg-side flick, a bent-leg straight drive, and his version of Sachin's back-foot push through cover.

He looked in good nick. In fact, he looked more like a Test match batsman than Suresh Raina, but then so would an inanimate shop window mannequin (dressed in ice-white shoes, ice-white socks with Navy cadet stripes and a t-shirt with chevron action flash) with a cricket bat wedged in its hands. Poor old Suresh – talented though he is – should probably leave the Test match stuff to VVS and Rahul.

I spun the ball in my fingers and looked down the impromptu pitch. There was a patch of decaying leaves on a good length. You didn't get that at the Gabba, or Trent Bridge. Headingley back in the good old days, definitely, (according to Boycs) but it certainly wouldn't have passed muster with the ICC. You could probably have played better cricket on the pitch at New Road in Worcestershire when it was under three feet of flood water.

A dozen or more yards away, Rosh was standing upright and unflinching, like a smartly-dressed, poncey-shoed Tendulkar – like Tendulkar if he listened to Talking Heads rather than the Eagles, and watched French cinema instead of Eddie Murphy flicks.

"Ready?" he shouted.

"Yeah," I bellowed back. I spun the ball between my hands once more. I started my run-up and began to leap into my delivery stride. My mind was completely blank. I'd decided to stop trying to work out what was going on. The sun was out, and I was playing cricket with my best mate. There were worse ways (Infernos nightclub in Clapham to name one) to spend a picture-perfect early evening in the capital.

"Woah, woah, woah! Stop!"

Just as I was about to absent-mindedly release the ball, Rosh had hurriedly reeled away from his position in front of the stumps, his bat waving wildly in all directions. In a split second, he had dropped his bat and scurried over to his weird little briefcase, leaning forlornly against the roots of a nearby tree. From it, he pulled a dog-eared piece of paper, neatly folded it up and jogged over towards me at the other end of the 'pitch'.

"Sorry," he puffed, "I just thought you should probably see this before you bowl at me. It might make you think a bit more seriously about it all."

My brow furrowed again. I had set a new personal best for most number of frowns in a day. Nobody had looked this moody and confused since Ricky Ponting caught Mitchell Johnson starting a fight with himself in the mirror (*'this bloke keeps staring at me skip'*) and Shane Watson taking bets on the winner during the fourth Ashes Test in Melbourne in 2010. Mitchell's money went on himself, everyone else lumped on the bloke in the mirror. He looked harder, somehow. Mitch is now banned from being around reflective surfaces. Which might explain his haircuts.

I took the piece of paper from Rosh. It was the most bizarre thing I'd seen that day.

It was a deed poll certificate. A deed poll certificate confirming that Rosh's name was...*bollocks*. Well, no, not that his name was 'bollocks'. His point about people growing into their name held particularly true if your name was 'bollocks'. Not even *Generous* would go near you with a name like that. And people would always be expecting you to be one of a set of identical twins.

"What do you think?" he said, his eyes wide and a toothy grin on his face.

"You're shitting me," I said. "What is this?"

"You can read, can't you?" His grin was reaching *Cheshire*-ish levels.

"Well yes, but…" I whimpered.

"Why do you think Big Gun was so sure that number he gave you earlier – *my number,* remember – was the right number for Tendulkar?"

I stared at him, mouth open, looking completely gormless.

"I am," he announced grandly, inching closer to me, "*Roshan Tendulkar.*"

Roshan Tendulkar. Inspired. Rosh grabbed me by the front of my jumper.

"You, my friend," he panted, "are just about to bowl the all-important ball – the one ball that may or may not hit the stumps – at Tendulkar. I wanted to make sure you succeeded." He let a wry grin form on his face. "Sort of succeeded, anyway. This is it, man."

I was blown away. It still wasn't clear why, or how, but it certainly seemed like Rosh had done something utterly insane, and something that had taken organisation and deviousness in equal measures – but something wonderful, kind and above the call of duty, too.

"But why have you…?" I spluttered.

"I'll explain it all later," said Rosh, grabbing me by the shoulders and shaking me as I limply clung to the deed poll sheet, a little tear forming in my eye. (Honestly, it was *very* little, and I reckon the tight crotch of those friggin' shorts had something to do with it anyway. And I was very tired. And I'm a right soppy git.)

"Ad," he said, looking me in the eyes, "focus. You are about to bowl that one ball at Tendulkar, *right now*. This is it. If you reckon you can get Tendulkar – *any* Tendulkar – with one cherry…then this is it."

Gulp.

"Oh, and if you do manage to skittle me," he continued, walking slowly backwards, "we can finally settle this argument about you bowling me once and for all. I will be doing my best Tendulkar impression, and I am not going to be doing you any favours. It's simple – you either knock me over, or you don't. Ready?"

I tossed the ball up in the air, took a huge breath in through my nose and let a slightly cocky smirk form on my lips. I was so fucking ready. Excuse my French, but I was.

"Ready," I said (told you). Rosh turned on his heel and picked up his bat and settled into his best Tendulkar pose, his bat perfectly perpendicular to the turf, his stance upright and statue-still.

My mind was whirring at a million miles an hour – it didn't matter that Rosh wasn't *really* Sachin Tendulkar; he represented the end of a journey – maybe not the journey I'd expected, but an important one nonetheless. All through these mad few months, I'd rolled with the punches and the wrong turnings. This was just another one. However I looked at it, this was the conclusion of something important, something that had shaped me and changed me.

But more than that, this was a chance to finally shut him up. This was for bragging rights for all eternity. This was to finally win the argument, after 15 years. I tossed the ball into the air, spinning my fingers under it and sending it fizzing into my opposite hand. I tried to clear my mind of all thoughts.

But there he was. Utterly immovable.

Roj Whelan.

Roj, my spiritual guide on this quest to bowl out Sachin;

Roj, my learned Sherpa who had already achieved the impossible;

Roj, the man who had told me how I could follow in his footsteps.

His words came flooding back to me as I watched Rosh stood in wait:

"Before I bowled Sachin, he had told me, *I hadn't even thought about it. I just ran in like I was playing cricket with my mates at home. You've just got to think about it that way – just imagine it's you and your best mate…and make sure you celebrate properly when you bowl him…"*

Roj, you brilliant, *brilliant* man. What a piece of advice! It ranked up there with '*I think we should change the name of the show from 'Annoying Twats' to 'Friends'* in the annals of great bits of advice. I didn't even have to pretend, either – I really was bowling at my best mate. I could freestyle the bits of the Soulja Boy dance I hadn't mastered. Success was seconds away.

"Come on, get on with it," bellowed Rosh, lifting his sunglasses off his head and re-focusing my mind on his upright, perfectly balanced stance just yards away from me.

I tensed my shoulders up and let them slump back down, hoping to rid my body of any lingering tensions. I needed to be as relaxed as possible. I spun the ball into the air in front of me, really ripping my fingers across it, but keeping my focus on Rosh. The ball landed, alive with spin, back in my hand. I was ready.

I thought back to my first net session with Josh – the horrid balls I had chucked down; the agonising feeling of knowing how crap I was; the mocking jeers of those little shits who had decided to sit and watch. *Go Grease Lightning* briefly began playing in my head. *Cheers, Josh.* It seemed my brother had the capacity to be a nuisance (a loveable one, but a nuisance all the same) when he wasn't even in the same city as me. But it didn't last long. A strange calm immediately descended on me.

I was in an almost Zen state. I ran up to the makeshift bowling crease, my mind free from distractions. I leapt into my action, my eyes trained on nothing but the three stumps Rosh was trying to protect. I didn't think about what I was doing, or what was to come. I was running on auto-pilot. My head dipped as my momentum took me forward and the ball zipped from my hand. In an instant, I looked up to see where the ball was headed. In the millisecond since the ball had become airborne, my calm, trance-like state had vanished.

As the ball headed towards Rosh, his bat now raised higher in readiness to attack, Sachin was utterly absent from my thoughts. There was, at that precise moment, only one

Tendulkar who existed in my world – and he didn't have 99 international hundreds to his name. He was clutching a tatty old bat and itching to finish playing cricket so he could have a fag and a pint.

He may not have been the real deal, but in some ways – actually, in almost *all* ways, besides cricketing ability – I realised Rosh was the more important one to me. This Tendulkar – the phony, ridiculously-dressed, hipster-moustachioed Dalston *'Tendulkar'* – was the one I really wanted to knock over the most.

I wanted his stump out of the ground more than anyone else's in the world, for one simple reason. It really, truly meant something. Not just to me, but to Rosh too.

Sach might have been my childhood hero – the cricketer who had inspired me to take up the game, and an icon I had dreamed of sharing a moment or two with – but Rosh, far more importantly, was my best mate. My one-off duel in a net somewhere with Sachin would have been like a passionate fling – one that sent my pulse racing skywards, but quickly fizzled out. If I'd knocked Sachin's off peg out, he would have chuckled, taken his gloves off and shaken my hand, while some lackey coolly replaced the disturbed stump. It would have been like it never even happened. Sach would have disappeared through a door marked *players and officials only* and forgotten about the whole thing. We wouldn't swap mocking texts about it. We wouldn't reminisce over pints in the pub. It would have mattered to me, but not to him.

But my duel with Rosh was a decade-and-a-half in the making – and still threatened to spill over into a full-blown hair-pulling, face-slapping, whacking-each-other-with-our-man-bags bitch fight after all that time. Cricket – and our own battles playing the game – meant something to both of us. It was the reason England vs. Australia meant more than England vs. New Zealand.

If I bowled him with this ball, the image of my celebrating

face would haunt his dreams. He would know it meant constant jeering text messages until he got the opportunity to inflict his own humiliation. This ball might not castle one of the game's all-time legends – it was more important than that. It was at one of the true legends I knew. There was no contest in the importance stakes.

The ball was on its way, arcing sweetly through golden rays of sunlight. This was the moment my whole summer had been building towards. 'Tendulkar' was facing. He would either miss or hit.

The ball was straight.

The ball was true.

Rosh swung.

Rosh *missed*.

"Well," Rosh began with a sigh, as we sipped our first pints of the evening. "I should probably explain everything, shouldn't I?"

I nodded, my mouth full of ice-cold beer. The day had been one of the most baffling and exhausting of my life. Still, I'd had an easier time of it than Mr Chopra. Turns out he wasn't even real. I do hope he wasn't married. His wife would be furious.

"It became clear a few weeks ago," began Rosh, "that despite your best efforts, the greatest batsman to have ever played the game probably wasn't that bothered about letting a chubby little…"

"What?" *Chubby?* How rude.

"Sorry," said Rosh, suitably chastised, "but it became clear that Sachin and all the people around him weren't particularly bothered about helping a *slightly* chubby little chap from Portsmouth bowl at him, childhood dream or not. So Mr Chopra was born. I knew if all your hope of bowling to Sachin was gone, you might throw the towel in, and I really didn't want you to do that. I wanted you to see this through, come hell or high water. I wanted you to succeed, somehow; *anyhow.*"

I sipped at my pint again and smiled to myself. Rosh had gone to extraordinary lengths. He had seen that things were going down the pan, and he'd stepped in to resurrect my hopes of (sort of, at least) fulfilling my childhood dream. He hadn't wanted me to get to the end of the summer and come away empty-handed. Bloody hell. The nicest thing I'd ever done for him was apologising to him (through gales of laughter) after I had accidentally reversed over his foot in my car years ago.

It was a brilliant little wheeze. Rosh could tease and humiliate me, safe in the knowledge that, eventually, he was going to do something incredibly kind and brilliant for me. It was the perfect plan; the most evilly benevolent plan imaginable. It was like he had been punching me in the face for weeks with his fist in a plush velvet glove. I was right about Mr Chopra; he really was *exactly* like the most peculiar best mate I'd ever had.

"Once I had the plan," Rosh continued, "it was just a case of telling everyone what I was up to, and getting them involved – Josh, Big Gun, Jono, Ed at the stag do – they were all pulling the strings for me at various points. They'd let me know what you were up to, when I needed to call, what I needed to say or where I should send you to maximise your frustration – all of that stuff. We had a few nervous moments along the way – times like today when we thought you might *actually* run onto the pitch and get yourself blacklisted by the ECB, or the time when you seemed to want to ring Mr Saidu and…"

Boom. It hit me right away. A crucial detail I should have noticed which would have alerted me, from the very first bloody time I spoke to 'Mr Chopra', that he was a joker and a fraud.

"*Naidu,*" I chuckled to myself. "It's bloody Naidu."

"What?"

"His name, Rosh. It's Mr *Naidu*. I called him Mr *Saidu* by accident the first time I spoke to him and I must have said the wrong name to you as well. You – or rather 'Mr Chopra' didn't correct the obvious mistake. *Bollocks*. I should have known then that you didn't work for Sachin…"

"I *never* said I did," Rosh said briskly, shaking his head. "Or that I knew Mr Sai…sorry, *Naidu*. I was very careful about that. All I asked was whether you wanted to interview him and have a bowl at him. You just assumed I worked for him. I was just a man making conversation. You took it as something else. You should be more thorough," he smirked.

We both sipped our beers and chuckled at the ridiculousness of the situation.

"Oh, and sorry about sending you up to The Oval at silly-o-clock, by the way. I just know how much you hate mornings. The pubs are shut, the telly is shit, and…"

"…And Chris Moyles is on the radio, yes, yes, yes. I know," I laughed.

"But come on," he said wryly. "You'd have done the same thing."

He was right. I would have.

"It's funny, now that I think about it. I've been to Northampton almost *twice* because of you. I have humiliated myself in all manner of ways in front of numerous people around the country – including Sachin," I said, fixing him with an evil stare. "I've slept in my car in bloody *Greenwich,* someone mistook me for a Paul McCartney fan – and I have had to drink beer from a rubber chicken foot. And that's not even the half of it. And it's all because of you. Sort of."

"Yup. All my fault. Sort of," smiled Rosh impishly. "I heard the second forfeit at The Oval was pretty wild, too…"

I shuddered at the thought of it and pretended Rosh hadn't mentioned it.

"But do you know what Rosh?"

"What?"

"Thanks."

The night passed in a flurry of nostalgia. Empty pint glasses soon snaked around us as, once more, we relived our childhood cricketing adventures. It was another nice jog (again, we were too drunk to have driven) down memory lane.

After a few hours' hard drinking, we sank the dregs of our final pints and wobbled to our feet. It was time to go home. It had been a long, and strangely successful day. But one thing from the day's madness was still bothering me.

"Rosh, that deed poll thing…" I said, stifling a beery burp. "It's bollocks isn't it?"

"Erm…well…I got it off the internet," he slurred. "I'm sure it's kosher. They wouldn't put dodgy things on the internet."

"My mate Ian has a certificate which says he has a degree in Philosophy from the University of Cairo," I sloshed. "And he got that off the internet. That doesn't make it official…"

Rosh and I looked at each other, beers in our bellies and eyelids growing heavy. We both spontaneously combusted into fits of giggles.

"Forget about it," hiccupped Rosh. "Let's just agree that you have *definitely* bowled at Tendulkar today. Alright?"

I chuckled to myself. I was in no mood to quibble. I was happy. And drunk. *Very* drunk.

"Oh yeah," said Rosh, as we tumbled out of the pub door and onto the chitter-chattering Dalston streets, "I almost forgot. You owe Jono a bottle of champagne. He says there is an asterisk next to 'point one' of the plan he gave you, which meant that if you didn't bowl at the real Sachin, you had to do a forfeit. And he wants some booze. And he said if you quibbled, I should point out that you signed it."

Eugh. What a sneaky bastard. He had me over a barrel. Or more specifically over a magnum of champagne.

"But that's it now, yeah?" I whispered. "No more late

surprises? No more twists in the tale?"

"Oh, shit. Yes, actually," Rosh said, reaching into his little briefcase once more. "There's one more thing. This…" he said, handing me a tatty-looking sheet of paper. It looked like it had been through the wash a few times, crumpled up in the pocket of someone's jeans. My drunken eyes could make out the words '*Chicken chow mein*'.

"It's a *list to the cosmos…*" said Rosh.

"The cosmos…? Oh, *no way*," I said, with genuine surprise. Geno's Cosmic Ordering list had returned.

"I added something to the list after you'd left," spluttered Rosh. "It's right there in black and white."

There it was. The phrase 'help Adam bowl at Tendulkar'.

"What about the Chinese takeaway?" I slurred. "And what about '*Emma Watson wearing nothing but a jaunty little hat?*'

"Nope," he said sadly.

"Maybe tonight's the night," I said cheerily.

"I hope not," chuckled Rosh. "I haven't changed my sheets in two weeks."

PART EIGHTEEN

I finally knew the truth about Mr Chopra, and the incredible
lengths to which my friends would go to both annoy, amuse
and best of all, actually help me. In a manner of speaking, I'd
succeeded, thanks to them. Sort of. *Ish.*

But the fact remained that the real Sachin was well and
truly off my radar. How much he'd ever been on it was open
to debate. His demi-god status had only been enhanced by
just how inaccessible he was to mere mortals like me. I'd tried
almost everything and nothing had worked.

Sachin's tour was over just a few days later. A recurrence
of an old toe injury meant he would have to return to India
and miss the ODI series. It was hard not to feel as though he'd
done it on purpose, just to avoid me. It was hard to blame
him. Maybe he'd seen me in the chicken outfit at The Oval
and decided an early flight back home was the safest course
of action.

But there was still one thing that might put me in touch
with him. It was the longest of long shots. Until now, I'd
viewed it as the ultimate in back-up plans – something only
to be used when all else had failed. That moment was now.

And so, as I tumbled back to Rosh's place and he tumbled
off to bed, I opened his laptop, plonked myself down on his
sofa, and surfed to my email inbox.

I drunkenly punched in an address that I'd long-since

memorised and kept mentally stored away for a rainy day – an email address that was undoubtedly my last, desperate roll of the dice…**Sachin Tendulkar's**.

I stared, one-eyed, at the computer screen, took a deep breath and began to type:

Dear Mr Tendulkar,

My name is Adam Carroll-Smith.

You won't have heard of me (unless you happen to have been a very diligent follower of low-quality schools cricket in the south of England in the late 1990s and early 2000s, or been a fan of 'Five Day Weekend', my band when I was 15) but for the past few months, I have been trying, by hook or by crook, to find a way of getting in contact with you.

I have travelled the length and breadth of the country (sometimes in the wrong direction, but that's another story) and I got within touching distance of meeting you on a number of occasions. Or at least I felt like I did. I certainly got to within the width of a phone line away. But sadly, you have proved beyond my reach.

I'm sure I'm not the first fan to have tried to gain such precious access to you, nor will I be the last. But my reasons for contacting you were a bit different from the norm – I didn't want a signed photograph, or one of your old bats, and nor was I some hungry journalist eager for a scoop. All I wanted was the opportunity to bowl one ball at you.

Just one. Not a whole over, just one ball.

But why, I hear you ask, would I be so obsessed by such a pursuit? Why would anyone be so determined to get the opportunity to bowl just one delivery at you? Well Sachin (excuse me being forward and calling you Sachin – by all means feel free to call me Adam/Ad/LL Cool A in your reply), I shall tell you.

Bowling at you would have been an incredible thrill, but

*really, I wanted to bowl one ball at you because I believed –
and on some level, I still do – that with that one delivery, I
could clean bowl you.*

*Obviously, chances were that I wouldn't. You are a legend
of the game, and my best bowling figures of 5-35 came in an
under 14s game more than a decade ago. I think my cricket
has been deteriorating ever since that moment.*

*People told me I was running down a blind alley when
I told them I could knock your off-stump over, but as my
brother said: sometimes blind alleys do lead somewhere,
even if they might not appear to (there's an unsavoury story
attached to this Sachin, but trust me, away from the smut,
there's a moral in there, somewhere).*

*But even so, I thought simply having that sort of belief
was a positive thing. I knew it was a foolhardy, grandiose
thing to try and achieve, but I wanted to do it anyway. Sure,
it was a pipe dream, but every once in a while, it's only right
to go chasing one of those. Even if you don't succeed. Because
if you never try to do the improbable, you never really work
out just how much is possible, do you?*

*It would only have taken a minute or two. On paper, it
seemed such an obvious, achievable aim. After all, you have
spent years of your life in the nets, padded up and facing
bowlers of all shapes and sizes. How difficult could it be, I
thought to myself, to just trundle up and bowl one ball to
you?*

*The answer turned out to be very bloody difficult indeed.
I'll spare you the details, but suffice to say, it's been fun
and frustrating, tedious and exciting, even pointless and
rewarding at different points, and often a combination of all
those elements at the same time, too. I've learned a lot about
myself, and about what – and who – is important.*

*But anyway, you're probably wondering how I've
managed to obtain your email address, but don't worry, it
was nothing nefarious – I was handed it a number of weeks*

ago by Professor Shetty at the BCCI. He mentioned I should drop you a line and tell you about my quest, and see what you thought.

And so here I am. I am emailing you – one of my biggest childhood heroes – and asking if you would consider letting me run up and bowl one delivery at you sometime soon.

It's that simple. My brother had a few ideas on how to spice the whole thing up, but don't worry – I'll keep him a safe distance away and closely monitored by a few trustworthy friends. It really would just be a case of me throwing one down at you, and seeing if you miss, and I hit.

Anyway, thanks for reading, and I hope to hear from you soon.

Adam Carroll-Smith

P.S. Coming To America *is now my favourite film too.*
P.P.S. It's never too late to learn to swim.

I sent the email, and fell asleep with Sachin's innings at Edgbaston in 1996 playing on the laptop. It was the only right and proper way to end the day.

"It's been a privilege to be here today…" said the commentator as I tried to get to sleep. I couldn't have agreed more.

****

I had two new emails and a stonking hangover the next morning. I dealt with the hangover first, before schlepping back to the laptop screen.

One of the new messages was from a very recognisable name – a name I'd grown to love and fear in equal measures in recent months. More specifically, it was a name I had grown to love and fear over many *years*. It was the name of a man who had shaped the person I was today, whether he knew it or not.

He was someone I had grown up with; someone whose

successes and failures had become inextricably linked with my own as I had grown from a boy into a (feckless, immature, rather short) man.

In some ways, this email was from a person I knew very well – but in many more ways, it represented a rare, thrilling communiqué from a very special person about whom there was still so much I wanted to learn. My pulse climbed with anticipation as I clicked open the email.

Adam,

You owe me for the cost of that all-over spray tan I got done back at the start of August. I only got it done because I thought I might have had to streak in front of Sachin.

Lots of love, Josh x

P.S. I told Mum and Dad about what happened with Rosh/Tendulkar/etc. Dad's words? 'Wasn't Adam more of a batsman?' Joker. Oh, and I spoke to Dave. He says to tell you that 'He's proud of you, you dickhead'. He said the 'you dickhead' was necessary and you'd know what he meant by that.

The other email? A bounceback.

But you're not getting away that easily, Sachin. I *will* get you one day. I'll still dream of being there, ball in hand, watching you poised and ready to face me at the other end of a cricket pitch somewhere. I'll still dream of watching at close quarters while you clobber one of my dreadful deliveries.

Not that you will of course, because if I ever do get that chance, I **am** going to knock your off stump over.

Probably.

Oh bugger, I almost forgot: you're probably wondering what happened with that first ball to Roshan 'Tendulkar', right? He did miss. But so did I, by the width of one of wee Stuey Broad's bumfluff moustache hairs.

But don't worry. I knocked him over with the third ball. I nailed the first half of the Soulja Boy dance, but then did myself a mischief. Those shorts really were **very** tight. Bragging rights had been secured; my point had been proven; the argument was over. I had finally bowled him. *

He says it was a no-ball. It wasn't.

The biggest of thanks to: Paul and Jane at *Pitch* for everything; the main man Rosh, for so much (I owe you one, two, maybe ten); Jono, for being a top lad; all at M & Y (except DC – only joking mate); Tim, for putting up with my frequent absences; Mucka (and Stef and Alfie), obviously, for being part of team M4L; Ed for being the funniest man in the world; Chickenpockets, for loving cricket (*sorry, cruckutt*) as much as I do; BG – for reasons unknown; KT, for just being tremendous; Naomi for all the patience and advice; Roj Whelan for being brilliant (check out his new band The Roj Light at www.therojlight.com); my family, for being the most supportive, amazing and loving people on the planet; and finally Sachin and anyone else who has made this so much fun. There are probably people I've missed, and if I have, I owe you a pint. There, it's in writing!